Treatment Protocols for Stuttering

Treatment Protocols for Stuttering

M. N. Hegde, Ph.D., CCC-SLP

PLURAL
PUBLISHING
INC.
SAN DIEGO
OXFORD
BRISBANE

KH

5521 Ruffin Road
San Diego, CA 92123

e-mail: info@pluralpublishing.com
Web site: http://www.pluralpublishing.com

49 Bath Street
Abingdon, Oxfordshire OX14 1EA
United Kingdom

Typeset in 11/13 Bookman by Flanagan's Publishing Services, Inc.
Printed in the United States of America by Bang Printing

ISBN-13: 978-1-59756-050-4
ISBN-10: 1-59756-050-2

Library of Congress Cataloging-in-Publication Data:

Hegde, M. N. (Mahabalagiri N.),
    Treatment protocols for stuttering / M.N. Hegde.
        p. ; cm.
    Includes bibliographical references and index.
    ISBN-13: 978-1-59756-050-4 (softcover)
    ISBN-10: 1-59756-050-2 (softcover)
    1. Stuttering. 2. Speech therapy.   I. Title.
    [DNLM: 1. Stuttering—therapy. 2. Clinical Protocols. 3. Speech
Therapy—methods.   WM 475 H462t 2007]
    RC424.H442 2007
    616.85'5406—dc22
                                            2006023214

9/8/15

Contents

Preface   ix
Overview of Stuttering Treatment   xi
Introduction to Stuttering Treatment Protocols and the CD Resource   xv
How to Use the Accompanying CD   xvii

Part 1. Baserating Stuttering in Children   **1**
 Baserate Protocol for Sentences   4
 Baserates for Continuous and Conversational Speech   6
 Baserate Protocol for Continuous and Conversational Speech   7
 Baserates for Narrative Speech   9
 Baserate Protocol for Narrative Speech   10
 Baserate Recording Sheet   13

Part 2. Treatment of Stuttering in Preschoolers   **15**
 Treatment Options   16
   I. Fluency Reinforcement   **17**
   Treatment at the Sentence Level   18
   Treatment Protocol for Sentences   19
   Treatment at the Continuous Speech Level   23
   Treatment Protocol for Continuous Speech   24
   Treatment at the Narrative Speech Level   26
   Treatment Protocol for Narrative Speech   27
   Treatment at the Conversational Speech Level   30
   Treatment Protocol for Conversational Speech   31
   Treatment Recording Sheet   33
   Probe Protocol   34
   Probe Recording Sheet   35
   II. Fluency Reinforcement Plus Corrective Feedback   **36**
   Treatment at the Sentence Level   37
   Treatment Protocol for Sentences   39
   Treatment at the Continuous Speech Level   43
   Treatment Protocol for Continuous Speech   44
   Treatment at the Narrative Speech Level   46
   Treatment Protocol for Narrative Speech   47
   Treatment at the Conversational Speech Level   50
   Treatment Protocol for Conversational Speech   51
   Treatment Recording Sheet   53
   Probe Protocol   54
   Probe Recording Sheet   55
   III. Response Cost   **56**
   Treatment at the Sentence Level   57

Treatment Protocols for Sentences   60
Treatment at the Continuous Speech Level   66
Treatment Protocol for Continuous Speech   67
Treatment at the Narrative Speech Level   70
Treatment Protocol for Narrative Speech   71
Treatment at the Conversational Speech   74
Treatment Protocol for Conversational Speech   75
Treatment Recording Sheet   78
Probe Protocol   79
Probe Recording Sheet   80
IV. Promoting Maintenance of Fluency   **81**
Maintenance Strategies   81
Maintenance Probe Recording Sheet   82

Part 3. Treatment of Stuttering in School-Age Children   **83**
Treatment Options   84
I. Comprehensive Fluency Shaping Procedure   **85**
Establishing Stutter-Free Conversational Speech   88
Treatment Protocol for Stutter-Free Conversational Speech   90
Establishing Stutter-Free Narrative Speech   100
Treatment Protocol for Stutter-Free Narrative Speech   101
Stabilizing Natural-Sounding Fluency   106
Treatment Protocol for Natural-Sounding Fluency   107
Treatment Recording Sheet   111
Probe Protocol   112
Probe Recording Sheet   113
II. Prolonged Speech   **114**
Establishing Stutter-Free Conversational Speech   116
Treatment Protocol for Conversational Speech   118
Establishing Stutter-Free Narrative Speech   125
Treatment Protocol for Narrative Speech   126
Stabilizing Natural-Sounding Speech   131
Treatment Protocol for Natural-Sounding Speech   132
Treatment Recording Sheet   136
Probe Protocol   137
Probe Recording Sheet   138
III. Pause-and-Talk (Time-out)   **139**
Treatment at the Conversational Speech Level   141
Treatment Protocol for Conversational Speech   143
Treatment at the Narrative Speech Level   148
Treatment Protocol for Narrative Speech   149
Treatment Recording Sheet   155
Probe Protocol   156
Probe Recording Sheet   157

IV. Response Cost   **158**
Treatment at the Sentence Level   159
Treatment Protocol for Sentences   163
Treatment at the Continuous Speech Level   168
Treatment Protocol for Continuous Speech   169
Treatment at the Narrative Speech Level   172
Treatment Protocol for Narrative Speech   173
Treatment at the Conversational Speech Level   180
Treatment Protocol for Conversational Speech   181
Treatment Recording Sheet   184
Probe Protocol   185
Probe Recording Sheet   186

V. Promoting Maintenance of Fluency   **187**
Maintenance Strategies   187
Maintenance Probe Recording Sheet   188

Part 4. Baserating Stuttering in Adults   **189**
The Need for Baserates in Conversational Speech   190
Baserate Protocol for Conversational Speech   191
The Need for Baserates in Oral Reading   195
Baserate Recording Sheet   196

Part 5. Treatment of Stuttering in Adults   **197**
Treatment Options   198

I. Comprehensive Fluency Shaping Procedure   **200**
Establishing Stutter-Free Conversational Speech   203
Treatment Protocol for Conversational Speech   205
Establishing Stutter-Free Narrative Speech   214
Treatment Protocol for Narrative Speech   215
Stabilizing Normal-Sounding Fluency   218
Treatment Protocol for Natural-Sounding Fluency   219
Treatment Recording Sheet   222
Probe Protocol   223
Probe Recording Sheet   224

II. Prolonged Speech   **225**
Establishing Stutter-Free Conversational Speech   228
Treatment Protocol for Conversational Speech   230
Establishing Stutter-Free Narrative Speech   238
Treatment Protocol for Narrative Speech   239
Stabilizing Natural-Sounding Fluency   242
Treatment Protocol for Natural-Sounding Fluency   243
Treatment Recording Sheet   246
Probe Protocol   247
Probe Recording Sheet   248

III. **Pause-and-Talk (Time-Out)**   **249**
    Treatment in Conversational Speech   251
    Treatment Protocol for Conversational Speech   253
    Establishing Fluency in Narrative Speech   257
    Treatment Protocol for Narrative Speech   258
    Treatment Recording Sheet   263
    Probe Protocol   264
    Probe Recording Sheet   265

IV. **Minimal Prolongation Plus Pause-and-Talk**   **266**
    Establishing Fluency in Conversational Speech   268
    Treatment Protocol for Conversational Speech   270
    Establishing Fluency in Narrative Speech   276
    Treatment Protocol for Narrative Speech   277
    Fading Syllable Prolongation   280
    Treatment Protocol for Fading Syllable Prolongation   281
    Treatment Recording Sheet   283
    Probe Protocol   284
    Probe Recording Sheet   285

 V. **Promoting Maintenance of Fluency**   **286**
    Maintenance Strategies   286
    Maintenance Probe Recording Sheet   288

Glossary   289
References   293
Appendixes   297
    Baserate Recording Work Sheet   298
    Baserate of Stuttering [*file form*]   299
    Treatment Recording Work Sheet   300
    Progress in Treatment [*file form*]   301
    Stuttering Probe Results Work Sheet   302
    Stuttering Probe Results [*file form*]   303
Index   305

Preface

The *Webster's II New College Dictionary* defines a protocol as "a plan for a scientific experiment or treatment." An effective plan for treatment needs to be as clear and precise as a scientific experiment. The concept of protocols, therefore, is eminently suitable for treatment plans in speech-language pathology.

Treatment in communication disorders is primarily a matter of planned social interaction. These interactions can be envisioned as dynamic relationships in which the clinician and the client affect each other. A single observation of a treatment session will convince us that, in any treatment session, the clinician and the client play out their respective roles and come out of successful treatment as changed people. It is this view of treatment that has inspired these protocols.

If treatment is a set of scenarios in which the clinician and the client play out their roles, protocols are the scripts they follow to achieve improved patterns of communication. Therefore, these protocols are written as scripts that help the clinician and the client play their roles effectively, efficiently, and with a reasonable expectation of positive outcome for the child and his or her family.

Another in a series of protocols for treating various communication disorders, this book offers treatment protocols for stuttering in children and adults. The book follows the general pattern established in the two first protocols: *Treatment Protocols for Language Disorders in Children, Volume I (Essential Morphological Skills)* and *Volume II (Social Communication)*.

These protocols for treating stuttering in preschool-children, school-age children, and adults, as well as adolescents, include a variety of treatment options based on treatment efficacy research. In treating stuttering in clients of all ages, the clinician now has good choices. Clinicians also have an exciting potential of eliminating stuttering in young children and reducing it to manageable levels in most adults. The protocols are offered with the optimistic view that there has never been a better time to treat stuttering in clients of all ages.

Overview of Stuttering Treatment

There are many treatment procedures advocated for treating stuttering in children and adults. Evidence of effectiveness of these procedures varies greatly. Although some procedures are supported by a very high level of evidence, others are supported only by theory or clinical experience. In selecting a treatment procedure for a client, the clinician should consider the level of evidence as well as the suitability of the procedure for the client and the family.

Criteria for Selecting Treatment Procedures

A range of evidence may be found for various treatment procedures. A particular treatment procedure may be based on a specific level. Treatment evidence may be gathered by group experimental design studies or single-subject experimental design studies. Levels of evidence should not be biased against any acceptable research strategy. *Experimental control* and *replication* are the two important methodological aspects of treatment evaluation. Experimental control is necessary to show that a treatment was effective by comparing treatment with no treatment; it helps rule out the influence of such extraneous variables as maturation or spontaneous recovery. Replication helps establish the generality of treatment effects. Direct replications are those in which the same investigator repeats a previous study with new clients. Systematic replications are those in which other investigators in other settings repeat a study published in the literature. Replications demonstrate treatment generality. If a treatment yields similar results in different settings when used by different clinicians, then the treatment has generality. Controlled and systematically replicated evidence supports widespread application of a technique. Therefore, unlike other levels of evidence advocated in the literature, the following hierarchy is neutral to research methods, and based on the degree of control and the extent of replication. This hierarchy of evidence results in six levels of evidence:

Level 1. The treatment procedure is supported by a an uncontrolled and unreplicated case study. If a procedure has been researched in a single (not yet replicated) case study (uncontrolled), the researcher may have shown that the treatment produces improvement. But effectiveness for the treatment cannot be claimed at this level.

Level 2. The treatment procedure is based on an uncontrolled but directly replicated case study. If a case study has been replicated with positive results by the same clinician, the technique may be judged to produce improvement more reliably than without replication. Still, effectiveness cannot be claimed.

Level 3. The treatment procedure is based on an uncontrolled but systematically replicated case study. If a case study has been replicated with positive results by different clinicians in different settings, the technique may be judged to produce improvement more reliably than with direct replication. Nonetheless, effectiveness is not yet evident.

Level 4. The treatment procedure is based on controlled but unreplicated experimental evidence. This is the level at which treatment effects (not just improvement) are demonstrated by comparing treatment with no treatment in a controlled experimental study. Not just improvement, effectiveness may be claimed for the procedure. Because this is the first experimental study and the procedure has not been replicated, generality (wider applicability) will not have been demonstrated. But the evidence is better than those in the previous levels.

Level 5. The treatment is based on controlled and directly replicated evidence. At this level, treatment effects are shown to be reliable by the same investigator who replicates his or her study in the original setting in which level 4 evidence was demonstrated. The evidence at this level is superior to that in level 4 because of increase confidence in the effectiveness demonstrated for the techniques.

Level 6. The treatment is based on controlled and systematically replicated evidence. This is the final and the best evidence for a treatment technique. Other investigators in other professional settings have demonstrated that the treatment is effective with varied clients. Successful systematic replication confirms that the procedure may be used in varied setting with different clients to obtain the same effectiveness as the original investigators. The procedure with level 6 evidence may be recommended for general practice with known limitations to the technique.

Unfortunately, many stuttering treatment procedures do not meet any of the listed criteria or level of evidence. They are practiced because experts advocate them or they have been historically used. Expert advocacy and historical trends are no basis to use a technique. If a procedure lacks even case study evidence (level 1), it should be rejected. If a technique with a higher level of evidence is available, the one with a lower level of evidence should not be offered. It is the clinician's responsibility to select a procedure that is based on the highest level of efficacy research evidence.

Although experimental evidence is a paramount consideration in selecting treatment procedures, other variables, especially those related to the client and the family, cost, duration of treatment, need for expensive equipment, generalization and maintenance of treatment gains, and ethnocultural variables that may affect treatment should be considered. Elements of certain effective procedures may be unnecessary, needlessly costly, and introduce additional treatment steps that can be avoided to increase the treatment's efficiency and social acceptance. For instance, delayed auditory feedback (DAF) and masking noise are both reasonably effective procedures (Bloodstein, 1995). The DAF procedure, by inducing syllable prolongations, results in stutter-free speech. There is evidence to support the use of DAF machines in treatment. However, a slower rate of speech that virtually eliminates stuttering can be induced just by instructions, frequent modeling, positive reinforcement, and corrective feedback. Therefore, the expensive DAF machines are unnecessary; when used, the machines have to be carefully faded in multiple small steps, lengthening treatment duration. Consequently, slower speech induced by behavioral techniques is cost-effective, efficient, and affordable to many more clients than when the DAF machines are used. The masking noise procedure also reliably reduces stuttering in the initial stages of treatment. Nonetheless it is not recommended because of its poor long-term effects and the potential health hazard associated with continued use.

Clinicians should self-evaluate their own expertise in administering techniques. No clinician can ethically use a procedure for which she or he is not trained. However, if the clinician's repertoire does not include effective procedures, there is no license to use ineffective procedures based on past clinical experience. In such cases, either the clinician refrains from treating disorders for which he or she cannot offer effective services or, if required to offer services, gets the needed training in effective procedures.

Effective techniques, even those with the highest level of positive evidence (level 6, controlled and systematically replicated) have their limitations. Individual differences in reaction to treatment may limit otherwise effective procedures. In a particular client, a procedure known to be effective may be ineffective or not as effective as expected. Treatment research sometimes may have identified such limitations of specific techniques. This is more likely to happen if the treatment researchers had used a single-subject design, and consequently, provided profiles of clients who improved as well as of those who did not. In any case, even when using a procedure known to be effective, the clinician should carefully monitor the client's progress with reliably established baselines that are frequently compared against measures of dysfluencies (or stuttering) recorded in each treatment session. If there is no expected improvement, the clinician should immediately make a self-evaluation of whether the technique was used correctly. If there are no errors in treatment administration, the clinician should abandon the technique in favor of another effective procedure.

Organization of Stuttering Treatment Protocols

These protocols for stuttering in children and adults are written as scenarios that unfold in teaching either certain fluency skills that indirectly reduce stuttering or for reducing stuttering directly. In selecting treatment procedures for the protocols, the overriding concern has been efficacy. The protocols include a set of treatment procedures for which there is plenty of replicated positive evidence.

In recent years, treating children who stutter, especially preschool children who stutter, has gained much philosophical, ethical, clinical, and treatment research attention (Conture, 2001; Cordes & Ingham, 1998; Curlee, 1999a; Guitar, 2006; Hegde, 2004; Onslow, 1993; Ryan, 1998; Shapiro, 1999; Yairi & Ambrose, 2005). Many clinicians believe that stuttering is effectively treated in young children, perhaps even more effectively than in adults (Curlee, 1999a; Gregory & Hill, 1999; Harris & Onslow, 1999). In recent years, experimental and clinical data on effectiveness of certain treatments offered to preschool and school-age children are emerging (Cordes & Ingham, 1998; Curlee, 1999b; Hegde, 2004; Onslow, 1993). Generally, behavioral treatments, with little or no concern for emotional or attitudinal components of stuttering in young children, have been shown to be effective. Therefore, the protocols include behavioral procedures known to be effective in treating both preschool and school-age children.

Systematic treatment of stuttering in adults has even a longer history than treatment in young children (Bloodstein, 1995; Conture, 2001; Manning, 1999; Shapiro, 1999; Guitar, 2006). Nonetheless, significant problems remain in effective treatment of stuttering in adults. Maintenance of fluency over time and across situations has been a major problem. The fluency shaping procedure, which is most often offered to adults who stutter, induces unnatural-sounding speech, possibly leading to a relapse of stuttering. Nonetheless, the protocols offer a more optimistic view of treating stuttering in adults. The key to promote maintenance of fluency in adults treated for stuttering is regular follow-ups and additional booster treatments when the follow-up data warrant.

The treatment protocols included in the book for treating adults who stutter are based on both uncontrolled (case studies) and controlled replicated treatment research (Conture, 2001; Cordes & Ingham, 1998; Curlee, 1999a; Guitar, 2006; Shapiro, 1999). In addition to a comprehensive fluency shaping procedure, which includes airflow management, gentle phonatory onset, and syllable prolongation, the protocols offer the following alternatives for clinicians to consider in treating adults who stutter: an exclusive syllable prolongation method (without airflow and gentle phonatory onset), pause-and-talk (time-out), and an experimental procedure that combines a slight syllable prolongation with pause-and-talk.

The protocols do not include mere counseling, psychotherapy, and related treatment approaches that particularly focus on feelings, emotions, attitudes, and cognitive dispositions of people who stutter. There is plenty of observational evidence that strong emotions, feelings, and certain negative thoughts about self are a part of the stuttering symptom complex (Bloodstein, 1995, Curlee, 1999a; Shapiro, 1999). Nonetheless, there is no strong, independent, and experimentally verified evidence that suggests that an approach exclusively concerned only with emotions, feelings, and negative thoughts of people who stutter will help reduce stuttering (Bloodstein, 1995; Cordes & Ingham, 1998; Onslow, 1993). When stuttering is not reduced with counseling and similar approaches, there is no reason to expect that the associated negative emotions, feelings, thoughts, and avoidance behaviors will be diminished because the latter are a consequence of stuttering. Clinicians who recommend emotionally based treatment to people who stutter almost always use other techniques that are known to be independently effective (e.g., syllable prolongation and airflow management). When two or more procedures are simultaneously applied to treat a disorder, it will not be clear which component had an effect and which one did not. Most experimental treatment of stuttering has been within the behavioral framework; most, if not all, currently experimentally supported behavioral treatments are included in the protocols.

Diagnostic and Measurement Issues

Clinicians use somewhat different criteria to diagnose stuttering. It also implies that clinicians assess or measure stuttering somewhat differently. Nonetheless, most parents and clinicians can readily agree that a child stutters. Although there may be some doubt and debate about a few borderline cases, theoretical differences on what stuttering is have not been detrimental to diagnosis and treatment.

The author prefers to measure all types of dysfluencies and then diagnose stuttering if the percent dysfluency rate is at least 5%. The author is aware that different clinicians measure different sets of behaviors to diagnose stuttering and often use clinical judgment, not objective criteria. Different theories advocate different approaches as well. The author is also aware that most clinicians will bypass theoretical differences and recognize, diagnose, and treat stuttering in children and adults. Therefore, the protocols are written for treatment of stuttering, not for its diagnosis. Measurement of stuttering, however defined, is crucial for demonstrating improvement under treatment. Therefore, it is recommended that the clinician define stuttering according to his or her own criteria, and measure it in all treatment sessions to claim improvement. Generally speaking, clinicians either measure stuttering globally (based on judgment) or measure it more specifically in terms of dysfluency types. The treatment and probe recording sheets allow for this variation.

Introduction to Stuttering Treatment Protocols and the CD Resource

Treatment protocols are common in medicine, where such protocols are more prescriptive. Treatment plans in speech-language pathology need to be flexible and adaptable to individual clients. Nonetheless, a general pattern of baserate, treatment, and probe sequence is basic to treating all communication disorders, including stuttering. Such protocols may easily be modified to suit individual children and adults. The protocols described in this book leave much room for the clinician's innovation, adaptation, and modification. The protocols for each form of treatment are described as separate, complete, and self-contained entities, even at the expense of sounding redundant and repetitive of certain information. The author did not want the clinician to have to thumb through different sections of the protocol to implement a particular procedure. Protocols are written such that once a treatment procedure is selected for a client, the clinician will have everything needed to treat the client with that procedure. Therefore, many of the conversational exchanges, narratives, and other aspects of treatment are repeated now and then to make each section as complete and self-contained as possible. These protocols, like those for child language and articulation and phonological disorders, require the following five elements:

- **A protocol to establish baserates** of stuttering or dysfluencies. The baserates help establish the need for treatment and provide an objective and quantitative basis to evaluate the child's progress in treatment.

- **A baserate recording sheet** that allows the clinician to record the rate of stuttering or dysfluency before treatment is started. Such baseline data help establish the need for treatment and provide a basis for evaluating the client's progress under treatment.

- **Various protocols to treat stuttering in children and adults** that provide unfolding scenarios for treatment. The protocols are detailed enough for the clinician to implement treatment with little or no modification. They are written in the form of scripts for both the clinician and the client. In essence, these treatment protocols allow the clinician and the client to play their respective roles.

- **A treatment recording sheet** that allows the clinician record dysfluency or stuttering rates in children and adults in all treatment sessions. When carefully measured and recorded, these protocols help evaluate the client's progress in treatment and help justify the clinical services to third-party payers.

- **A protocol to probe for and record generalized fluency** without an explicit monitoring of stuttering or fluency skills. One or more conversational speech samples in the clinic and in the client's natural environment will help establish generalized fluency. Guidelines to measure generalized fluency and a recording sheet to document the percent stuttering or dysfluency rates are both provided in the protocols.

The various recording sheets may be photocopied for clinical use. For instance, the clinician can photocopy the baserate, treatment, or probe recording sheet to document stuttering rates before, during, and after treatment. Templates for the baserate, treatment, and probe recording sheets are also provided in Appendixes that the clinician can photocopy for personal use. Furthermore, the clinician can use the accompanying CD to individualize the recording sheets to prepare for treatment sessions.

How to Use the Accompanying CD

The CD that accompanies the book contains the baserate, treatment, and probe recording sheets for the treatment procedures for which protocols have been written. All the files on the CD are modifiable. The clinician can type in new information or delete what is on them. This makes it possible for the clinician to individualize the identifying information for particular clients he or she serves. The clinician can type in the name of the clinic, the clinician, the client, client's family and address, and the treatment procedure offered. The forms thus modified and printed for the client's files will appear like the clinic stationary. While individualizing the recording sheets in this manner, the clinician can retain the standard recording sheet on the CD.

Because the clinician can individualize the forms given on the CD, they will not look like the typical forms given in resource books. The modifiable and printable forms on CD do not have page numbers, book chapter titles, and such other information that will make it inappropriate to place in a client's folder. Forms so modified and printed from the CD provided in the book will look like the clinician's clinic stationary.

For the clinician's convenience, the CDs are prepared in simple MS Word format that most clinicians are familiar with; the CD is not encrypted in any way to facilitate quick access and easy use of the documents on it. Once again, the use of the CD will help the clinician save planning time and effort involved in preparing for treatment sessions.

Part 1

Baserating Stuttering in Children

Baserating Stuttering in Children

The Need for Baserates

Even though an assessment will have been done on the child, it is essential to establish the pretreatment baserates of dysfluencies or stuttering, as defined by the clinician. A single assessment result may or may not be reliable. Furthermore, an assessment may have been made weeks or months prior to the initiation of treatment. Stuttering frequency may have changed since the assessment. Therefore, it is essential to baserate stuttering before starting treatment.

Overview

- With preschool and school-age children, it may be necessary to initially establish baserates of dysfluencies or stuttering in sentences evoked with the help of concrete stimulus materials. Asking simple questions about pictures shown or toys being manipulated will help evoke sentences. Often, children tend to produce single words or phrases when asked questions. Therefore, the clinician needs to prompt the production of full sentences. On occasion, the clinician may model a full sentence but the child is not asked to immediately imitate the modeled production. Imitation may improve fluency, but this improved fluency will not reflect the child's typical fluency levels (or stuttering rates).

- A few minutes of speech evoked at the sentence level should lead to more continuous and narrative speech. The child may be asked to talk about themes or topics most children know well (e.g., birthday parties). The child may be told a brief story and asked to retell it. The clinician keeps interruptions to a minimum; prompts the child to supply more details in sentences.

- Protocols illustrate the response evoking strategies and exemplars of dysfluencies. While baserating dysfluencies in a particular child, the clinician takes note of the specific kinds of responses and dysfluencies a child produces.

- The clinician always points to the relevant part of the picture before asking a question. Initially, the clinician prompts sentence productions and gradually fades prompts as shown in the protocols.

- The clinician selects child-specific and ethnoculturally appropriate storybooks that contain large and colorful pictures.

- The clinician selects a few toys the child can play with and talk about the play activity. The clinician tape-records the speech sample for later analysis of dysfluency or stuttering rates.

- The clinician counts the dysfluencies and the number of words in the sample to calculate the percent dysfluency rate. Alternatively, the clinician may count the number of stutterings as he or she defines it and calculate the percent syllables or words stuttered.

Clinic Baserate Procedures

The protocols for establishing baserates of stuttering include the following steps:

- **Session 1:** During the first session following assessment, clinician may tape-record a 15- to 20-minute speech sample to measure the dysfluency rates. The remainder of the session may be necessary to talk with the parents about changes in stuttering since assessment, their expectations regarding treatment, and to get more familiarized with the child.

- **Session 2:** At the beginning of the second session, the clinician may tape-record another 10-minute conversational speech sample, followed by an introduction to treatment. The clinician may describe the planned treatment for the child, justify the selected treatment to parents in terms of evidence, answer questions the parents may have about the offered and available alternative treatments, and discuss any other matter that concerns the child, the parents, and the treatment regimen.

- **Session 3:** At the beginning of the third session, the clinician may tape-record a third, 5- to 7-minute speech sample before starting treatment. The remainder of the session may be devoted to treatment.

If the first three baserates are divergent by a defined criterion (e.g., more than 3 or 5% variation across three measures), the clinician may take another baserate at the beginning of the next session.

Home Speech Samples

Whenever practical, the clinician may request parents to tape three speech samples at home, each 5 to 7 minutes in duration and submit them for analysis. The parents may be asked to do this after they have observed the first baserate session in which the clinician will have demonstrated the procedure of taping the child's speech sample.

Baserating Stuttering in Children
Baserate Protocol for Sentences

Scripts for Baserating Dysfluencies in Sentences		Note
Clinician	[*showing the picture of a farm scene*] "What do you see here? Do you see a farm or a home?"	The first trial
Child	"A farm."	Fluent production; no verbal praise
Clinician	"Yes, it's a farm. Can you say it in a sentence? You can say, *I see a farm, this is a farm*, or anything like that in a sentence."	Prompting a sentence production
Child	"I ssss-see a farm."	Sound prolongation; no corrective feedback
Clinician	"What is this animal? Can you say it in a sentence?"	The next trial
Child	"d-d-d-dog."	Sound repetition; no corrective feedback
Clinician	"Say it in a sentence. You can say, *it is a dog, this is a dog, that is a dog*, or anything like that."	Prompting a sentence production
Child	"This is a d-d-dog."	Sound repetition; no corrective feedback
Clinician	"What is this man doing here? Say, *he is . . .* "	The next trial; prompting a sentence production
Child	"Fffffeeding cow."	Sound prolongation; no corrective feedback; prompt did not work
Clinician	"What is the man doing? Start with, *he is . . .* "	The next trial; new prompt
Child	"He is ffffeeding cow."	Sound prolongation; no corrective feedback; effective prompt
Clinician	"What is this calf doing here?"	The next trial; no prompts
Child	"um-um j-j-jumping."	Interjection and sound repetition; no corrective feedback
Clinician	"Can you say it in a sentence? Say, *the calf . . .* "	The next trial; prompting a sentence production
Child	"The calf is jumping." praise	Fluent production; no verbal
Clinician	"This is hay. What is it? Say it in a sentence."	The next evoked trial; instruction only

Baserating Dysfluencies in Sentences, continued

Scripts for Baserating Dysfluencies in Sentences		Note
Child	"This is hay."	Fluent production; no verbal praise; effective instruction
Clinician	"Who likes to eat hay? Say, *the cow* . . . "	The next trial; prompting a sentence production
Child	"The cow-cow-cow lllllikes to eat hay."	Word repetition and sound prolongation; no corrective feedback
Clinician	"What is she doing here? Start with, *she is* . . . "	The next trial; prompting a sentence production
Child	"She is mmmmilking cow."	Sound prolongation; no corrective feedback
Clinician	"What is this pig doing here? Start with, *the pig* . . . "	The next evoked trial
Child	"The p-p-p-pig is drinking wa-wa-water."	A sound and a syllable repetition; no corrective feedback (2 part-word repetitions)
Clinician	"What is this cat doing? Say it in a sentence."	The next evoked trial; prompting a sentence production
Child	"It is sleeping."	A fluent production; no verbal praise
Clinician	"What is this girl doing?"	The next trial
Child	"Chasing-chasing-chasing chickens."	Word repetition; no corrective feedback
Clinician	"What are these children doing here? Start with *they* . . . "	The next trial; prompting sentence productions
Child	"They are playing with hay."	Fluent production; no verbal praise
Clinician	"What are these two men doing here?"	The next trial; no prompts
Child	"They are c-c-c-carrying wood."	Sound repetition; no corrective feedback
Clinician	"What do you see here?"	The next trial; no prompts
Child	"I see-I see-I see boys riding horses."	Phrase repetition; no corrective feedback

Continue to baserate until a representative speech sample has been recorded.

Baserating Stuttering in Children

Baserates for Continuous and Conversational Speech

Overview

- The frequency of dysfluencies tends to be higher in connected, continuous speech than in isolated words, phrases, or even sentences. Therefore, it is essential to establish baserates of dysfluencies in continuous speech.

- An initial period of controlled sentence productions as illustrated previously will help lead the child to more continuous speech.

- To baserate dysfluencies in a child's continuous speech, the clinician asks open-ended questions the child answers.

- The clinician may describe a scene in a picture and ask the child to recount it.

- The clinician may suggest a script (e.g., birthday parties, Thanksgiving, Kwanza, Hanukkah, helping Mom make a sandwich, camping in a park, planting some seeds, etc.) and ask the child to describe the event or a sequence of events. The clinician may use pictures as prompts for the stories or scene descriptions.

- The clinician facilitates conversation but does not provide models for imitation. The clinician lets the child talk continuously with minimal interruptions.

- The clinician prompts complete sentences, longer productions, and additional descriptions only when the child stops talking or when the child appears unsure of what to say.

- The pictures used to evoke isolated sentences may be reused; this time, the clinician may ask more open-ended questions; if this is not productive, new stimulus materials may be selected.

Baserating Stuttering in Children

Baserate Protocol for Continuous and Conversational Speech

Scripts for Baserating Dysfluencies in Continuous Speech		Note
Clinician	[*showing the picture of a farm scene*] "I want you to tell me what is happening in this picture. First tell me what these people are doing here. Remember to talk in long sentences. You can start with, *these people are working on the farm.*"	The first trial; prompting a sentence production
Child	"These people are working on the farm."	Fluent production; no verbal praise
Clinician	"OK, now I will point to all these people and you tell me what they are doing. Start with these kids here. Tell me about everything they are doing." [*points to children; continues to point to different parts of the picture to prompt more continuous speech*]	Next trial; instructions to evoke more continuous speech
Child	"The kids are p-p-playing with hay. They are throwing hay everywhere. They-they-they are climbing on this. They are chasing all the ch-ch-ch-chickens."	Describes various parts of the picture as the clinician points to them Two sound repetitions and one word repetition; no corrective feedback
Clinician	"Tell me all about what these big people are doing. Say it in long sentences like you just did." [*points to various adults; continues to point to different parts of picture to prompt more continuous speech*]	Next trial; instructions to evoke more continuous speech
Child	"These mmmen are working. She is mmmilking the cow. He is ffffeeding the cow. They are c-c-c-arrying wood. They are sitting on the-on the-on the grass. They are eating something."	Describes various parts of the picture as the clinician points to them Three sound prolongations, one sound repetition, and one phrase repetition; no corrective feedback
Clinician	"Have you ever seen a farm? Answer me in a whole sentence."	Evoking conversational speech
Child	"I have seen one."	A fluent answer
Clinician	"Whose farm was it? Who took you there?"	An open-ended question
Child	"My cousin's farm. My mom and d-d-d-dad took me there."	A sound repetition

Baserates in Continuous and Conversational Speech, continued

Scripts for Baserating Dysfluencies in Continuous Speech		Note
Clinician	"What did you see there?"	Another open-ended question
Child	"I saw some chickens. They have mmm-many cows there. Some ponies, too."	A sound prolongation
Clinician	"Did you see any baby cows? Did you pet them?"	Another question
Child	"I saw baby cows there. I pet them."	Fluent production
Clinician	"What else did you do there?"	Open-ended question
Child	"We had a picnic."	Fluent production
Clinician	"Who were all there?"	Open-ended question
Child	"My aunt and uncle were there. um . . . my two um . . . cousins. [*clinician asks: tell me their names*] Two. One is Jane. The other is Tom. Some other people were there. I don't know them."	Two syllable interjections
Clinician	"What did you eat? What did you drink?"	Open-ended questions
Child	"We had hot dogs. We had some lemonade. We ate some watermelon."	Fluent production
Clinician	"What else did you do on the farm?"	Open-ended question
Child	"We took a ride on a pony."	Fluent production
Clinician	"Were you scared or was it a lot of fun?"	Another question
Child	"I-I-I was not scared. It was a lot of fun."	A word repetition
Clinician	"Are your cousins older or younger than you?"	Another question
Child	"One is older. [*clinician asks: who*] Jane is older. Tom is a baby."	Fluent production
Clinician	[*continues conversation in this manner to obtain a representative speech sample to establish the dysfluency baserates*]	

Baserating Stuttering in Children

Baserates for Narrative Speech

Overview

- To establish the baserates of dysfluencies in narrative speech, the clinician may tell stories to children and ask them to retell them. In some cases, story retelling may reveal a number of dysfluencies or dysfluencies of certain kinds that may not be evident in short conversational exchanges in which the child produces brief utterances.
- A variety of strategies may be used to select stories. Children react differently to different kinds of stories. The clinician may have to experiment to find out what kinds of stories provoke the greatest interest in a child, leading to better (lengthier) narration. For instance:
  - ➢ The stories selected may be of universal appeal. Fairy tales and tales from the past may be of interest to children of all ethnocultural backgrounds.
  - ➢ Stories that demand some thinking or present a puzzle may be especially productive in evoking narratives as well as continuous speech from children.
  - ➢ The stories selected may also be unique to the child's experience. In such cases, the stories will be especially relevant to the child's ethnocultural background. For many ethnoculturally diverse children, stories from their particular backgrounds with matching illustrations may be needed to stimulate good narratives.
  - ➢ It is fine to tell stories from other cultures and lands if they seem to provoke greater curiosity and interest than the more commonly told stories.
- It is important to tell a story in such a manner that the child will remember the details. To help promote better retelling of the story, the clinician may pause and ask questions during the storytelling.
- Important details may be repeated to draw the child's attention.
- The child may be asked to repeat crucial elements *during* storytelling.
- The story gist may be provided at the end to have the child remember the most important elements of the story.
- The clinician my prompt and ask brief questions to keep the child on track.
- The clinician may redirect the child's attention to missing details.
- The clinician may stop the child when the sequence is wrong and redirect the child to correct sequence of events.

Baserating Stuttering in Children

Baserate Protocol for Narrative Speech

Scripts for Baserating Dysfluencies in Narrative Speech		Note
Clinician	"Now, I will tell you a story and I want you to remember everything I tell you. When I am finished, I want **you** to tell **me** the same story. Okay?"	Introducing the storytelling task
Child	"Okay."	Child understands the task
Clinician	"Once upon a time, a man worked in a king's palace. One day he came to work very late. The king was mad at the man. He asked him, 'why are you so late? You should have been here two hours ago.' The man began to tremble with fear because he thought he was going to lose his job.	Clinician tells the first of the 3 stories to baserate dysfluencies in narrative speech
	"Now where did the man work? Why was the king mad at him? What was the man afraid of?"	Asks questions so the child will learn parts of the story before retelling all of it
Child	"The mmman worked in a palace. The k-k-k-ing was mad because the man came late to work. The man was afraid because he may lose the job."	The child tells part of the story; a sound prolongation and a sound repetition
Clinician	"Good, you remember. Also remember to tell me that the man came to work two hours late.	Reiterates certain points and continues with the story
	"Now, the king asked again, 'tell me why are you so late to work?' The man said, 'Oh my kind king! I have a 4-year-old son at home! You know he lost his mother! I am the only one to take care of him.'	
	"Are you listening? What did the king ask and what did the man say?"	Checks the child's understanding of the story
Child	"The king asked, 'why-why-why are you so late?' The man said, 'oh my kind king! I have a I have a 4-year-old son at home! You know he lllost his mother! I am taking care of him.'"	The child tells part of the story; word repetition Sound prolongation
Clinician	"That's good! Remember everything so you can tell me the whole story again!	Reinforcers for telling the story; no contingencies on fluency or stuttering
	"The man said, 'This morning, when I was ready to leave for work, my son wanted a banana. I did not have one at home. So I ran to the store and got him a banana. Then he began to cry, saying he wants the banana cut into pieces. So I cut the banana into pieces.'	Continues with the story
	"What happened that morning, when the man wanted to leave for work?"	Asks the child to retell parts of the story

Baserating Stuttering in Narrative Speech, continued

Scripts for Baserating Dysfluencies in Narrative Speech		Note
Child	"His boy wa-wa-wanted a banana. The man didn't have any. So he went to store to get one. Then, the boy wanted his Dad to cut the banana into pieces. D-d-d-dad cut it into pieces."	The child tells parts of the story; syllable repetition Sound repetition
Clinician	"Excellent! You are a good storyteller! You remember everything! "Then the man told his king. 'Oh my kind king! My son began to cry very loudly. He was screaming! He was very sad. My boy was sad because the banana was cut into pieces. Now he wanted a whole banana. But I didn't have another banana. So I had to put the banana pieces together to make it a whole banana. It took me two hours!' "Tell me what happened."	Continues with the story Asks the child to retell parts of the story
Child	"Wh-wh-when Dad cut banana into pieces, the boy began to cry! He wanted the whole banana. Man had no banana. P-p-p-putting all the pieces together, he tried to make a whole banana. It-it-it took him two hours!"	Retells parts of the story; sound repetition Sound repetition Word repetition
Clinician	"Good job! Now I want you to tell me the whole story. Then we will talk about how the man put the banana pieces together to make it a whole banana. "Start at the very beginning. Once upon a time . . . "	Asks the child to narrate the entire story Prompts the story beginning
Child	"Once upon a time, a man was working in a palace. He-he-he came to work very late one day. He was two hours late that day. The k-k-king became very mad! He asked him, 'why are you so late? You are two hours late.' The mmmman began to tremble. He was afraid because the king was angry. He thought he-he-he-he may not have his job. The king wanted to know why he was lllate. The man said, 'Oh my kind king! I have a 4-year-old son at home! He has no mother! I-I-I am taking care of him.'"	Narrates the story Word repetition Sound repetition Sound prolongation Word repetition Sound prolongation Word repetition
Clinician	"Good storytelling! I like it. Okay, then what happened?"	Reinforces storytelling, but not fluency

Baserating Stuttering in Narrative Speech, continued

Scripts for Baserating Dysfluencies in Narrative Speech		Note
Child	The man wanted to come to work, but the boy wanted a banana. Mmmman didn't have a banana at home. So he ran to the store and got him a banana. Then the boy b-b-b-egan to cry, saying he wanted the banana cut into pieces. Sssso the man cut the banana into pieces. But now, the boy began to cry very loudly. He began to scream. He-he-he was ssssad. The boy was sad because the banana was cut into pieces. Now he-he-he wanted a whole banana! But the man didn't have another [*an unusual pause*] banana. So the man had to make a whole banana with all the little pieces! It-it-it took him two hours!"	Continues the narration Sound prolongation Sound repetition Sound prolongation Word repetition and sound prolongation Word repetition A pause Word repetition
Clinician	"Excellent! You are a good storyteller! Now tell me, how did the man put the banana pieces together to make a whole banana?"	Reinforces narrative behaviors, not fluency; initiates conversational speech
Child	"I d-d-don't know! You didn't t-t-t-ell me!"	Sound repetition
Clinician	"I don't know either! The story didn't say! But let's guess! How would you put banana pieces together to make a whole banana?"	
Child	"Mmmmaybe with scotch tape?"	Sound prolongation
Clinician	"That's one way of doing it. What if you didn't have scotch tape? In olden times, they didn't have it."	
Child	"um-um You can do it with glue!"	interjections
Clinician	"But you can't eat banana with glue on it, can you? How about a long toothpick? You can stick all the pieces onto a toothpick?"	
Child	"Yeah. You can also use a string!"	Fluent production
Clinician	"Yes. I wish the man told us how he put the banana pieces together!"	

Have the child retell additional stories if more narrative speech samples are needed.

Baserating Stuttering in Children

Baserate Recording Sheet

Personalize and print this page from the CD.

Name of the child:	DOB:
Name of the parents:	Phone:
Diagnosis: Stuttering	Session date(s):
Clinician:	Comments:

Types of Dysfluencies	Frequency		
	Sentence Productions	Continuous Speech	Narratives
Prolongations			
Sound or syllable prolongations			
Silent prolongations			
Broken words			
Pauses			
Silent pauses			
Repetitions			
Sound or syllable repetitions			
Word repetitions			
Phrase repetitions			
Interjections			
Schwa or *um* interjections			
Word interjections			
Phrase interjections			
Revisions			
Incomplete phrases			
Total number of dysfluencies			
Total number of words spoken			
Percent dysfluency rate			
Total percent dysfluency/stuttering rate			

If considered unnecessary to calculate percent dysfluency rates separately for sentence productions, continuous speech, and narration, calculate a single percentage for all samples combined.

Part 2

Treatment of Stuttering in Preschoolers

Treatment of Stuttering in Preschoolers

Treatment Options

Stuttering may be effectively treated in preschool children. Fairly simple yet effective procedures are available to treat stuttering in preschoolers. The clinician and the parents may be trained to administer treatment with moderate training effort. Choices for effectively treating stuttering in preschool children include:

- **Fluency Reinforcement.** This is the most minimal and simplest of all treatments available to treat stuttering in preschoolers. Parents and clinicians may be trained to administer this procedure with minimum time and effort. In this procedure, the clinician simply verbally praises the child for speaking fluently. No corrective feedback is offered for stuttering. In other words, stuttering is completely ignored. The clinician may, however, frequently model sentences and longer productions for the child to imitate. This is an exclusive positive reinforcement strategy for fluent productions. In this strategy, the clinician and the parents offer such verbal reinforcers as the following:
  - ➤ "Excellent! I like your smooth speech!"
  - ➤ "Very good! That was very smooth!"
  - ➤ "Your speech is so smooth!"
  - ➤ "You are working hard! Your speech is smooth and nice!"

- **Fluency Reinforcement Plus Corrective Feedback.** This is the next, slightly more complex treatment that may be offered to preschoolers who stutter. In addition to verbal praise for fluency, the clinician offers corrective feedback for dysfluent productions. The corrective feedback may take the form of such verbal statements as the following:
  - ➤ "No! that was bumpy!"
  - ➤ "Oops! You had a bump there!"
  - ➤ "Oh No! you were a bit bumpy!"
  - ➤ "Stop! Your speech is not smooth!"

  The clinician may immediately fluently model the child's dysfluent productions. The child is expected to imitate the fluent modeling. The clinician enthusiastically reinforces all correctly imitated and spontaneous fluent productions.

- **Response Cost.** This is a highly effective procedure with both preschool and school-age children. The procedure includes positive reinforcement for fluent productions by presenting tokens and reinforcement withdrawal for stuttering by removing tokens. Token presentation is typically accompanied by verbal praise; token withdrawal, by corrective feedback. The procedure does not target such fluency skills as airflow management, gentle phonatory onset, or slower rate of speech. Consequently, the procedure does not induce unnatural-sounding speech. Therefore, it is unnecessary to spend time on restoring natural-sounding fluency. This is an efficient procedure to treat stuttering in preschool as well as school-age children.

The protocols that follow describe these procedures for treating stuttering in preschool children.

Treatment of Stuttering in Preschoolers:
I. Fluency Reinforcement

Overview

Fluency reinforcement, perhaps the simplest of the effective procedures available to treat stuttering, is especially useful with preschoolers. Most student clinicians can be trained in the method with relative ease. Parents of children who stutter learn to praise the child for fluency by clinical observations and short training sessions. The parents may be trained to administer the procedure at home. They may be trained to hold informal sessions with storybook reading, story telling, picture descriptions, and planned play activities during which the parent praises the child for fluent speech. Subsequently, in more spontaneous and naturalistic situations, the procedure may be administered in a subtle manner. A smile, a nod, a thumbs-up or similar gesture, or a gentle touch for fluent productions may be sufficient to help maintain fluency in natural settings.

If verbal praise does not systematically increase fluency in the child, the clinician may select another procedure. At all times, the clinician should measure the rate of stuttering or dysfluencies to make sure the verbal praise is a functional reinforcer: that is, it does increase fluent productions and as a side effect, decrease dysfluencies. If two or three sessions do not evidence acceptable progress, the clinician may combine verbal praise with corrective feedback for stuttering and frequent fluent modeling of dysfluent productions. Response cost may be another procedure to consider.

Treatment protocols are offered at four levels of training:

1. Treatment at the sentence level
2. Treatment at the continuous speech level
3. Treatment at the narrative speech level
4. Treatment at the conversational speech level

Treatment of Stuttering in Preschoolers: I. Fluency Reinforcement

Treatment at the Sentence Level

Overview

- With preschoolers, fluency reinforcement may be initiated at the sentence level, although the child is likely to produce many single words and phrases when asked questions about the stimulus materials.

- As in the baserate session, the clinician may prompt, instruct, or otherwise encourage the child to produce shorter and longer sentences.

- Unlike in the baserate session, however, the clinician may model and immediately ask the child to imitate shorter and longer sentences. Children often are fluent when they immediately imitate a production, which gives an opportunity for the clinician to reinforce fluency. Frequent modeling in the beginning stages of treatment is essential to stabilize fluency at the sentence level.

- The clinician may initially use the same stimulus materials used in baserating dysfluencies in sentences. The child may more readily respond to the same and familiar storybook pictures, toys, or activities that were used to establish the baserates of dysfluencies.

- If the child appears bored with the previously used stimulus materials, the clinician may introduce novel stimuli that will sustain the child's interest.

- Each session may be tape-recorded to later analyze dysfluencies or stutterings (as the clinician defines them) so that a percent dysfluency or stuttering may be calculated. Such an objective measurement of dysfluencies or stutterings is essential to evaluate the child's progress in treatment.

- If the child does not seem to make satisfactory progress when the procedure is used correctly, the clinician may consider alternative procedures (e.g., response cost). To be judged satisfactory progress, fluency should improve significantly from the baserate in a matter of few sessions, although individual differences are important to consider.

- The clinician should praise the child immediately following every fluent production in the beginning stage of treatment. The clinician should be spontaneous and natural-sounding in praising the child. A pleased and pleasant disposition and facial expression should accompany verbal praise. Verbal praise should be enthusiastic and varied.

- The clinician should be careful not to accidentally reinforce dysfluent productions.

- In this exclusive fluency reinforcement program, no corrective feedback is given for dysfluencies, which are completely ignored.

- The clinician should be careful not to induce slow speech, which also may reduce stuttering. In this exclusive fluency reinforcement program, no fluency shaping takes place. No fluency skills are targeted.

- In some cases, the child may begin to speak very slowly to earn the reinforcers; in such cases, the clinician may instruct the child to speak faster. A normally fast rate may be modeled for the child to imitate.

Treatment of Stuttering in Preschoolers:
I. Fluency Reinforcement

Treatment Protocol for Sentences

Scripts for Reinforcing Fluency in Sentences		Note
Clinician	"Sometimes our speech may be bumpy, instead of smooth. I will show you what is bumpy speech. When I say *t-t-t-time*, instead of *time*, my speech is bumpy. What kind of speech is it when I say *t-t-t-time* instead of *time*? Say, it is bumpy speech."	The clinician introduces the concepts of *bumpy speech* and *smooth speech*
Child	"It is bumpy speech."	
Clinician	"Yes, that's what it is called! It is called *bumpy speech*. Our speech can be bumpy in other ways. When I say *I llllike it*, it is bumpy isn't it?"	
Child	"Yes."	The clinician illustrates instances of bumpy speech by producing various types of dysfluencies
Clinician	"When I say, *I-I-I want it*, what do you call it?"	
Child	"Bumpy speech."	
Clinician	"You are right! When I say, *um-um-um I had a birthday party*, what do you call it?"	
Child	"Bumpy speech."	
Clinician	"You are right again! It is all bumpy speech. When we talk without bumps, we call it smooth speech. When I say, *I had a birthday party*, what do you call that?"	
Child	"Smooth speech."	
Clinician	"You are right about that, too! When we talk without bumps, we have smooth speech. Do you sometimes have bumpy speech?"	Probing the child's awareness of his or her bumpy speech
Child	"Sometimes."	
Clinician	"Yes, you do have bumpy speech sometimes. Do you like to have smooth speech instead of bumpy speech?"	Setting the stage for treatment
Child	"Yes."	

Fluency Reinforcement at the Sentence Level, continued

Scripts for Reinforcing Fluency in Sentences		Note
Clinician	"You can do it. You can have smooth speech, I want to help you talk smoothly. Is that Okay?"	Reassures the child
Child	"Okay."	
Clinician	[*showing the picture of a farm scene*] "Okay, let's begin then! You know we have talked about this picture before. You can talk about this again, only this time, I want you to talk smoothly. What do you see here? Do you see a farm or a home? Tell me in a sentence and make it smooth."	The first treatment trial
Child	"I see a farm."	Fluent production
Clinician	"That's great! You said it smoothly! No bumps! Now, what is this animal here? Say it in a smooth sentence."	Verbal praise for fluency; initiates the next trial
Child	"d-d-d-dog."	Sound repetition
Clinician	"Say, *it is a dog.*"	No corrective feedback, but models a sentence production for the child to imitate
Child	"It is a dog."	Fluent imitation of the model
Clinician	"You are excellent! It was smooth speech! I heard no bumps! Now see this man. What is this man doing here? Say, *he is . . .*"	Verbal praise for fluency; initiates the next trial
Child	"Fffffeeding cow."	Sound prolongation; the prompt did not work
Clinician	"Say, *he is feeding the cow.*"	Models a fluent sentence production
Child	"He is feeding the cow."	Fluent imitation of modeled speech
Clinician	"Great! Your speech was smooth. Now, what is this calf doing here? Say, *the calf is jumping.*"	Reinforces the child and initiates the next modeled trial
Child	"The calf is jumping."	Fluent imitation of modeled speech
Clinician	"Fantastic! Your speech was smooth! No bumps, you see! Now let's look at this part here. What is this? Say, *this is hay.*"	Reinforces the child and initiates the next modeled trial
Child	"This is hay."	Fluent imitation of modeled speech

Fluency Reinforcement at the Sentence Level, continued

Scripts for Reinforcing Fluency in Sentences		Note
Clinician	"I like how you are talking! You are really smooth! Now let's see. Who likes to eat hay? Say, *the cow likes to eat hay.*"	Reinforces fluency and initiates the next modeled trial
Child	"The cow lllikes to eat hay."	Sound prolongation
Clinician	"Say, *the cow likes to eat hay.*"	Gives no corrective feedback but initiates the next modeled trial
Child	"The cow likes to eat hay."	Fluent imitation
Clinician	"You are very smart! It was smooth again! Now look here. What is she doing here? Say, *she is milking the cow.*"	Reinforces the child and initiates the next modeled trial
Child	"She is mmmmilking the cow."	Failed imitation; sound prolongation
Clinician	"Say, *she is milking the cow.*"	No corrective feedback; models fluent production
Child	"She is mmmmilking the cow"	Second failed attempt at imitation
Clinician	"What is this pig doing here? Say, *the pig is drinking water.*"	Ignores the previous two failed attempts and moves on; models a new sentence on this next trial
Child	"The pig is drinking water."	Fluent imitation
Clinician	"You are super! Nice, smooth, speech! Now let's look here. What is this cat doing? Say, *the cat is sleeping.*"	Reinforces the child and initiates the next modeled trial
Child	"The cat is sleeping."	A fluently imitated production
Clinician	"Wonderful! You are working really hard to say it smoothly! Okay, what is this girl doing here? Say, *she is chasing the chicken.*"	Reinforces the child and initiates the next modeled trial
Child	"She is chasing the chicken."	Fluent imitation
Clinician	"That was smooth again! You are doing really well! Now look at this part here. What are these children doing here? Say, *they are playing with hay.*"	Reinforces the child and initiates the next modeled trial
Child	"They are playing with hay."	Fluently imitated production
Clinician	"Very nice! I like that smooth speech! Now look at these two men here. What are they doing here? Say, *they are carrying wood.*"	Reinforces the child and initiates the next modeled trial

Fluency Reinforcement at the Sentence Level, continued

Scripts for Reinforcing Fluency in Sentences		Note
Child	"They are c-c-c-carrying wood."	Sound repetition
Clinician	"Say, *they are carrying wood.*"	No corrective feedback; modeling
Child	"They are carrying wood."	Fluently imitated production
Clinician	"You are smooth again! Okay, what are these boys doing here?"	Reinforces the child; omits modeling to initiate an evoked trial
Child	"They are-they are-they are riding horses."	Phrase repetition; failed evoked trial
Clinician	"Say, *they are riding horses.*"	Gives no corrective feedback, models fluent production
Child	"They are riding horses."	Fluently imitated production
Clinician	"Fantastic! I like your smooth speech! Now let us look at another picture. See, this is a picture of a fair going on. Have you ever been to a fair?"	**Introduction of a brief conversational exchange**
Child	"Yes."	
Clinician	"Who took you to the fair? Tell me in a sentence."	A more open-ended question and a request for description
Child	"My mom and d-d-dad took me to the fair."	A part-word (sound) repetition
Clinician	"Say, *my mom and dad took me to the fair.*"	Models a fluent production
Child	"My mom and dad took me to the fair."	A fluent sentence production
Clinician	"That's great! Your speech was smooth! Now look here. What are these kids doing?"	Verbal praise and the next trial
Child	"They are taking a ride."	A fluent production
Clinician	"Wonderful! I like your smooth speech! Did you take a ride when you went to the fair?"	Verbal praise; an open-ended question
Child	"Yes."	
Clinician	"Very good! What kind of ride was it? Tell me in a sentence."	Verbal praise; open-ended question
Child	"It was a roller-coaster ride."	A fluent production
Clinician	"That was smooth speech! You are doing great! Who went on the ride with you? Don't forget to say it in a sentence."	Verbal praise; open-ended question
Child	"My brother went on the ride."	A fluent production
Clinician	"Nice, smooth speech again!"	Verbal praise

Continue to evoke speech and reinforce fluency as shown on the protocols. After two or three sessions in which the child is consistently fluent in evoked sentences (without modeling), shift treatment to the continuous speech level.

Treatment of Stuttering in Preschoolers: I. Fluency Reinforcement

Treatment at the Continuous Speech Level

Overview

- With preschoolers, fluency reinforcement initiated at the isolated sentence level should be shifted to the continuous speech level as soon as practical. When fluency is systematically reinforced at the isolated sentence level in two or three sessions, the child may be ready to move on to the continuous speech level.

- If the child's fluency drops significantly when continuous speech is evoked, the clinician can move back to the sentence level for additional training.

- Continuous speech may be reintroduced after a period of additional training at the level of evoked individual sentences.

- To begin with, the clinician may use the same stimulus materials that were used in baserating fluency at the continuous speech level. The protocols reflect this strategy. Familiar stimuli may evoke continuous speech more readily than unfamiliar stimuli. Eventually, the clinician may introduce new materials to reinforce fluency.

- At this stage, the clinician encourages the child to produce more continuous speech with such prompts as "tell me about everything you see here," "say it in longer sentences," "talk about all that is happening" and so forth.

- As before, in this exclusive fluency reinforcement program, the clinician promptly and enthusiastically reinforces fluent production with verbal praise. No corrective feedback is offered for stuttering, although stuttered sentences may be fluently modeled for the child to imitate.

- The clinician should model all fluent productions at normal rate. Clinician should not induce slow speech by instructions or modeling.

- The clinician may initiate maintenance strategies when the child's fluency in continuous speech is stabilized in the clinic. Family members who initially observe the sessions may join the clinician to evoke and reinforce fluency in the child. Additional information is offered on maintenance strategies in a later section of the protocols.

- The duration of treatment at the continuous speech level will depend on the individual child. The criterion of treatment success and the individual child's progress in treatment will help determine when to dismiss the child from services. A suggested criterion is less than 2% dysfluency or stuttering rate (based on the number of words spoken) in the clinic sessions and well under 5% in natural settings.

Treatment of Stuttering in Preschoolers:
I. Fluency Reinforcement

Treatment Protocol for Continuous Speech

Scripts for Reinforcing Fluency in Continuous Speech		Note
Clinician	[*showing the picture of a farm scene*] "Remember, we talked about this picture before? You told me stories about this picture. I want you to do the same again. This time, I want you to tell me everything in smooth speech. First tell me what these people are doing here. Remember to talk in long and smooth sentences. You can start with, *these people are working on the farm.*"	The first trial; prompting a sentence production
Child	"These people are working on the farm."	Fluent production
Clinician	"Excellent! That was a long and smooth sentence! Okay, now I will point to all these people and you tell me what they are doing. Start with these kids here. Tell me about everything they are doing." [*points to children; continues to point to different parts of the activity to prompt more continuous speech*]	Next trial; instructions to evoke more continuous speech
Child	"The kids are playing with hay. They are throwing hay everywhere."	Fluent production
Clinician	"Good job! I like that smooth speech!"	Gives verbal praise; points to another part of the picture
Child	"They-they-they are climbing on this."	Word repetition
Clinician	"Say, *the children are climbing on this ladder.*"	Models extended fluent production
Child	"The children are climbing on this ladder."	Fluent production
Clinician	"Excellent! Smooth speech! What about this part here?"	Gives verbal praise; points to another part of the picture
Child	"They are chasing all the ch-ch-ch-chickens."	Part-word repetition
Clinician	"Who are chasing all the chickens? I want you to say the whole thing. Say it smoothly this time. Start with *the children . . .* "	Prompting a longer production
Child	"The children are chasing all the chickens."	Fluent production
Clinician	"Great job! You said it smoothly. Tell me all about what these big people are doing. Say it in long sentences like you just did."	Next trial; points to different parts of the picture to evoke more continuous speech

Fluency Reinforcement in Continuous Speech, continued

Scripts for Reinforcing Fluency in Continuous Speech		Note
Child	"These men are working. Woman is milking the cow. This man is feeding the cow. They are carrying wood. They are sitting on the grass. They are eating something."	Continuous fluent speech as the clinician pointed to different parts of the picture
Clinician	"That was fantastic! You said so many sentences smoothly! That's what I want you to do. Now let us look at another picture. Here. You have seen this before. It shows a fair, doesn't it? I will point to different parts of the picture. You tell me all you see and everything that is happening in this picture. Now start here. What do you see and what are they doing?"	Verbal praise for fluent and continuous speech; introduction of new picture stimulus (scene at a fair); points to a portion of the picture
Child	"I see a lot of kids. They are riding on a roller coaster. People here are eating hot dogs. They are taking a ride on this big wheel. They are eating cotton candy."	Produces multiple sentences as the clinician points to different parts of the picture
Clinician	"Excellent! You talked smoothly. I didn't hear any bumps! You said many sentences! Okay, tell me more about this part here. Like you just did, tell me a lot. Say it in many sentences."	Verbal praise; shows another part of the picture
Child	"I see a little zoo here. Kids are petting a . . . [*the clinician prompts: "Lamb"*] lamb. They are looking at the baby cow. The mommy cow is licking the baby cow. He is brushing that horse. The girls are feeding some chickens. Here the boy is taking a ride on a [*the clinician prompts: "Pony"*] pony."	The clinician may prompt a word the child doesn't seem to know
Clinician	"How wonderful! You are saying a lot and still your speech is so smooth! I am so proud of you! Now let's look at this new picture. It shows a birthday party. Tell me what is going on here. First tell me whose birthday is being celebrated."	If the child were to stutter, the clinician would and model the sentence fluently
Child	"This girl's birthday is being celebrated . . . [*the clinician gestures the child to continue*] She is wearing a pink hat. She is opening presents. There are many kids here. They are wearing pink and blue hats. Dad is sitting at the table. Mom is . . . [*the clinician prompts: "pouring"*] pouring juice. These two boys are playing ball. These girls are dancing."	May point to different parts of the picture only when the child hesitates May fluently model a stuttered production for the child to imitate
Clinician	"That was great! You said so many sentences smoothly!"	Verbal praise for fluent speech

Treatment of Stuttering in Preschoolers:
I. Fluency Reinforcement

Treatment at the Narrative Speech Level

Overview

- With preschoolers, fluency reinforcement completed at the continuous speech level should be shifted to the narrative speech level as soon as practical. When 98% or better fluency is sustained at the continuous speech level across several sessions, the child may be ready to move on to the narrative speech level.

- If the child's fluency drops significantly when narrative speech is evoked, the clinician can move back to the continuous speech level for additional training.

- Narrative speech may be reintroduced after a period of additional training at the lower level (continuous speech).

- At this stage, the clinician tells stories to the child and asks the child to retell them. The clinician selects simple stories for preschoolers; storybooks written for preschool children may be selected for treatment sessions. In selecting the stories, the clinician may consider the ethnocultural background of the child. The selected stories may be of universal appeal, but the clinician may consider stories from the child's cultural background.

- The clinician encourages the child to tell the story in all its details and prompts story elements when the child is unsure. Various other strategies to promote good narrative speech are specified in the protocols that follow.

- As before, in this exclusive fluency reinforcement program, the clinician promptly and enthusiastically reinforces fluent production with verbal praise. No corrective feedback is offered for stuttering, and modeling of fluent productions is kept to a minimum.

- The clinician should tell the story at normal rate and should not inadvertently induce a slower rate in the child.

- The clinician may continue to use the maintenance strategies introduced in the previous level of treatment. The child may be taken out of the treatment room to informally monitor fluency as the child narrates stories or bits of experiences.

The duration of treatment at the narrative speech level will depend on the individual child. The criterion of treatment success and the individual child's progress in treatment will help determine when to dismiss the child from services. A suggested criterion is less than 2% dysfluency or stuttering rate (based on the number of words spoken) in the clinic sessions and well under 5% in natural settings.

Treatment of Stuttering in Preschoolers:
I. Fluency Reinforcement

Treatment Protocol for Narrative Speech

Scripts for Reinforcing Fluency in Story Retelling		Note
Clinician	"Now, I will tell you a story and I want you to remember everything I tell you. When I am finished, I want **you** to tell **me** the same story. I want you to talk smoothly as you tell me the stories. Okay?" "Now listen carefully. Once upon a time there was a little boy. Every time he saw a big moon in the sky, he would ask his Mom, 'Mom can I touch the moon?' Mom would say, 'it is too far! If you are a bird, you can fly to the moon to touch it.' Then one morning, the boy got up from the bed, ran to Mom, and told, 'Mom, last night I flew to the moon and touched it!' The Mom said, 'yes, I saw you touch the moon.' The end. Now you tell me the same story. You can start with, *once upon a time* . . ."	Introducing the storytelling task
Child	"Once upon a t-t-time . . ."	Sound repetition
Clinician	"Say, *once upon a time* . . ."	Models fluent production; prompts the child when the child hesitates
Child	"Once upon a time, there was a little boy. When he saw a big moon in the sky, he wanted to touch it. [*the clinician prompts: "He asked Mom . . ."*] He asked 'Mom, can I touch it?' Mom said, 'if you are a bird, you can touch it.' [*the clinician prompts: "Then one morning . . ."*] Then one morning, the boy got up from the bed, ran to Mom, and said, 'Mom, last night I flew to the moon and touched it!' [*the clinician prompts: "and the Mom said . . ."*] The Mom said, 'I saw you touch the moon.' The end."	A fluent production Receives prompts from the clinician whenever there is a bit of a hesitation in the flow of speech
Clinician	"What a nice story you told me! I liked that smooth speech you had! You are a good storyteller! I will tell you another story. Listen carefully. I want you to tell me the story again." "You know what a crow is? It is black bird. One hot day a crow was very thirsty. He was looking for water. He flew here. He flew there, looking for water. Then he saw a pot with *(continued)*	Verbal praise Tells a new story to the child Prompts the child whenever the child is unsure of what to say

Fluency Reinforcement in Story Telling, continued

Scripts for Reinforcing Fluency in Story Retelling		Note
Clinician *(continues)*	"a little bit of water in it. He sat on the top of the pot and put his head into it to drink the water. But he couldn't reach the water. He tried and tried, but he couldn't reach the water. He then looked around and saw some pebbles on the ground. He put one pebble into the pot. He put another pebble into the pot. He put some more pebbles into the pot. He saw the water coming up! He put a lot more pebbles into the pot. The water came all the way up and the crow drank the water! The end. Now you tell me the story. Remember smooth speech."	
Child	"There was a crow. He was thirsty. He wanted water. [*the clinician prompted: "He flew . . . "*] He flew here. He flew there. Then he saw a pot. There was water in it. The c-c-crow [*the clinician interrupts the child with modeling "the crow"*] The crow sat on the pot and put his head inside. He couldn't reach the water. He saw pebbles. He put one pebble in the pot. He p-p-put [*the clinician interrupts the child with modeling "he put"*] He put another pebble. He put some more pebbles in the pot. The water came up. The crow drank water. The end!"	The child tells the story The clinician models fluent production without giving corrective feedback for stuttering
Clinician	"Thank you! You told me a nice story! Your speech was smooth, too! "Do you like these stories? Are you ready for another story?"	Verbal praise
Child	"Yes."	
Clinician	"Once upon a time, there was a big ant. One day, the ant was creeping along in the forest. It was a hot day. The ant was very thirsty. Remember the thirsty crow? The ant had the same problem. While moving along, he saw a little pond. The ant was very happy to see the pond full of water! But when he tried to drink some water, he fell into the pond. He was drowning! He was going to die! He cried out help, help! Who is there to help? Well, there was a bird sitting on a tree. She was watching the sad ant. To save the ant, the bird dropped a big leaf to the pond! The ant climbed on to the leaf. The leaf floated to the shore and the *(continued)*	Tells a longer story, but stops in the middle to have the child tell the first part

Fluency Reinforcement in Story Telling, continued

Scripts for Reinforcing Fluency in Story Retelling		Note
Clinician *(continues)*	"ant climbed out of the pond. The story is not finished, but you tell me what I just told you. I will tell you the rest after I hear this much from you. Don't forget smooth speech."	Reminds *smooth speech*
Child	"A big ant was thirsty like the crow. He was creeping in the forest. It was a hot day. He then saw a little pond. He wanted to drink water. But he fell into the pond. He was going to die! So he cried, help! help! There was no one there to help. But a bird was sitting in a tree. She saw the ant. She dropped a big leaf to the pond. The ant climbed on to the leaf and came out of the pond!"	Child retells the first part of the story
Clinician	"That was excellent! You remembered everything! You did not have a single bump! It was all so smooth! "Now I will tell you the rest of the story. The ant was tired from his adventure in the pond. He wanted to go home. As he was going home, he saw a hunter. The hunter was trying to catch the bird with a net. The bird did not see the hunter, so he was still happily sitting there! Just when the hunter was ready to throw the net on the bird to catch it, the big ant bit him hard on his toe! What did the hunter do? He just screamed 'Ouch!' The bird heard the scream and quickly flew away! The bird saved the ant first and then the ant saved the bird! The end. "Now you tell me the rest of the story I just told you. Tell me in your smooth speech."	Verbal praise Tells the rest of the story
Child	"The ant was tired. He was going home. He then sss-saw [*the clinician models* "he then saw . . . "] He then saw a hunter. Hunter was trying to catch the bird. [*clinician prompts: How?*] He tried to catch the bird with a net. The bird did not see the hunter. He was happily sitting on the tree. When the hunter was going to catch the bird, the big ant bit his toe! The hunter screamed 'Ouch!' The bird heard it. He flew away. [*the clinician prompts: "Who saved whom?"*] The bird saved the ant. Then, ant saved the bird."	Retells the story; gets prompted and receives corrective feedback for dysfluencies
Clinician	"That was great! Again you remembered the story! I liked your smooth speech, too!"	Verbal praise for fluent narration

Give additional training at the narrative speech level if necessary.

Treatment of Stuttering in Preschoolers:
I. Fluency Reinforcement

Treatment at the Conversational Speech Level

Overview

- With preschoolers, fluency reinforcement completed at the narrative speech level should be shifted to the conversational speech level as soon as practical. When 98% or better fluency is sustained at the narrative speech level across several sessions, the child may be ready to move on to the conversational speech level.

- At this stage, the clinician simply talks with the child and reinforces all fluent productions with verbal praise.

- At this level of training, the clinician asks questions and encourages longer sentence productions in the conversational format. Initially, the clinician may ask questions about the child's family, names of parents, siblings, and friends, while encouraging complete sentence productions.

- As before, in this exclusive fluency reinforcement program, the clinician promptly and enthusiastically reinforces fluent production with verbal praise. No corrective feedback is offered for stuttering, and modeling of fluent productions is kept to a minimum.

- The clinician should talk to the child at a normal rate and should not inadvertently induce a slower rate in the child.

- The clinician may continue to use the maintenance strategies introduced in the previous level of treatment. The child may be taken out of the treatment room to informally monitor fluent conversational speech.

The duration of treatment at the conversational speech level will depend on the individual child. The criterion of treatment success and the individual child's progress in treatment will help determine when to dismiss the child from services. A suggested criterion is less than 2% dysfluency or stuttering rate (based on the number of words spoken) in the clinic sessions and well under 5% in natural settings.

Treatment of Stuttering in Preschoolers:
I. Fluency Reinforcement

Treatment Protocol for Conversational Speech

Scripts for Reinforcing Fluency in Conversational Speech		Note
Clinician	"You have been doing great! You speak in smooth speech most of the time. I liked the way you told me some stories last time. Now we are going to just talk for a while. I want you to practice smooth speech as we talk. Okay?"	Introduces the conversational speech task
Child	"Okay!"	
Clinician	"What's your Mom's name? You should start with *My Mom's . . .* and tell me in a complete, long sentence."	Asks simple questions, prompts the production of complete sentences
Child	"My Mom's name is Lydia."	A fluent, spontaneous production
Clinician	"Excellent! Your speech was very smooth! It was a long sentence! Now tell me, what's your Dad's name?"	Verbal praise
Child	"My Dad's name is Carlos."	Fluent production
Clinician	"You are working very hard! I like your smooth speech and long sentences! How many brothers do you have? Remember the sentence."	Verbal praise Next question
Child	"Two." [*the clinician prompts "I have . . ."*] I have two brothers."	Fluent production, prompted longer sentence
Clinician	"Great job! Are they both older than you?"	Verbal praise Next question
Child	"No. One brother is my baby brother. Another is older."	Verbal praise Next question
Clinician	"How nice! Smooth speech and good sentences! Tell me the name of your baby brother and the name of your older brother. Use complete sentences. You should start, *the name of my . . .*"	Verbal praise Next question
Child	"The name of my baby brother is Antonio. The name of my older brother is Noah."	Fluent production
Clinician	"That was fantastic. You know your speech was smooth, right? You are doing really well!"	Verbal praise Continues this line of conversation

Fluency Reinforcement in Conversational Speech, continued

Scripts for Reinforcing Fluency in Conversational Speech		Note
Clinician	"Is your birthday coming up?"	Introduces a new topic for conversation
Child	"I already had my birthday."	Fluent production
Clinician	"Oh you did? When was it? Did you have a big party? Tell me all about the party. Tell me how many kids attended, what kind of gifts you got, what kind of cake did you have, and all that."	Prompts more continuous speech
Child	"I had a party yesterday. It was a big party. Many friends came . . . [*the clinician prompts: "Tell me some names of your friends."*] My friend Cindy came. Timmy came also. Jennifer, Erick, and Alicia also came. [*the clinician prompts: "Tell me about gifts."*] I got lots of gifts. I got a toy car, storybooks, some chocolate. [*the clinician prompts: "What did you get from your Mom and Dad?"*] I got a T-shirt from Mom and Dad. I also got a big dump truck! And a big puzzle. My brother gave me crayons."	Fluent, relatively more spontaneous production
Clinician	"Yes, you did get a lot of nice gifts! And your speech was very smooth!" "Now tell me, what did you all eat and drink?"	Verbal praise Open-ended question
Child	"We ate chocolate cake. [*the clinician prompts: "Is that your favorite kind? What other kinds of cakes do you like?"*] Yeah, I like chocolate cake. I also like cheesecake. [*the clinician prompts: "What about drinks?"*] We had lemonade. Cindy wanted milk. Erick wanted coke."	Fluent production
Clinician	"Thank you, that was smooth speech! "Did you guys play any games? Tell me how you played it"	Verbal praise Next question
Child	"I played with my dump truck. They all worked on the puzzle I got. I also worked on the puzzle. Timmy played with my dump truck."	Fluent, continuous speech
Clinician	"Nice, smooth speech! Did you give something to your friends?"	Verbal praise Next question
Child	"Yeah. They all got a hat, balloons, and candy."	Fluent production
Clinician	"Great talking! Looks like you guys had a great time!"	Verbal praise
Child	"It was fun!"	Fluent production

Give additional training at the conversational speech level if necessary.

Treatment of Stuttering in Preschoolers:
I. Fluency Reinforcement

Treatment Recording Sheet

Personalize and print this page from the CD.

Name of the child:	DOB:
Name of the parents:	Phone:
Diagnosis: Stuttering	Session date(s):
Clinician:	Comments:

Chart the child's progress for each session with your preferred method. You may calculate a percent dysfluency or stuttering rate based on the number of words spoken. If more detailed data are warranted, score the individual dysfluency types and add them up to calculate the dysfluency rate.

Essential Measures		Optional Measures: Frequency of Specific Dysfluency Types					
Dates of Service	Percent Stuttering	Prolongations	Pauses	Repetitions	Interjections	Revisions	Incomplete Phrases

Treatment of Stuttering in Preschoolers: I. Fluency Reinforcement

Probe Protocol

Probe Procedure

- Record two conversational speech samples, each 5 to 7 minutes in duration
- Record a 3-minute monologue; ask the child to talk about a topic such as:
  - ➢ Birthday parties
  - ➢ Vacations
  - ➢ Visit to a zoo or a theme park
  - ➢ Favorite games or TV shows
  - ➢ Weekend activities
  - ➢ Any other child-specific topic
- Obtain a 5-minute home speech sample
- Record one or more extraclinic speech samples in such places as the child's home, and if relevant, the classroom, cafeteria, and the playground
- Analyze the percent dysfluency or stuttering rate
- Personalize the *Probe Recording Sheet* on the CD and record the dysfluency or stuttering rates; print the sheet for child's clinical file

Treatment of Stuttering in Preschoolers:
I. Fluency Reinforcement
Probe Recording Sheet

Personalize and print this page from the CD.

Name of the child:	DOB:
Name of the parents:	Phone:
Diagnosis: Stuttering	Session date(s):
Clinician:	Comments:

Analyze the probe speech samples with your preferred method. You may calculate a percent dysfluency or stuttering rate based on the number of words spoken. If more detailed data are warranted, score the individual dysfluency types and add them up to calculate the dysfluency rate.

Take at least three clinic probe samples. If possible, obtain three extraclinic probe samples.

Essential Measures		Optional Measures: Frequency of Specific Dysfluency Types					
Dates/Setting of Probe	Percent Stuttering	PRO	PAU	REP	INT	REV	INC
1. /mm/dd/yy/ Clinic							
2. /mm/dd/yy/ Clinic							
3. /mm/dd/yy/ Clinic							
1. /mm/dd/yy/ Home							
2. /mm/dd/yy/ Classroom							
3. /mm/dd/yy/ Playground							

PRO (Prolongations); PAU (Pauses); REP (Repetitions); INT (Interjections); REV (Revisions); INC (Incomplete phrases).

Dismiss the child from current services when the child's stuttering or dysfluency rate stays below the target percentage in conversational probes. Suggested criterion is less than 2% dysfluency rate in the clinic and less than 5% in natural settings. Schedule follow-ups and booster treatments as needed.

Treatment of Stuttering in Preschoolers:
II. Fluency Reinforcement Plus Corrective Feedback

Overview

Fluency reinforcement, described in the previous section to treat stuttering in preschool children, is the most minimal of all treatment procedures in that only the positive reinforcement for fluent productions is implemented. Dysfluencies are completely ignored. Therefore, a single positive reinforcement contingency is placed on fluent productions.

The clinician may, however, offer reinforcement for fluent productions *and* corrective verbal feedback for dysfluent productions in treating preschool children. In this procedure, the clinician places contingencies on fluent as well as dysfluent productions. A combination of fluency reinforcement and corrective feedback for dysfluencies may be more effective, although the combination has not been experimentally evaluated against each of the single procedures. Nonetheless, in doing so, the clinician will have combined two procedures known to be effective in their own right. Therefore, clinicians may ethically use a combination of reinforcement and corrective feedback procedures.

Before starting treatment with a combination of reinforcement and corrective feedback, the clinician should establish the baserates of dysfluencies in sentences, conversational speech, and narratives as described in Section I. Regardless of the treatment procedures used, the baserate protocols remain the same for preschool children. After establishing the baserates, the clinician may chose either the exclusive fluency reinforcement procedure, the fluency reinforcement plus corrective feedback procedure, or the response cost method.

Student clinicians and parents can be relatively easily trained in reinforcing fluency and providing corrective feedback for stuttering. Most parents may be trained to give subtle hints and prompts to help maintain fluency in their children.

Treatment protocols are offered at four levels of training:

1. Treatment at the sentence level
2. Treatment at the continuous speech level
3. Treatment at the narrative speech level
4. Treatment at the conversational speech level

Treatment of Stuttering in Preschoolers:
II. Fluency Reinforcement Plus Corrective Feedback

Treatment at the Sentence Level

Overview

- With preschoolers, fluency reinforcement plus corrective feedback may be initiated at the sentence level.

- When the child produces single words and phrases in response to questions about the stimulus materials, the clinician may prompt, instruct, or otherwise encourage the child to produce shorter and longer sentences.

- In contrast to the baserate sessions, however, the clinician may model and immediately ask the child to imitate shorter and longer sentences. Stuttering frequency typically decreases when children immediately imitate a fluent production, which gives an opportunity for the clinician to reinforce fluency. Frequent modeling in the beginning stages of treatment is essential to stabilize fluency at the sentence level.

- With most children, verbal reinforcement may be effective. A small gift at the end of the session may help sustain the child's interest in the treatment session.

- Positive reinforcement should be prompt, natural, and should follow all fluent productions in the beginning stage of treatment. Subsequently, reinforcement may be intermittent and approximate more natural conversational exchanges.

- The clinician may reinforce fluent productions with a variety of verbal statements:
  - ➤ That was great! You said it smoothly!
  - ➤ Wonderful! You are such a smooth talker!
  - ➤ That was nice smooth speech!
  - ➤ I like your smooth speech!
  - ➤ You are doing a great job!

- When the child produces a dysfluency, the clinician gives verbal corrective feedback. The feedback should be prompt, clear, and objective in tone. The clinician may use several forms of corrective feedback:
  - ➤ Stop, that was bumpy!
  - ➤ Oh no! You didn't say it smoothly!
  - ➤ That was bumpy!
  - ➤ Stop, you are having trouble saying it!
  - ➤ No, that was not smooth!

- The same stimulus materials used in baserating dysfluencies in sentences may be appropriate for treatment sessions. Familiar stories and pictures may more readily evoke speech from the child.

- If previously used stimuli fail to provoke interest in the child, the clinician may introduce novel stimuli that will sustain the child's interest.

- To evaluate the child's progress in treatment, the clinician may tape-record each session and later calculate the percent dysfluency or stuttering rate.

- If a correctly implemented combination of positive reinforcement and corrective feedback does not produce satisfactory results, the clinician may consider alternative procedures (e.g., response cost). Although there will be individual differences, stuttering frequency should be significantly reduced in a matter of few sessions. If not, the progress may be judged unsatisfactory, leading to a change in the treatment procedure.

- In the beginning stage of treatment, the clinician should praise the child immediately following every fluent production and offer corrective feedback for each dysfluency or stuttering. The clinician should be careful not to reinforce a dysfluent production, nor to punish a fluent production. Each type of consequence should be strictly contingent on the specified response topography. The verbal praise should be delivered in a spontaneous and enthusiastic manner. The corrective feedback should be objective and without unfavorable emotional overtones.

- The clinician should take note that in this combination of reinforcement for fluency and corrective feedback for dysfluencies, such fluency shaping skills as gentle phonatory onset, airflow management, and slower rate of speech are not targeted. A common error to be avoided is to inadvertently induce slower speech. Fluent productions should be modeled at a normal rate of speech.

- If the child begins to speak slowly to minimize stuttering, earn the reinforcers, and to avoid corrective feedback for stuttering, the clinician may instruct the child to speak faster. A normally fast rate may be modeled for the child to imitate.

- The same introductory scenario given for an exclusive fluency reinforcement program is replicated for fluency reinforcement plus corrective feedback. Only the actual treatment procedures include both reinforcement and corrective feedback.

Treatment of Stuttering in Preschoolers:
II. Fluency Reinforcement Plus Corrective Feedback

Treatment Protocol for Sentences

Scripts for Reinforcement Plus Corrective Feedback in Sentences		Note
Clinician	"Sometimes our speech may be bumpy, instead of smooth. I will show you what is bumpy speech. When I say *t-t-t-time*, instead of *time*, my speech is bumpy. What kind of speech is it when I say *t-t-t-time* instead of *time*? Say, it is bumpy speech."	The clinician introduces the concepts of *bumpy speech* and *smooth speech*
Child	"It is bumpy speech."	
Clinician	"Yes, that's what it is called! It is called *bumpy speech*. Our speech can be bumpy in other ways. When I say *I llllike it*, it is bumpy isn't it?"	The clinician illustrates instances of bumpy speech by producing various types of dysfluencies
Child	"Yes."	
Clinician	"When I say, *I-I-I want it*, what do you call it?"	
Child	"Bumpy speech."	
Clinician	"You are right! When I say, *um-um-um I had a birthday party*, what do you call it?"	
Child	"Bumpy speech."	
Clinician	"You are right again! It is all bumpy speech. When we talk without bumps, we call it smooth speech. When I say, *I had a birthday party*, what do you call that?"	
Child	"Smooth speech."	
Clinician	"You are right about that, too! When we talk without bumps, we have smooth speech. Do you sometimes have bumpy speech?"	Probing the child's awareness of his or her bumpy speech
Child	"Sometimes."	
Clinician	"Yes, you do have bumpy speech sometimes. Do you like to have smooth speech instead of bumpy speech?"	Setting the stage for treatment
Child	"Yes."	

Reinforcement Plus Corrective Feedback in Sentences, continued

Scripts for Reinforcement Plus Corrective Feedback in Sentences		Note
Clinician	"You can do it. You can have smooth speech, I want to help you talk smoothly. Is that Okay?"	Reassures the child
Child	"Okay."	
Clinician	[*showing the picture of a farm scene*] "Alright, let's begin then! You know we have talked about this picture before. You can talk about this again, only this time, I want you to talk smoothly. What do you see here? Do you see a farm or a home? Tell me in a sentence and make it smooth."	The first treatment trial
Child	"I see a farm."	Fluent production
Clinician	"That's great! You said it smoothly! No bumps! Now, what is this animal here? Say it in a smooth sentence."	Verbal praise for fluency; initiates the next trial
Child	"d-d-d-d . . . "	Sound repetition
Clinician	"Oops! That was bumpy. Say, *it is a dog.*"	Offers corrective feedback and models fluent production of the child's dysfluent speech; **note the child is not allowed to continue the dysfluent speech**
Child	"It is a dog."	Fluent imitation of the model
Clinician	"You are excellent! It was smooth speech! I heard no bumps! Now see this man. What is this man doing here? Say, *he is . . .* "	Verbal praise for fluency; initiates the next trial
Child	"Fffffee . . . "	Sound prolongation; the prompt did not work; **the child gets stopped**
Clinician	"Stop! That was a bump, wasn't it? Say, *he is feeding the cow.*"	Gives corrective feedback and models fluent production of the child's dysfluent speech
Child	"He is feeding the cow."	Fluent imitation of modeled speech
Clinician	"Great! Your speech was smooth. Now, what is this calf doing here? Say, *the calf is jumping.*"	Reinforces the child and initiates the next modeled trial
Child	"The calf is jumping."	Fluent imitation of modeled speech
Clinician	"Fantastic! Your speech was smooth! No bumps, you see! Now let's look at this part here. What is this? Say, *this is hay.*"	Reinforces the child and initiates the next modeled trial
Child	"This is hay."	Fluent imitation of modeled speech

Reinforcement Plus Corrective Feedback in Sentences, continued

Scripts for Reinforcement Plus Corrective Feedback in Sentences		Note
Clinician	"I like how you are talking! You are really smooth! Now let's see. Who likes to eat hay? Say, *the cow likes to eat hay.*"	Reinforces fluency and initiates the next modeled trial
Child	"The cow lllli . . ."	Sound prolongation
Clinician	"No, that was bumpy. Say, *the cow likes to eat hay.*"	Gives corrective feedback and models fluent production
Child	"The cow likes to eat hay."	Fluent imitation
Clinician	"You are very smart! It was smooth again! Now look here. What is she doing here? Say, *she is milking the cow.*"	Reinforces the child and initiates the next modeled trial
Child	"She is mmmmil . . ."	Failed imitation; sound prolongation
Clinician	"Oops! Bumpy speech. Say, *she is milking the cow.*"	Gives corrective feedback and models fluent production
Child	"She is mmmmil . . ."	Second failed attempt at imitation
Clinician	"Stop! That was bumpy. Now look here! What is this pig doing here? Say, *the pig is drinking water.*"	Ignores the previous two failed attempts and moves on; models a new sentence on this next trial
Child	"The pig is drinking water."	Fluent imitation
Clinician	"You are super! Nice, smooth, speech! Now let's look here. What is this cat doing? Say, *the cat is sleeping.*"	Reinforces the child and initiates the next modeled trial
Child	"The cat is sleeping."	A fluently imitated production
Clinician	"Wonderful! You are working really hard to say it smoothly! Okay, what is this girl doing here? Say, *she is chasing the chicken.*"	Reinforces the child and initiates the next modeled trial
Child	"She is chasing the chicken."	Fluent imitation
Clinician	"That was smooth again! You are doing really well! Now look at this part here. What are these children doing here? Say, *they are playing with hay.*"	Reinforces the child and initiates the next modeled trial
Child	"They are playing with hay."	Fluently imitated production
Clinician	"Very nice! I like that smooth speech! Now look at these two men here. What are they doing here? Say, *they are carrying wood.*"	Reinforces the child and initiates the next modeled trial
Child	"They are c-c-c-ca . . ."	Sound repetition; gets stopped

Reinforcement Plus Corrective Feedback in Sentences, continued

Scripts for Reinforcement Plus Corrective Feedback in Sentences		Note
Clinician	"Stop! That was bumpy. Say, *they are carrying wood.*"	Corrective feedback; modeling
Child	"They are carrying wood."	Fluently imitated production
Clinician	"You are smooth again! Okay, what are these boys doing here?"	Reinforces the child; omits modeling to initiate an evoked trial
Child	"They are-they are-they are . . ."	Phrase repetition; failed evoked trial
Clinician	"That was bumpy. Say, *they are riding horses.*"	Gives corrective feedback, models fluent production
Child	"They are riding horses."	Fluently imitated production
Clinician	"Fantastic! I like your smooth speech! See, this shows a fair. Have you ever been to a fair?"	Introduction of a brief conversational exchange
Child	"Yes."	
Clinician	"Who took you to the fair?"	An open-ended question
Child	"My Mom and D-d-d . . ."	A part-word (sound) repetition
Clinician	"No, that was bumpy. Say, *my Mom and Dad took me to the fair.*"	Models a fluent production
Child	"My Mom and Dad took me to the fair."	A fluent sentence production
Clinician	"That's great! Your speech was smooth! Now look here. What are these kids doing?"	Verbal praise and the next trial
Child	"They are taking a ride."	A fluent production
Clinician	"Wonderful! I like your smooth speech! Did you take a ride when you went to the fair?"	Verbal praise; an open-ended question
Child	"Yes."	
Clinician	"Very good! What kind of ride was it?"	Verbal praise; open-ended question
Child	"It was a roller-coaster ride."	A fluent production
Clinician	"That was smooth speech! You are doing great! Who went on the ride with you? Don't forget to say it in a sentence."	Verbal praise; open-ended question
Child	"My brother went on the ride."	A fluent production
Clinician	"Nice, smooth speech again! Thanks for working so hard!"	Verbal praise

Continue to evoke speech with reinforcement for fluency and corrective feedback for stuttering as shown on the protocols. After two or three sessions in which the child is consistently fluent in evoked sentences (without modeling), shift treatment to the continuous speech level.

Treatment of Stuttering in Preschoolers:
II. Fluency Reinforcement Plus Corrective Feedback

Treatment at the Continuous Speech Level

Overview

- With preschoolers, reinforcement plus corrective feedback initiated at the isolated sentence level should be shifted to the continuous speech level as soon as practical. When fluency systematically increases at the isolated sentence level in two or three sessions, the child may be ready to move on to the continuous speech level.

- If the child's fluency drops significantly when continuous speech is evoked, the clinician can move back to the sentence level for additional training.

- Continuous speech may be reintroduced after a period of additional training at the level of evoked individual sentences.

- To begin with, the clinician may use the same stimulus materials that were used in baserating fluency at the continuous speech level. The protocols reflect this strategy. Familiar stimuli may evoke continuous speech more readily than unfamiliar stimuli. Eventually, the clinician may introduce new materials to reinforce fluency.

- At this stage, the clinician encourages the child to produce more continuous speech with such prompts as "tell me about everything you see here," "say it in longer sentences," "talk about all that is happening" and so forth.

- As before, the clinician promptly and enthusiastically reinforces fluent production with verbal praise. The clinician equally promptly offers corrective feedback for stuttering and fluently models stuttered sentences for the child to imitate.

- The clinician should model all fluent productions at normal rate. Clinician should not induce slow speech by instructions or modeling.

- The clinician may initiate maintenance strategies when the child's fluency in continuous speech is stabilized in the clinic. Family members who initially observe the sessions may join the clinician to evoke and reinforce fluency in the child. Additional information is offered on maintenance strategies in a later section of the protocols.

- The duration of treatment at the continuous speech level will depend on the individual child. The criterion of treatment success and the individual child's progress in treatment will help determine when to dismiss the child from services. A suggested criterion is less than 2% dysfluency or stuttering rate (based on the number of words spoken) in the clinic sessions and well under 5% in natural settings.

Treatment of Stuttering in Preschoolers:
II. Fluency Reinforcement Plus Corrective Feedback

Treatment Protocol for Continuous Speech

Scripts for Reinforcement Plus Corrective Feedback in Continuous Speech		Note
Clinician	[*showing the picture of a farm scene*] "Remember, we talked about this picture before? You told me stories about this picture. I want you to do the same again. This time, I want you to tell me everything in smooth speech. First tell me what these people are doing here. Remember to talk in long and smooth sentences. You can start with, *these people are working on the farm.*"	The first trial; prompting a sentence production
Child	"These people are working on the farm."	Fluent production
Clinician	"Excellent! That was a long and smooth sentence! Okay, now I will point to all these people and you tell me what they are doing. Start with these kids here. Tell me about everything they are doing." [*points to children; continues to point to different parts of the activity to prompt more continuous speech*]	Next trial; instructions to evoke more continuous speech
Child	"The kids are playing with hay. They are throwing hay everywhere."	Fluent production
Clinician	"Good job! I like that smooth speech!"	Gives verbal praise; points to another part of the picture
Child	"They-they-they . . . "	Word repetition
Clinician	"Oops! That was bumpy. Say, *the children are climbing on this ladder.*"	Gives corrective feedback; models extended speech
Child	"The children are climbing on this ladder."	Fluent production
Clinician	"Excellent! Smooth speech! What about this part here?"	Gives verbal praise; points to another part of the picture
Child	"They are chasing all the ch-ch-ch . . . "	Part-word repetition
Clinician	"No, that was bumpy. Who are chasing all the chickens? I want you to say the whole thing. Say it smoothly this time. Start with *the children . . .*"	Gives corrective feedback; prompts a longer production
Child	"The children are chasing all the chickens."	Fluent production
Clinician	"Great job! You said it smoothly. Tell me all about what these big people are doing. Say it in long sentences like you just did."	Next trial; points to different parts of the picture to evoke more continuous speech

Fluency Reinforcement Plus Corrective Feedback in Continuous Speech, continued

Scripts for Reinforcement Plus Corrective Feedback in Continuous Speech		Note
Child	"These men are working. Woman is milking the cow. This man is feeding the cow. They are carrying wood. They are sitting on the grass. They are eating something."	Continuous fluent speech as the clinician pointed to different parts of the picture
Clinician	"That was fantastic! You said so many sentences smoothly! That's what I want you to do. Now let us look at this new picture here. You have seen this before. It shows a fair, doesn't it? I will point to different parts of the picture. You tell me all you see and everything that is happening in this picture. Now start here. What do you see and what are they doing?"	Verbal praise for fluent and continuous speech; introduction of new picture stimulus (scene at a fair); points to a portion of the picture
Child	"I see a lot of kids. They are riding on a roller coaster. People here are eating hot dogs. They are taking a ride on this big wheel. They are eating cotton candy."	Produces multiple sentences as the clinician points to different parts of the picture
Clinician	"Excellent! You talked smoothly. I didn't hear any bumps! You said many sentences! Okay, tell me more about this part here. Like you just did, tell me a lot. Say it in many sentences."	Verbal praise; shows another part of the picture
Child	"I see a little zoo here. Kids are petting a . . . [*the clinician prompts: "Lamb"*] lamb. They are looking at the baby cow. The mommy cow is licking the baby cow. He is brushing that horse. The girls are feeding some chickens. Here the boy is taking a ride on a [*the clinician prompts: "Pony"*] pony."	The clinician may prompt a word the child doesn't seem to know
Clinician	"How wonderful! You are saying a lot and still your speech is so smooth! I am so proud of you! Now let's look at this new picture. It shows a birthday party. Tell me what is going on here. First tell me whose birthday is being celebrated."	If the child were to stutter, the clinician would give corrective feedback and model the sentence fluently
Child	"This girl's birthday . . . [*the clinician gestures the child to continue*] She is wearing a pink hat. She is opening presents. There are many kids here. They are wearing pink and blue hats. Dad is setting the table. Mom is . . . [*the clinician prompts: "pouring"*] pouring juice. These two boys are playing ball. These girls are dancing."	Gets prompted
Clinician	"That was great! You said so many sentences smoothly!"	Verbal praise for fluent speech

Treatment of Stuttering in Preschoolers: II. Fluency Reinforcement Plus Corrective Feedback

Treatment at the Narrative Speech Level

Overview

- With preschoolers, reinforcement plus corrective feedback completed at the continuous speech level should be advanced to the narrative speech level as soon as practical. When fluency systematically increases at the continuous speech level across several sessions, the child may be ready to move on to the narrative speech level.

- If the child's fluency drops significantly when narrative speech is evoked, the clinician can move back to the lower level for additional training.

- Narrative speech may be reintroduced after a period of additional training at the lower level.

- At this stage, the clinician tells stories to the child and asks the child to retell them. The clinician selects simple stories for preschoolers; storybooks written for preschool children may be selected for treatment sessions. In selecting the stories, the clinician should consider the ethnocultural background of the child. The selected stories may be of universal appeal, but the clinician should, in addition, select stories from the child's cultural background.

- The clinician encourages the child to tell the story in all its details and prompts story elements when the child is unsure. Various other strategies to promote good narrative speech are specified in the protocols that follow.

- The clinician promptly and enthusiastically reinforces fluent production with verbal praise. The clinician equally promptly offers corrective feedback for stuttering. The need for modeling at this level of treatment should be minimal.

- The clinician should tell the stories at the normal rate. Clinician should not induce slow speech by instructions, modeling, or the manner of storytelling.

- The clinician may continue to implement the maintenance strategies introduced in the earlier level. Family members who initially observe the sessions may join the clinician to evoke and reinforce fluency in the child. Additional information is offered on maintenance strategies in a later section of the protocols.

- The duration of treatment at the narrative speech level will depend on the individual child. The criterion of treatment success and the individual child's progress in treatment will help determine when to dismiss the child from services. A suggested criterion is less than 2% dysfluency or stuttering rate (based on the number of words spoken) in the clinic sessions and well under 5% in natural settings.

Treatment of Stuttering in Preschoolers:
II. Fluency Reinforcement Plus Corrective Feedback

Treatment Protocol for Narrative Speech

Scripts for Reinforcement Plus Corrective Feedback in Story Retelling		Note
Clinician	"Now, I will tell you a story and I want you to remember everything I tell you. When I am finished, I want **you** to tell **me** the same story. I want you to talk smoothly as you tell me the stories. Okay?	Introducing the storytelling task
	"Now listen carefully. Once upon a time there was a little boy. Every time he saw a big moon in the sky, he would ask his Mom, 'Mom, can I touch the moon?' Mom would say, 'it is too far! If you are a bird, you can fly to the moon to touch it.' Then one morning, the boy got up from the bed, ran to Mom, and told, 'Mom, last night I flew to the moon and touched it!' The Mom said, 'yes, I saw you touch the moon.' The end. Now you tell me the same story. You can start with once upon a time . . . "	
Child	"Once upon a t-t-t . . . "	Sound repetition
Clinician	"Stop! That was bumpy. Say, *once upon a time* . . . "	Corrective feedback and modeling
Child	"Once upon a time, there was a little boy. When he saw a big moon in the sky, he wanted to touch it. [*the clinician prompts: "He asked Mom . . . "*] He asked 'Mom, can I touch it?' Mom said, 'if you are a bird, you can touch it.' [*the clinician prompts: "Then one morning . . . "*] Then one morning, the boy got up from the bed, ran to Mom, and said 'Mom, last night I flew to the moon and touched it!' [*the clinician prompts: "and the Mom said . . . "*] The Mom said, 'I saw you touch the moon.' The end."	A fluent production Receives prompts from the clinician whenever there is a bit of a hesitation in the flow of speech
Clinician	"What a nice story you told me! I liked that smooth speech you had! You are a good storyteller! I will tell you another story. Listen carefully. I want you to tell me the story again.	Verbal praise
	"You know what a crow is? It is black bird. One hot day a crow was very thirsty. He was looking for water. He flew here. He flew there, looking for water. Then he saw a pot with a little *(continued)*	Tells a new story to the child Prompts the child whenever the child is unsure of what to say

Fluency Reinforcement Plus Corrective Feedback in Story Telling, continued

Scripts for Reinforcement Plus Corrective Feedback in Story Retelling		Note
Clinician *(continues)*	"bit of water in it. He sat on the top of the pot and put his head into it to drink the water. But he couldn't reach the water. He tried and tried, but he couldn't reach the water. He then looked around and saw some pebbles on the ground. He put one pebble into the pot. He put another pebble into the pot. He put some more pebbles into the pot. He saw the water coming up! He put a lot more pebbles into the pot. The water came all the way up and the crow drank the water! The end. Now you tell me the story. Remember smooth speech."	
Child	"There was a crow. He was thirsty. He wanted water. [*the clinician prompted: "He flew . . . "*] He flew here. He flew there. Then he saw a pot. There was water in it. The c-c-crow [*the clinician stopped the child: "Oops! That was bumpy, say it again smoothly"*] The crow sat on the pot and put his head inside. He couldn't reach the water. He saw pebbles. He put one pebble in the pot. He p-p-put [*the clinician stopped the child: "Oops! That was bumpy, say it again smoothly"*] He put another pebble. He put some more pebbles in the pot. The water came up. The crow drank water. The end!"	The child tells the story The clinician gives corrective feedback for stuttering
Clinician	"Thank you! You told me a nice story! Your speech was smooth, too! "Do you like these stories? Are you ready for another story?"	Verbal praise
Child	"Yes."	
Clinician	"Once upon a time, there was a big ant. One day the ant was creeping along in the forest. It was a hot day. The ant was very thirsty. Remember the thirsty crow? The ant had the same problem. While moving along, he saw a little pond. The ant was very happy to see the pond full of water! But when he tried to drink some water, he fell into the pond. He was drowning! He was going to die! He cried out, 'help, help!' Who is there to help? Well, there was a bird sitting on a tree. She was watching the sad ant. To save the ant, the bird dropped a big leaf to the pond! The ant climbed on to the leaf. The leaf floated and the ant climbed *(continued)*	Tells a longer story, but stops in the middle to have the child tell the first part

Fluency Reinforcement Plus Corrective Feedback in Story Telling, continued

Scripts for Reinforcement Plus Corrective Feedback in Story Retelling	Note
Clinician *(continues)* "out of the pond. The story is not finished, but you tell me what I just told you. I will tell you the rest after I hear this much from you. Don't forget smooth speech."	Reminds *smooth speech*
Child "A big ant was thirsty like the crow. He was creeping in the forest. It was a hot day. He then saw a little pond. He wanted to drink, water. But he fell into the pond. He was going to die! So he cried, 'help! help!' There was no one there to help. But a bird was sitting in a tree. She saw the ant. She dropped a big leaf to the pond. The ant climbed on to the leaf and came out of the pond!"	Child retells the first part of the story
Clinician "That was excellent! You remembered everything! You did not have a single bump! It was all so smooth! "Now I will tell you the rest of the story. The ant was tired from his adventure in the pond. He wanted to go home. As he was going home, he saw a hunter. The hunter was trying to catch the bird with a net. The bird did not see the hunter, so he was still happily sitting there! Just when the hunter was ready to throw the net on the bird to catch it, the big ant bit him hard on his toe! What did the hunter do? He just screamed 'Ouch!' The bird heard the scream and quickly flew away! The bird saved the ant first and then the ant saved the bird! The end. "Now you tell me the rest of the story I just told you. Tell me in your smooth speech."	Verbal praise Tells the rest of the story
Child "The ant was tired. He was going home. He then sss-saw [*the clinician stopped the child: Oops! That was bumpy, say it again smoothly*] He then saw a hunter. Hunter was trying to catch the bird. [*clinician prompts: "How?"*] He tried to catch the bird with a net. The bird did not see the hunter. He was happily sitting on the tree. When the hunter was going to catch the bird, the big ant bit his toe! The hunter screamed 'Ouch!' The bird heard it. He flew away. [*the clinician prompts: "Who saved whom?"*] The bird saved the ant. Then, ant saved the bird."	Retells the story; gets prompted and receives corrective feedback for dysfluencies
Clinician "That was great! Again you remembered the story! I liked your smooth speech, too!"	

Treatment of Stuttering in Preschoolers:
II. Fluency Reinforcement Plus Corrective Feedback

Treatment at the Conversational Speech Level

Overview

• With preschoolers, fluency reinforcement plus corrective feedback completed at the narrative speech level should be shifted to the conversational speech level as soon as practical. When 98% or better fluency is sustained at the narrative speech level across several sessions, the child may be ready to move on to the conversational speech level.

• At this level of training, the clinician simply talks with the child. The clinician asks questions and encourages longer sentence productions in the conversational format. Initially, the clinician may ask questions about the child's family, names of parents, siblings, and friends, while encouraging complete sentence productions.

• As before, in this fluency reinforcement plus corrective feedback program, the clinician promptly and enthusiastically reinforces fluent production with verbal praise. Equally promptly, but in an objective tone, the clinician offers corrective feedback for stuttering. The need for modeling at this stage of treatment should be minimum.

• The clinician should talk to the child at a normal rate and should not inadvertently induce a slower speech rate in the child.

• The clinician may continue to use the maintenance strategies introduced in the previous level of treatment. The child may be taken out of the treatment room to informally monitor fluent conversational speech.

The duration of treatment at the conversational speech level will depend on the individual child. The criterion of treatment success and the individual child's progress in treatment will help determine when to dismiss the child from services. A suggested criterion is less than 2% dysfluency or stuttering rate (based on the number of words spoken) in the clinic sessions and well under 5% in natural settings.

Treatment of Stuttering in Preschoolers:
II. Fluency Reinforcement Plus Corrective Feedback

Treatment Protocol for Conversational Speech

Scripts for Reinforcement Plus Corrective Feedback in Conversational Speech		Note
Clinician	"You have been doing great! You speak in smooth speech most of the time. I liked the way you told me some stories last time. Now we are going to just talk for a while. I want you to practice smooth speech as we talk. Okay?"	Introduces the conversational speech task
Child	"Okay!"	
Clinician	"What is your Mom's name? You should start with *My Mom's* . . . and tell me in a complete, long sentence."	Asks simple questions, prompts the production of complete sentences
Child	"My Mom's name is Lydia."	A fluent, spontaneous production
Clinician	"Excellent! Your speech was very smooth! It was a long sentence! Now tell me, what is your Dad's name?"	Verbal praise
Child	"My Dad's name is Carlos."	Fluent production
Clinician	"You are working very hard! I like your smooth speech and long sentence! How many brothers do you have? Remember the sentence."	Verbal praise Next question
Child	"Two." [*the clinician prompts "I have. . ."*] I have two brothers."	Fluent production, prompted longer sentence
Clinician	"Great job! Are they both older than you?"	Verbal praise Next question
Child	"No. One brother is my baby brother. Another is older."	Verbal praise Next question
Clinician	"How nice! Smooth speech and good sentences! Tell me the name of your baby brother and the name of your older brother. Use complete sentences. You should start, *the name of my* . . . "	Verbal praise Next question
Child	"The name of my baby brother is Antonio. The name of my older brother is Noah."	Fluent production
Clinician	"That was fantastic. You know your speech was smooth, right? You are doing really well!"	Verbal praise Continues this line of conversation

Reinforcement Plus Corrective Feedback in Conversational Speech, continued

Scripts for Reinforcement Plus Corrective Feedback in Conversational Speech		Note
Clinician	"Is your birthday coming up?"	Introduces a new topic for conversation
Child	"I already had my birthday."	Fluent production
Clinician	"Oh you did? When was it? Did you have a big party? Tell me all about the party. Tell me how many kids attended, what kind of gifts you got, what kind of cake did you have, and all that."	Prompt more continuous speech
Child	"I had a party yesterday. It was a big party. Many friends came. . . [*the clinician prompts:* "Tell me some names of your friends."] My friend Cindy came. Timmy came also. Jennifer, Erick, and Alicia also came. [*clinician prompts:* "Tell me about gifts."] I got lots of gifts. I got a toy car, storybooks, some chocolate. [*the clinician prompts:* "What did you get from your Mom and Dad?"] I got a T-shirt from Mom and Dad. I also got a big dump truck! And a big puzzle. My brother gave me crayons."	Fluent, relatively more spontaneous production
Clinician	"Yes, you did get a lot of nice gifts! And your speech was very smooth!" "Now tell me, what did you all eat and drink?"	Verbal praise Open-ended question
Child	"We ate chocolate cake. [*the clinician prompts:* "Is that your favorite kind? What other kinds of cakes do you like?"] Yeah, I like chocolate cake. I also like cheesecake. [*the clinician prompts:* "What about drinks?"] We had lemonade. Cindy wanted milk. Erick wanted coke."	Fluent production
Clinician	"Thank you, that was smooth speech!" "Did you guys play any games? Tell me how you played it"	Verbal praise Next question
Child	"I played with my dump truck. They all worked on the puzzle I got. I also worked on the puzzle. Timmy played with my dump truck."	Fluent, continuous speech
Clinician	"Nice, smooth speech! Did you give something to your friends?"	Verbal praise Next question
Child	"Yeah. They all got a hat, balloons, and candy."	Fluent production
Clinician	"Great talking! Looks like you guys had a great time!"	Verbal praise
Child	"It was fun!"	Fluent production

Treatment of Stuttering in Preschoolers:
II. Fluency Reinforcement Plus Corrective Feedback

Treatment Recording Sheet

Personalize and print this page from the CD.

Name of the child:	DOB:
Name of the parents:	Phone:
Diagnosis: Stuttering	Session date(s):
Clinician:	Comments:

Chart the child's progress for each session with your preferred method. You may calculate a percent dysfluency or stuttering rate based on the number of words spoken. If more detailed data are warranted, score the individual dysfluency types and add them up to calculate the dysfluency rate.

Essential Measures		Optional Measures: Frequency of Specific Dysfluency Types					
Dates of Service	Percent Stuttering	Prolongations	Pauses	Repetitions	Interjections	Revisions	Incomplete Phrases

Treatment of Stuttering in Preschoolers:
II. Fluency Reinforcement Plus Corrective Feedback

Probe Protocol

Probe Procedure

* Record two conversational speech samples, each 5 to 7 minutes in duration
* Record a 3-minute monologue; ask the child to talk about a topic such as:
  > Birthday parties
  > Vacations
  > Visit to a zoo or a theme park
  > Favorite games or TV shows
  > Weekend activities
  > Any other child-specific topic
* Obtain a 5-minute home speech sample
* Record one or more extraclinic speech samples in such places as the child's home, and if relevant, classroom, cafeteria, and the playground
* Analyze the percent dysfluency or stuttering rate
* Personalize the *Probe Recording Sheet* on the CD and record the dysfluency or stuttering rates; print the sheet for child's clinical file

Treatment of Stuttering in Preschooler:
II. Fluency Reinforcement Plus Corrective Feedback

Probe Recording Sheet

Personalize and print this page from the CD.

Name of the child:	DOB:
Name of the parents:	Phone:
Diagnosis: Stuttering	Session date(s):
Clinician:	Comments:

Analyze the probe speech samples with your preferred method. You may calculate a percent dysfluency or stuttering rate based on the number of words spoken. If more detailed data are warranted, score the individual dysfluency types and add them up to calculate the dysfluency rate.

Take at least three clinic probe samples. If possible, obtain three extraclinic probe samples.

Essential Measures		Optional Measures: Frequency of Specific Dysfluency Types					
Dates/Setting of Probe	Percent Stuttering	PRO	PAU	REP	INT	REV	INC
1. /mm/dd/yy/ Clinic							
2. /mm/dd/yy/ Clinic							
3. /mm/dd/yy/ Clinic							
1. /mm/dd/yy/ Home							
2. /mm/dd/yy/ Classroom							
3. /mm/dd/yy/ Playground							

PRO (Prolongations); PAU (Pauses); REP (Repetitions); INT (Interjections); REV (Revisions); INC (Incomplete phrases).

Dismiss the child from current services when the child's stuttering or dysfluency rate stays below the target percentage in conversational probes. Suggested criterion is less than 2% dysfluency rate in the clinic and less than 5% in natural settings. Schedule follow-ups and booster treatments as needed.

Treatment of Stuttering in Preschoolers: III. Response Cost

Overview

An exclusive fluency reinforcement and reinforcement plus corrective feedback, described in the previous sections to treat stuttering in preschool children, depend on differential verbal consequences for fluency and stuttering. Another effective procedure to treat preschool children who stutter is *response cost*.

In response cost, the clinician offers a reinforcer for fluent productions *and* withdraws a reinforcer contingent on each stuttering. In this procedure, the clinician places contingencies on fluent as well as dysfluent productions. Early experimental studies on response cost method include those by Seigel, Lenske, and Broen (1969), Halvorson (1971), Kazdin (1973), and Salend and Andress (1984). These studies documented the effectiveness of response cost in reducing dysfluencies in nonstuttering and stuttering adults and children. A study by Ahlander and Hegde (2000) demonstrated that both time-out and response cost are effective alternatives in treating stuttering in children. An extended experimental treatment program involving 35 preschool children in the age range of 2.6 years to 5 years has demonstrated that response cost is an effective method for treating stuttering in preschool children (Hegde, 2004). The study used the ABAB withdrawal design to demonstrate that within the duration of treatment, improvement shown under treatment was not due to spontaneous recovery, because treatment withdrawal increased stuttering in all cases and treatment reinstatement reduced it. A four-year follow-up has documented excellent maintenance of fluency in all except two children who had discontinued treatment because their families had moved out of the area. Because of such controlled and replicated evidence that supports its use, response cost is an attractive alternative to treat preschool children.

Before starting treatment with response cost, the clinician should establish the baserates of dysfluencies in sentences, conversational speech, and narratives as described in a previous section. Regardless of the treatment procedures used, the baserate protocols remain the same for preschool children. After establishing the baserates, the clinician may choose either the exclusive fluency reinforcement procedure, the fluency reinforcement plus corrective feedback procedure, or the response cost method.

Student clinicians and parents can be relatively easily trained in administering the response cost method at home. After a period of formal response cost treatment at home, the parents may be trained to maintain fluency in their child by verbal reinforcement alone.

Treatment of Stuttering in Preschoolers:
III. Response Cost

Treatment at the Sentence Level

Overview

- With preschoolers, **response cost method** may be initiated at the sentence level.

- When the child produces single words and phrases in response to questions about the stimulus materials, the clinician may prompt, instruct, or otherwise encourage the child to produce shorter and longer sentences.

- In contrast to the baserate sessions, however, the clinician may model and immediately ask the child to imitate shorter and longer sentences. Stuttering frequency typically decreases when children immediately imitate a fluent production, which gives an opportunity for the clinician to reinforce fluency with token presentation. Modeling and the resulting reduction in stuttering also help minimize token withdrawal. Frequent modeling in the beginning stages of treatment is essential to stabilize fluency at the sentence level.

- The clinician will assemble a selection of back-up reinforcers (small gifts) for the child. The clinician also will have tokens to be given to the child for fluent productions.

- At the beginning of each treatment session, the clinician presents a variety of small gifts and asks the child to select one for the day. The gift should be prominently displayed as the child works during the session. The child may be told that he or she will get a token for talking smoothly and that the tokens earned are like money. He or she should have enough money to "buy" the gift at the end of the session. More than the instructions, the actual experience of earning, losing, and retaining enough tokens to "buy" the gift at the end of the session are what informs the child of the essence of treatment.

- Although flat, coin-like, plastic tokens are commonly used, the clinician can select tokens of any kind. Some plastic tokens are colorful and come in different shapes. Children are especially attracted to colorful tokens of unusual shapes.

- In the beginning stages of treatment, the clinician frequently models fluent production so the child accumulates tokens. As the child becomes more fluent, the clinician gradually reduces the frequency of modeling.

- The clinician ensures that the child does not run out of tokens at the end of a session (token bankruptcy), resulting in a failure to acquire the selected gift. The child should always get the selected gift, but the tokens earned should also be contingent on fluent productions. Tokens cannot be just given at the end of a session because the child is token-bankrupt. The child cannot be given the gift without tokens, although a set number of tokens is not necessary. Some tokens still left with the child are a good reason to give the gift.

- The clinician uses a few strategies to avoid token bankruptcy. Obviously, token bankruptcy is likely when the child earns too few tokens and loses too many. To avoid this problem, clinician increases the frequency of token presentation and decreases the frequency of token withdrawal. In other words, the clinician increases opportunities for fluent productions and decreases the chances of stuttering. To accomplish this, the clinician:
  - ➢ Models fluent production more often, resulting in increased fluency and higher level of token earning

> ➤ Requires single words or phrases, instead of sentences, that also result in increased fluency and higher level of token earning
>
> ➤ Presents two tokens, instead of the typical single token, for *longer* fluent productions; the clinician in such cases should point out the reason for giving an extra token (e.g., "here is an extra token, because you said a very long sentence smoothly")
>
> ➤ Extends the treatment session by a few minutes to give a few extra tokens for fluency

- On occasion, a child may **react negatively** to the first token withdrawal. In the study described earlier (Hegde, 2004), three of the 35 preschool children reacted negatively when the clinician withdrew the first token. A 3-year-old girl said "I don't want to talk" (before the treatment, a strategy she had used at home when the parents gave corrective feedback), a 4-year-old boy declared that he was not going to cry because "he was a big boy" (but the crying seemed imminent), and a 2.6-year-old girl showed reluctance to continue with the treatment. Although these examples are from preschool children, the possibility of a school-age child exhibiting negative reactions cannot be discounted. In all three cases involving preschool children, the negative reaction was eliminated with **role-reversal**. Each child was given an opportunity to give tokens to the clinician for smooth speech and withdraw tokens for bumpy speech. Such a role-reversal, conducted for 2 to 3 minutes in a session completely eliminated the negative reaction and the child was enthusiastically ready for continued treatment with response cost. None of the three children ever again exhibited any form of negative reaction. Similar role-reversal might work well with school-age children.

- In all treatment sessions, the clinician gives a token for fluent productions and takes one away for each stuttering or dysfluency. The clinician makes sure that the child accumulates some tokens to buy the gift. If it appears the child seems to be losing tokens at a faster rate than gaining them, the clinician should use strategies to prevent token bankruptcy. For each longer fluency, the clinician may give two tokens, instead of the typical single token. The clinician may model fluent productions for the child, so the child will be more fluent and earn more tokens.

- While presenting a token, the clinician verbally praises the child for smooth speech. Similarly, while removing a token, the clinician offers corrective verbal feedback. Pairing verbal reinforcement with token presentation and corrective feedback with token withdrawal helps fade out tokens and maintain fluency with the help of verbal reinforcement alone.

- The clinician presents tokens and reinforces fluent productions with a variety of verbal statements:
  - ➤ That was great! You said it smoothly, here is a token for you!
  - ➤ Wonderful! You are such a smooth talker! Another token!
  - ➤ Nice smooth speech! [*presents a token*]
  - ➤ I like your smooth speech! So you get another token!
  - ➤ You are doing a great job! [*presents a token*]

- The clinician withdraws tokens and gives corrective feedback with several forms of verbal statements:
  - ➤ That was bumpy! I need to take one token back!
  - ➤ Oh no! You didn't say it smoothly; I am taking one token from you!
  - ➤ That was bumpy! [*removes a token*]
  - ➤ You are having trouble saying it, I get a token back!
  - ➤ No, that was not smooth! [*removes a token*]

- The same stimulus materials used in baserating dysfluencies in sentences may be appropriate for treatment sessions. Familiar stories and pictures may more readily evoke speech from the child.

- If previously used stimuli fail to provoke interest in the child, the clinician introduces novel stimuli that will sustain the child's interest.

- To evaluate the child's progress in treatment, the clinician tape-records each session and later calculates the percent dysfluency or stuttering rate.

- If a correctly implemented response cost procedure does not produce satisfactory results, the clinician considers alternative procedures (e.g., simple fluency reinforcement). Although there will be individual differences, stuttering frequency should be significantly reduced in a matter of few sessions. If not, the progress may be judged unsatisfactory, leading to a change in the treatment procedure.

- The clinician makes sure that in the response cost procedure, such fluency shaping skills as gentle phonatory onset, airflow management, and slower rate of speech are not targeted. A common error to be avoided is to inadvertently induce slower speech. The clinician models fluent productions at a normal rate of speech.

- If the child begins to speak slowly to earn the reinforcers and to avoid token loss for stuttering, the clinician instructs the child to speak faster. The clinician also models a normally fast rate for the child to imitate.

Treatment protocols are offered at four levels of training:

1. Treatment at the sentence level
2. Treatment at the continuous speech level
3. Treatment at the narrative speech level
4. Treatment at the conversational speech level

Treatment of Stuttering in Preschoolers:
III. Response Cost

Treatment Protocol for Sentences

Scripts for Response Cost in Sentences		Note
Clinician	"Sometimes our speech may be bumpy, instead of smooth. I will show you what is bumpy speech. When I say *t-t-t-time*, instead of *time*, my speech is bumpy. What kind of speech is it when I say *t-t-t-time* instead of *time*? Say, it is bumpy speech."	The clinician introduces the concepts of *bumpy speech* and *smooth speech*
Child	"It is bumpy speech."	
Clinician	"Yes, that's what it is called! It is called *bumpy speech*. Our speech can be bumpy in other ways. When I say *I llllike it*, it is bumpy isn't it?"	The clinician illustrates instances of bumpy speech by producing various types of dysfluencies
Child	"Yes."	
Clinician	"When I say, *I-I-I want it*, what do you call it?"	
Child	"Bumpy speech."	
Clinician	"You are right! When I say, *um-um-um I had a birthday party*, what do you call it?"	
Child	"Bumpy speech."	
Clinician	"You are right again! It is all bumpy speech. When we talk without bumps, we call it smooth speech. When I say, *I had a birthday party*, what do you call that?"	
Child	"Smooth speech."	
Clinician	"You are right about that, too! When we talk without bumps, we have smooth speech. Do you sometimes have bumpy speech?"	Probing the child's awareness of his or her bumpy speech
Child	"Sometimes."	
Clinician	"Yes, you do have bumpy speech sometimes. Do you like to have smooth speech instead of bumpy speech?"	Setting the stage for treatment
Child	"Yes."	
Clinician	"You can do it. You can have smooth speech, I want to help you talk smoothly. Is that Okay?"	Reassures the child
Child	"Okay."	

Response Cost in Sentences, continued

Scripts for Response Cost in Sentences		Note
Clinician	Alright, let's get going then! [*showing a collection of small gifts*] You see all these goodies here? Select a gift you want to work for today. If you work real hard, speak smoothly, you can get this gift at the end."	Let the child select a back-up reinforcer (small gift)
Child	[*Selects a gift*]	
Clinician	"That will be your gift if you try to talk smoothly. But you have to buy that gift from me. I will show you how easily you can buy it. [*shows a collection of plastic tokens*] You see these plastic tokens? They are like money! I will give you a token every time you say something smoothly, without any bumps. Do you understand?"	Introduces the token procedure
Child	"Yes."	
Clinician	"Remember, this is a simple game we will be playing. You talk smoothly, [*placing a cup in front of the child*] I place a token into this cup. It's your cup. You talk bumpy, I will take a token from your cup and put it into my cup [*points to another cup*]. If you talk smoothly, your cup will get filled up fast! You lose tokens if you talk bumpy. When we are done, you can buy that gift [*points to the gift*] with the token money. If your token cup is empty, you can't buy that gift from me. Now tell me, how do you get the gift?"	Instructs the child about the response cost procedure
Child	"With the token money."	Child understands
Clinician	"You are right! You give me your tokens at the end, I give you your gift. But how do you get the tokens?"	Checks the child's understanding of token earning
Child	"By talking smoothly."	Child understands
Clinician	"What happens when you are bumpy?"	Checks the child's understanding of token loss
Child	"You take a token from my cup."	Child understands
Clinician	"That's right! You understand everything. Talk smoothly, you get a token. Talk bumpy, you lose a token. At the end, give me your tokens, you get this gift. Remember, you should work hard to get the gift. Working hard here means talking smoothly. Okay?"	Summarizes the procedure
Child	"Okay."	

Response Cost in Sentences, continued

Scripts for Response Cost in Sentences		Note
Clinician	"Alright, let's begin then! I want you to get that gift today! [*showing the picture of a farm scene*] You know we have talked about this picture before. You can talk about this again, only this time, I want you to talk smoothly. What do you see here? Do you see a farm or a home? Tell me in a sentence and make it smooth."	The first treatment trial
Child	"I see a farm."	Fluent production
Clinician	"That's great! [*presents a token*] You said it smoothly! Here is your first token! Now, what do you see here? Say it in a fluent sentence."	The **first token presentation along with verbal praise for fluency**; initiation of the next trial
Child	"I-I-I . . ."	Sound repetition
Clinician	"Oh no! That was bumpy. [*withdraws a token*] I am taking your token back. Say, *I see a dog.*"	The **first token removal along with verbal corrective feedback**; models a fluent sentence production at normal rate
Child	"I see a dog."	Fluent imitation of the model
Clinician	"Excellent! This is your token! Now see this man. What is this man doing here? Say, *he is . . .*"	Token presentation and verbal praise for fluency; initiates the next trial
Child	"He is feeding the cow."	Fluent production
Clinician	"Great! Smooth speech! You get another token. Now, what is this calf doing here? Say, *the calf is jumping.*"	Reinforces the child with verbal praise and a token; initiates the next modeled trial
Child	"The calf is jumping."	Fluent imitation of modeled speech
Clinician	"Fantastic! Another token for you! You see, how you are getting more tokens! Now let's look at this part here. What is this? Say, *this is hay.*"	Reinforces the child with a token and verbal praise; initiates the next modeled trial
Child	"This is hay."	Fluent imitation of modeled speech
Clinician	"I like how you are talking! Here is a token for your smooth speech! Now let's see. Who likes to eat hay? Say, *the cow likes to eat hay.*"	Token presentation and verbal praise; next modeled trial
Child	"The cow llllikes . . ."	Sound prolongation
Clinician	"No, that was bumpy. I get a token back. Say, *the cow likes to eat hay,* and say it smoothly."	Token withdrawal, corrective feedback; modeling fluent production

Response Cost in Sentences, continued

Scripts for Response Cost in Sentences		Note
Child	"The cow likes to eat hay."	Fluent imitation
Clinician	"That was wonderful! You get another token! "Now look here. What is she doing here? Say, *she is milking the cow.*"	Verbal and token reinforcement; initiation of next modeled trial
Child	"She is mmmmilking . . ."	Sound prolongation
Clinician	"No, that was a bump. I take a token back. Say, *she is milking the cow.*"	Immediate corrective feedback and token withdrawal; modeling fluent production
Child	"She is mmmmilking . . ."	Second failed attempt at fluent imitation
Clinician	"Oops! I have to take a token back from you. Say, *she is milking the cow.*"	Prompt corrective feedback and token withdrawal; modeling of a fluent production
Child	"She is milking the cow."	Successful third attempt
Clinician	"That was smooth! Here is a token for that. See, you can talk smoothly! Now look here. What is this pig doing here? Say, *the pig is drinking water.*"	Praises the child for the fluent production and models a new sentence on this next trial
Child	"The pig is drinking water."	Fluent imitation
Clinician	"You are super! Nice, smooth, speech! Another token for you! Now let's look here. What is this cat doing? Say, *the cat is sleeping.*"	Reinforces the child with a token and verbal praise; initiates the next modeled trial
Child	"The cat is sleeping."	A fluently imitated production
Clinician	"Wonderful! You are working really hard to say it smoothly! Have this token! Okay, what is this girl doing here? Say, *she is chasing the chicken.*"	Reinforces the child with a token and verbal praise and initiates the next modeled trial
Child	"She is chasing the chicken."	Fluent imitation
Clinician	"That was smooth again! Another token for you. Now look at this part here. What are these children doing here? Say, *they are playing with hay.*"	Offers token and verbal reinforcement; initiates the next modeled trial
Child	"They are playing with hay."	Fluently imitated production
Clinician	"Very nice! I like that smooth speech! [*presents a token*] You see two men here? What are they doing here? Say, *they are carrying wood.*"	Reinforces the child and initiates the next modeled trial
Child	"They are c-c-c-carry . . ."	Sound repetition

Response Cost in Sentences, continued

Scripts for Response Cost in Sentences		Note
Clinician	"Stop! I have to take one of your tokens. Now, make it smooth, and say, *they are carrying wood,* and you will get your token back."	Gives corrective feedback and withdraws a token; models fluent sentence; promises a token for fluency
Child	"They are c-c-c-carry . . ."	Sound repetition; second failed attempt
Clinician	"No, that was bumpy again. [*withdraws a token without announcement*] Say, *they are carrying wood.*"	Corrective feedback and unannounced token withdrawal; fluent sentence modeling
Child	"They are carrying wood."	A fluent production
Clinician	"Wonderful! A token for that smooth speech! Look at this part of the picture now. What are these boys doing here?"	Reinforces and asks an evoking question (no modeling)
Child	"They are riding horses."	A fluent production
Clinician	"Excellent! Another token for you! Now let us look at this picture. See, this picture here shows a fair going on. Have you ever been to a fair?"	Offers verbal praise and a token, moves on to the next stimulus **Injects a brief conversational exchange**
Child	"Yes."	
Clinician	"Who took you to the fair? Tell me in a sentence."	A more open-ended question
Child	"My Mom and D-d-da . . ."	A part-word (sound) repetition
Clinician	"Oops! [*takes a token without announcement*] Say, *my Mom and Dad took me to the fair.*"	Corrective feedback and unannounced token withdrawal; models a fluent production
Child	"My mom and dad took me to the fair."	A fluent sentence production
Clinician	"That's great! A token for your smooth speech! Now look here. What are these kids doing?"	Verbal praise plus token **Reverts to picture description**
Child	"They are taking a ride."	A fluent production
Clinician	"Wonderful! [*presents a token without announcement*] Did you take a ride when you went to the fair?"	Verbal praise plus unannounced token presentation **Another conversational exchange**
Child	"Yes."	A fluent response
Clinician	"Very good! What kind of ride was it? Tell me in a sentence."	Verbal praise, no token for the single-word response; open-ended question

Response Cost in Sentences, continued

Scripts for Response Cost in Sentences		Note
Child	"It was a roller-coaster ride."	A fluent production
Clinician	"You are doing great! [*presents a token*] Who went on the ride with you? Don't forget to say it in a sentence."	Verbal praise plus unannounced token presentation; open-ended question
Child	"My brother went with me."	A fluent production
Clinician	"Nice, smooth speech! Another token, and your cup is filling up! Thanks for working so hard!"	Verbal praise plus token

Continue to evoke speech to reinforce fluency with tokens and verbal praise; offer prompt corrective feedback and withdraw tokens contingent on dysfluencies as shown on the protocols. After two or three sessions in which the child is consistently fluent in evoked sentences (without modeling), shift treatment to the continuous speech level.

Treatment of Stuttering in Preschoolers: III. Response Cost

Treatment at the Continuous Speech Level

Overview

- With preschool children, the response cost method initiated at the isolated sentence level with frequent modeling may be shifted to the continuous speech level as soon as possible. When the response cost method results in significant reduction in stuttering frequency in isolated sentences, observed across two sessions, the child may be ready to move on to the continuous speech level.

- If the child's fluency drops significantly when continuous speech is evoked, the clinician should move back to the sentence level for additional training.

- Continuous speech may be reintroduced after a period of additional training at the level of evoked individual sentences.

- To begin with, the clinician may use the same stimulus materials that were used in baserating fluency at the continuous speech level. The protocols reflect this strategy. Familiar stimuli may evoke continuous speech more readily than unfamiliar stimuli. Eventually, the clinician may introduce new materials to the response cost treatment sessions.

- At this stage, the clinician encourages the child to produce more continuous speech with such prompts as "tell me about everything you see here," "say it in longer sentences," "talk about all that's happening," "say more than one sentence at a time," and so forth.

- The clinician should promptly and enthusiastically reinforce fluent productions with verbal praise and tokens. The clinician should equally promptly withdraw tokens and offer corrective feedback in an objective tone. The clinician should model fluent sentences as often as found necessary and ask the child to imitate.

- The clinician should model all fluent productions at normal rate. The effects of the response cost method does not depend on a slower rate, airflow management, or gentle onset of phonation. Therefore, the clinician should not inadvertently induce any of these fluency shaping targets that negatively affect prosodic features.

- The duration of continuous speech treatment phase will depend on the individual child. The criterion of treatment success and the individual child's progress in treatment will help determine when to move on to the conversational phase of treatment. A suggested criterion is less than 2% dysfluency or stuttering rate (based on the number of words spoken) across at least three clinic sessions.

- Response cost treatment protocols that follow include continuous speech, narrative speech, and conversational speech.

Treatment of Stuttering in Preschoolers:
III. Response Cost

Treatment Protocol for Continuous Speech

Scripts for Response Cost in Continuous Speech		Note
Clinician	[*showing the picture of a farm scene*] "Remember, we talked about this picture before? You told me stories about this picture. I want you to do the same again. This time, I want you to tell me everything in smooth speech. First tell me what these people are doing here. Remember to talk in long and smooth sentences. You can start with, *these people are working on the farm.*"	The first trial; prompting a sentence production
Child	"These people are working on the farm."	Fluent production
Clinician	"Excellent! That was a long and smooth sentence! You deserve a token for that! OK, I will point to all these people and you tell me what they are doing. Start with these kids here. Tell me about everything they are doing." [*points to children; continues to point to different parts of the picture to prompt more continuous speech*]	Verbal praise and token presentation; instructions to evoke more continuous speech
Child	"The kids are playing. They are throwing hay."	Fluent production
Clinician	"Good job! I like that smooth speech! Here is your token."	Gives verbal praise and a token; points to another part of the picture
Child	"They-they-they . . ."	Word repetition
Clinician	"Oh no! That was bumpy. [*withdraws a token*] I have to take a token back. Make it smooth this time and make it a long sentence."	Gives prompt corrective feedback and withdraws a token
Child	"They are climbing on this ladder. But this boy here is about to fall down!"	Fluent productions
Clinician	"Excellent! A token for your fluent speech! What about this part here?"	Gives verbal praise and a token; points to another part of the picture
Child	"They are chasing all the ch-ch-ch- . . ."	Part-word repetition
Clinician	"No. [*withdraws a token*] Who are chasing all the chickens? I want you to say the whole thing. Start with *the children . . .*"	Gives corrective feedback and removes a token unannounced; prompts a longer production

Response Cost in Continuous Speech, continued

Scripts for Response Cost in Continuous Speech		Note
Child	"The children are chasing chickens."	Fluent production
Clinician	"I like that smooth speech! [*presents a token*] Tell me all about what these big people are doing. Say more sentences this time. I want you to say many long sentences."	Verbal praise and unannounced token presentation; points to different parts of the picture to evoke more continuous speech
Child	"These men are working. They are digging dirt. That woman is milking. Milking the cow. This man is feeding it. Some men are carrying wood. These girls are sitting on the grass. They are eating something."	Produced continuous fluent speech as the clinician pointed to different parts of the picture **Such lengthy and fluent responses are opportunities to offer two or more tokens to avoid token bankruptcy**
Clinician	"That was fantastic! You said so many sentences smoothly! [*presents a token*] That's what I want you to do. Now let us look at this new picture here. You have seen this before. It shows a fair, doesn't it? I will point to different parts of the picture. You tell me all you see and everything that is happening in this picture. Remember, you should say a lot of sentences. Now start here. What do you see and what are they doing?"	Verbal praise plus token for fluent and continuous speech; introduction of new picture stimulus (scene at a fair)
Child	"I-I-I . . ."	Begins with a word repetition
Clinician	"No. [*withdraws a token*] Start with, *I* . . ."	Corrective feedback, unannounced token withdrawal, and a prompt
Child	"I see a lot of kids. They are riding. It's a roller coaster. It is big. People here are eating hot dogs. Some kids here are taking a ride on this big wheel. The girls are sitting on a bench. They are eating cotton candy."	Continuous fluent speech production
Clinician	"Excellent! You talked smoothly. [*presents a token*] Okay, tell me more about this part here. Like what you just did, tell me a lot. Say it in many sentences."	Verbal praise and token presentation; shows another part of the picture
Child	"I see a little zoo here. Kids are petting a . . . [*the clinician prompts: "lamb"*] lamb. They are looking at the baby cow. The mommy cow is licking it. A man is brushing that horse. The girls are feeding some chickens. Here the boy is taking a ride on a p-p-p-"	The clinician may prompt a word the child does not know
Clinician	"No. [*withdraws a token*] Make it smooth and say the whole sentence, start with *here the* . . ."	Corrective feedback and token withdrawal; prompts
Child	"Here the boy is taking a ride on a pony."	Fluent production

Response Cost in Continuous Speech, continued

Scripts for Response Cost in Continuous Speech		Note
Clinician	"Wonderful! Token for your smooth speech! Now let's look at this new picture. It shows a birthday party. Tell me what is going on here. First tell me whose birthday is being celebrated."	Verbal praise, token presentation, and drawing attention to a new picture
Child	"This girl's birthday. . . [*the clinician gestures the child to continue*] She is wearing a pink hat. She is opening presents. There are many kids here. They are wearing pink and blue hats. D-d-dad . . ."	Five fluent sentences before a sound repetition
Clinician	"That was bumpy. [*withdraws a token*] Make it smooth and tell me what the Dad is doing."	Token withdrawal and corrective feedback. Continues to point to others in the picture
Child	"Dad is setting the table. Mom is . . . [*the clinician prompts: "pouring"*] pouring juice. These two boys are playing ball. These girls are dancing."	Fluent productions
Clinician	"That was great! [*presents a token*] You said so many sentences smoothly!"	Verbal praise and token presentation

Exchange the tokens with the child's preferred gift at the end of each session. Continue to treat in this manner until the child sustains 98% or better fluent speech across three sessions. When this or a similar criterion is met, shift treatment to the next stage in which fluency is targeted in conversational speech.

Treatment of Stuttering in Preschoolers: III. Response Cost

Treatment at the Narrative Speech Level

Overview

- With preschoolers, the response cost procedure completed at the continuous speech level should be advanced to the narrative speech level as soon as practical. When fluency systematically increases at the continuous speech level across several sessions, the child may be ready to move on to the narrative speech level.

- If the child's fluency drops significantly when narrative speech is evoked, the clinician can move back to the lower level for additional training.

- Narrative speech may be reintroduced after a period of additional training at the lower level.

- At this stage, the clinician tells stories to the child and asks the child to retell them. The clinician selects simple stories for preschoolers. Storybooks written for preschool children may be selected for treatment sessions. In selecting the stories, the clinician should consider the ethnocultural background of the child. The selected stories may be of universal appeal, but the clinician should, in addition, select stories from the child's cultural background.

- The clinician encourages the child to tell the story in all its details and prompts story elements when the child is unsure. Various other strategies to promote good narrative speech are specified in the protocols that follow.

- The clinician promptly and enthusiastically reinforces fluent production with verbal praise and a token presentation. The clinician equally promptly withdraws a token and offers corrective feedback for each stuttering. The need for modeling at this level of treatment should be minimal.

- The clinician should tell the stories at the normal rate to avoid inducing slow speech by instructions, modeling, or the manner of story telling.

- The clinician may continue to implement the maintenance strategies introduced in the earlier level. Family members who initially observe the sessions may join the clinician to present a token and verbal reinforcement for each fluent production and withdraw a token while giving corrective feedback for stuttering. Additional information is offered on maintenance strategies in a later section of the protocols.

- The duration of treatment at the narrative speech level will depend on the individual child. The criterion of treatment success and the individual child's progress in treatment will help determine when to dismiss the child from services. A suggested criterion is less than 2% dysfluency or stuttering rate (based on the number of words spoken) in the clinic sessions and well under 5% in natural settings.

Treatment of Stuttering in Preschoolers:
III. Response Cost

Treatment Protocol for Narrative Speech

Scripts for Response Cost in Story Retelling		Note
Clinician	"Now, I will tell you a story and I want you to remember everything I tell you. When I am finished, I want **you** to tell **me** the same story. I want you to talk smoothly as you tell me the stories. Okay?" "Now listen carefully. Once upon a time there was a little boy. Every time he saw a big moon in the sky, he would ask his Mom, 'Mom can I touch the moon?' Mom would say, 'it is too far! If you are a bird, you can fly to the moon to touch it.' Then one morning, the boy got up from the bed, ran to Mom, and told, 'Mom, last night I flew to the moon and touched it!' The Mom said, 'yes, I saw you touch the moon.' The end. Now you tell me the same story. You can start with *once upon a time* . . . "	Introducing the storytelling task
Child	"Once upon a t-t-time. . . "	Sound repetition
Clinician	"Oops! That was bumpy. [*withdraws a token*] Say, *once upon a time* . . . "	Corrective feedback and token withdrawal
Child	"Once upon a time, there was a little boy. When he saw a big moon in the sky, he wanted to touch it. [*the clinician prompts: "He asked Mom . . . "*] He asked 'Mom, can I touch it?' Mom said, 'if you are a bird, you can touch it.' [*the clinician prompts: "Then one morning . . . "*] Then one morning, the boy got up from the bed, ran to Mom, and said, 'Mom, last nnnn . . . "	A fluent production Receives prompts from the clinician whenever there is a bit of a hesitation in the flow of speech Sound prolongation
Clinician	"No, I heard a bump!" [*withdraws a token*] Make it smooth."	Token withdrawal; no modeling
Child	"He ran to Mom and said, 'Mom, last night I flew to the moon and touched it!' [*the clinician prompts: "and the Mom said . . . "*] The Mom said, 'I saw you touch the moon.' The end."	Fluent speech
Clinician	"What a nice story you told me! [*presents a token*] I liked your smooth speech! I will tell you another story. Listen, I want you to tell me the story again. "You know what a crow is? It is black bird. One hot day a crow was very thirsty. He was looking for water. He flew here. He flew there, *(continued)*	Verbal praise, token presentation Tells a new story to the child

Response Cost in Story Telling, continued

Scripts for Response Cost in Story Retelling		Note
Clinician *(continues)*	"looking for water. Then he saw a pot with a little bit of water in it. He sat on the top of the pot and put his head into it to drink the water. But he couldn't reach the water. He tried and tried, but he couldn't reach the water. He then looked around and saw some pebbles on the ground. He put one pebble into the pot. He put another pebble into the pot. He put some more pebbles into the pot. He saw the water coming up! He put a lot more pebbles into the pot. The water came all the way up and the crow drank the water! The end. Now you tell me the story. Remember smooth speech."	Narrates the rest of the story
Child	"There was a crow. He was thirsty. He wanted water. [*the clinician prompted: "He flew . . ."*] He flew here. He flew there. Then he saw a pot. There was water in it. The c-c-crow . . ."	The child tells the story The clinician models fluent production without giving corrective feedback for stuttering
Clinician	"That was bumpy. Make it smooth." [*withdraws a token*]	Token withdrawal, no modeling
Child	"The crow sat on the pot and put his head inside. He couldn't reach the water. He saw pebbles. He put one pebble in the pot. He put another pebble. He put some more pebbles in the pot. The water came up. The crow drank water. The end!"	Fluent narration
Clinician	"Thank you! You told me a nice story in smooth speech! [*presents a token*] "Do you like these stories? Are you ready for another story?"	Verbal praise and token presentation
Child	"Yes."	
Clinician	"Once upon a time, there was a big ant. One day, the ant was creeping along in the forest. It was a hot day. The ant was very thirsty. Remember the thirsty crow? The ant had the same problem. While moving along, he saw a little pond. The ant was very happy to see the pond full of water! But when he tried to drink some water, he fell into the pond. He was drowning! He was going to die! He cried out help, help! Who is there to help? Well, there was a bird sitting on a tree. She was watching the sad ant. To save the ant, the bird dropped a big leaf to the pond! The ant climbed on to the leaf. The leaf floated to the shore and the *(continued)*	Tells a longer story, but stops in the middle to have the child tell the first part

Fluency Reinforcement in Story Telling, continued

Scripts for Response Cost in Story Retelling		Note
Clinician *(continues)*	"ant climbed out of the pond. The story is not finished, but you tell me what I just told you. I will tell you the rest after I hear this much from you. Don't forget smooth speech."	Reminds *smooth speech*
Child	"A big ant was thirsty like the crow. He was creeping in the forest. It was a hot day. He then saw a little pond. He tried to drink water. But he fell into the pond. He was going to die! So he cried, help! help! There was no one there to help. But a bird was sitting in a tree. She saw the ant. She dropped a big leaf to the pond. The ant climbed on to the leaf and came out of the pond!"	Child retells the first part of the story
Clinician	"That was excellent! [*presents a token*] You remembered everything! You did not have a single bump! It was all so smooth! "Now I will tell you the rest of the story. The ant was tired from his adventure in the pond. He wanted to go home. As he was going home, he saw a hunter. The hunter was trying to catch the bird with a net. The bird did not see the hunter, so he was still happily sitting there! Just when the hunter was ready to throw the net on the bird to catch it, the big ant bit him hard on his toe! What did the hunter do? He just screamed 'Ouch!' The bird heard the scream and quickly flew away! The bird saved the ant first and then the ant saved the bird! The end. "Now you tell me the rest of the story I just told you. Tell me in your smooth speech."	Verbal praise and token presentation Tells the rest of the story
Child	"The ant was tired. He was going home. He then saw a hunter. Hunter was trying to catch the bird. [*clinician prompts: How?*] He tried to catch the bird with a net. The bird did not see the hunter. He was happily sitting on the tree! When the hunter was going to catch the bird, the big ant bit his toe! The hunter screamed 'Ouch!' The bird heard it. He flew away. [*the clinician prompts: "Who saved whom?"*] The bird saved the ant. Then, ant saved the bird."	Retells the story; gets prompted
Clinician	"That was great! [*presents a token*] Again you remembered the story! I liked your smooth speech, too!"	Verbal praise and token presentation

Give additional training at the narrative level if necessary. Then move on the conversational speech level.

Treatment of Stuttering in Preschoolers:
III. Response Cost

Treatment at the Conversational Speech Level

Overview

- With preschoolers, the response cost method completed at the narrative speech level should be shifted to the conversational speech level as soon as practical. When 98% or better fluency is sustained at the narrative speech level across several sessions, the child may be ready to move on to the conversational speech level.

- At this level of training, the clinician simply talks with the child. The clinician asks questions and encourages longer sentence productions in the conversational format. Initially, the clinician may ask questions about the child's family, names of parents, siblings, and friends, while encouraging complete sentence productions.

- The clinician promptly and enthusiastically offers verbal reinforcement and a token for all fluent productions. For each dysfluent production (stuttering), the clinician offers corrective feedback in an objective tone and simultaneously withdraws a token. The need for modeling fluent productions at this stage of treatment should be minimal.

- The clinician should talk to the child at a normal rate to avoid inadvertently inducing a slower speech rate in the child.

- The clinician may continue to use the maintenance strategies introduced in the previous level of treatment. The child may be taken out of the treatment room to informally monitor fluent conversational speech with only verbal praise for fluency and subtle corrective feedback for stuttering (no token presentation or withdrawal).

The duration of treatment at the conversational speech level will depend on the individual child. The criterion of treatment success and the individual child's progress in treatment will help determine when to dismiss the child from services. A suggested criterion is less than 2% dysfluency or stuttering rate (based on the number of words spoken) in the clinic sessions and well under 5% in natural settings.

Treatment of Stuttering in Preschoolers:
III. Response Cost

Treatment Protocol for Conversational Speech

Scripts for Response Cost in Conversational Speech		Note
Clinician	"You have been doing great! You are talking smoothly now. Not too many bumps in your speech! You got so many tokens last time! Now we are going to just talk for a while and practice smooth speech. Okay?"	Introduces the conversational speech task
Child	"Okay!"	
Clinician	"What is your Mom's name? You should start with *My Mom's* . . . and tell me in a complete, long sentence."	Asks simple questions, prompts the production of complete sentences
Child	"My Mom's nnnname . . ."	A sound prolongation
Clinician	"That was bumpy. [*withdraws a token*] Try that again."	Corrective feedback plus token removal
Child	"My Mom's name is Lydia."	Fluent production
Clinician	"Excellent! Smooth speech! [*presents a token*] Now tell me, what is your Dad's name?"	Verbal praise and token presentation
Child	"My Dad's name is Carlos."	Fluent production
Clinician	"I like your smooth speech and long sentence! [*presents a token*] How many brothers do you have?"	Verbal praise and token presentation Next question
Child	"Two." [*the clinician prompts* "I have . . ."] "I have two brothers."	Fluent production, prompted longer sentence
Clinician	"Great job! [*presents a token*] Are they both older than you?"	Verbal praise and token presentation
Child	"No. One brother is my baby brother. Another is older."	Fluent production
Clinician	"How nice! Smooth speech and good sentences! [*presents a token*] Tell me the name of your baby brother and the name of your older brother. Start with, *the name of my* . . ."	Verbal praise and token presentation Next question and a prompt
Child	"The name of my baby brother is Antonio. The name of my older brother is Noah."	Fluent production
Clinician	"That was fantastic. You know your speech was smooth, right? [*presents a token*] You are doing really well!"	Verbal praise and token presentation Continues this line of conversation

Response Cost in Conversational Speech, continued

Scripts for Response Cost in Conversational Speech		Note
Clinician	"Is your birthday coming up?"	Introduces a new topic for conversation
Child	"I already had my birthday."	Fluent production
Clinician	"Oh you did? When was it? Did you have a big party? Tell me all about the party. Tell me how many kids attended, what kind of gifts you got, what kind of cake did you have, and all that."	Prompts more continuous speech; did not present a token
Child	"I had a party yesterday. It was a big party. Many friends came . . . [*the clinician prompts:* "*Tell me some names of your friends.*"] My friend Cindy came. Timmy came also. Jennifer, Erick, and Alicia also came. [*the clinician prompts:* "*Tell me about gifts.*"] I got lots of gifts. I got a toy train, storybooks. I got chocolate. [*the clinician prompts:* "*What did you get from your Mom and Dad?*"] I got a T-shirt. My brother gave me a big puzzle."	Fluent, relatively more spontaneous production
Clinician	"Yes, you did get a lot of nice gifts! [*presents a token*] And your speech was very smooth!" "Now tell me, what did you all eat and drink?"	Verbal praise and token presentation Open-ended question
Child	"We ate chocolate cake. [*the clinician prompts:* "*Is that your favorite kind? What other kinds of cakes do you like?*"] Yeah, I like chocolate cake. I also like cheesecake. [*the clinician prompts:* "*What about drinks?*"] We had lemonade. Cindy wanted milk. Erick wanted coke."	Fluent production
Clinician	"Thank you! [*presents a token*] That was smooth speech!" "Did you guys play any games?"	Verbal praise; token presentation Next question
Child	"I tried to put the puzzle together. But it was hard. My brother helped me with it. I can p-p"	A sound repetition
Clinician	"Oops! You stuttered. [*withdraws a token*] Try that again. Start with *I can* . . ."	Corrective feedback plus token removal; sentence prompt
Child	"I can put it together now. My friends also worked on the puzzle I got. Some played my video game. Timmy and Erick just ran around!"	Fluent production

Response Cost in Conversational Speech, continued

Scripts for Response Cost in Conversational Speech		Note
Clinician	"Nice, smooth speech! [*presents a token*] Did you give something to your friends?"	Verbal praise and token presentation Next question
Child	"Yeah. They all got a hat, balloons. Also candy."	Fluent production
Clinician	"Great talking! [*presents a token*] Looks like you guys had a great time!"	Verbal praise and token presentation
Child	"It was fun!"	Fluent production

Continue to apply the response cost procedure in the manner described until the child sustain fluent speech at 98% or better across three or more sessions. Record the dysfluency rates in treatment sessions.

Treatment of Stuttering in Preschoolers: III. Response Cost

Treatment Recording Sheet

Personalize and print this page from the CD.

Name of the child:	DOB:
Name of the parents:	Phone:
Diagnosis: Stuttering	Session date(s):
Clinician:	Comments:

Chart the child's progress for each session with your preferred method. You may calculate a percent dysfluency or stuttering rate based on the number of words spoken. If more detailed data are warranted, score the individual dysfluency types and add them up to calculate the dysfluency rate.

Essential Measures		Optional Measures: Frequency of Specific Dysfluency Types						
Dates of Service	Percent Stuttering	Prolongations	Pauses	Repetitions	Interjections	Revisions	Incomplete Phrases

Treatment of Stuttering in Preschoolers: III. Response Cost

Probe Protocol

Probe Procedure

- Record two conversational speech samples, each 5 to 7 minutes in duration
- Record a 3-minute monologue; ask the child to talk about a topic such as:
  - ➢ Birthday parties
  - ➢ Vacations
  - ➢ Visit to a zoo or a theme park
  - ➢ Favorite games or TV shows
  - ➢ Weekend activities
  - ➢ Any child-specific topic
- Obtain a 5-minute home speech sample
- Record one or more extraclinic speech samples in such places as the child's classroom, cafeteria, and the playground
- Analyze the percent dysfluency or stuttering rate
- Personalize the *Probe Recording Sheet* on the CD and record the dysfluency or stuttering rates; print the sheet for child's clinical file

Treatment of Stuttering in Preschoolers:
III. Response Cost

Probe Recording Sheet

Personalize and print this page from the CD.

Name of the child:	DOB:
Name of the parents:	Phone:
Diagnosis: Stuttering	Session date(s):
Clinician:	Comments:

Analyze the probe speech samples with your preferred method. You may calculate a percent dysfluency or stuttering rate based on the number of words spoken. If more detailed data are warranted, score the individual dysfluency types and add them up to calculate the dysfluency rate.

Take at least three clinic probe samples. If possible, obtain three extraclinic probe samples.

Essential Measures		Optional Measures: Frequency of Specific Dysfluency Types					
Dates/Setting of Probe	Percent Stuttering	PRO	PAU	REP	INT	REV	INC
1. /mm/dd/yy/ Clinic							
2. /mm/dd/yy/ Clinic							
3. /mm/dd/yy/ Clinic							
1. /mm/dd/yy/ Home							
2. /mm/dd/yy/ Classroom							
3. /mm/dd/yy/ Playground							

PRO (Prolongations); PAU (Pauses); REP (Repetitions); INT (Interjections); REV (Revisions); INC (Incomplete phrases).

Dismiss the child from current services when the child's stuttering or dysfluency rate stays below the target percentage in conversational probes. Suggested criterion is less than 2% dysfluency rate in the clinic and less than 5% in natural settings. Schedule follow-ups and booster treatments as needed.

Treatment of Stuttering in Preschoolers: IV. Promoting Maintenance of Fluency

Maintenance Strategies

Maintenance of fluency in preschool children who have been treated for their stuttering is less complicated than that in adults. Generally, if stuttering is reduced to less than 1% and sustained across several treatment sessions, chances of maintenance in preschoolers are better than they are in the case of adults. Nonetheless, the possibility of relapse of stuttering cannot be ruled out. Therefore, the clinician should implement procedures designed to promote maintenance of fluency across situations and over time. The general strategies are common to most clients and applicable to all treatment procedures.

To promote maintenance of fluency, the clinician:

- Always selects the most effective procedure for the child; to improve chances of maintenance, the resulting fluency must be strong and the stuttering frequency should be well below 3%; preferably, it should be below 1% at the time of dismissal.

- Gives sufficient treatment at the level of conversational speech and narrative speech; fluency not strengthened at these levels of complex speech is unlikely to be maintained.

- Teaches self-monitoring skills to the child. Instead of saying, "Oh that was bumpy!" ask the child "Oops! What happened?" to promote self-evaluation. Uses similar strategies when the child is fluent so the child can evaluate fluent productions as well. In using response cost, the clinician encourages the child to give up a token when he or she stutters. The clinician also lets the child take a token when speech is fluent.

- Initially, has the parents observe the treatment sessions and understand how it is implemented; responds fully to their questions about the treatment procedure.

- Later, invites parents into the treatment sessions; points out the important aspects of the treatment. In subsequent sessions, trains parents in the administration of the treatment procedure that has worked well for the child. The clinician teaches parents to:
  - ➢ Model fluent productions for the child
  - ➢ Praise the child for fluent productions
  - ➢ Offer gentle corrective feedback for stutterings
  - ➢ Prompt fluent productions before the child begins to talk
  - ➢ Conduct home treatment at least twice a week; perhaps three times after dismissal

- Moves treatment to less structured, more naturalistic settings; takes the child out for a walk, and monitors the child's fluency by offering verbal reinforcement and corrective feedback in a subtle manner.

- Asks parents to contact the clinic if there is an increase in stuttering rate; lets them know that a few sessions of booster treatment at a later date may help sustain fluency.

- Follows-up the client and takes a brief conversational probe sample to assess maintenance of fluency.

- Calculates the percent dysfluency or stuttering rate; if the rate is unacceptable, offers booster treatment.

- Encourages parents to resume treatment sessions at home.

- Schedules further follow-ups.

Treatment of Stuttering in Preschoolers:
IV. Maintenance of Fluency

Maintenance Probe Recording Sheet

Personalize and print this page from the CD.

Name of the child:	DOB:
Name of the parents:	Phone:
Diagnosis: Stuttering	Session date(s):
Clinician:	Comments:

Analyze the follow-up speech samples with your preferred method. You may calculate a percent dysfluency or stuttering rate based on the number of words spoken. If more detailed data are warranted, score the individual dysfluency types and add them up to calculate the dysfluency rate.

Essential Measures		Optional Measures: Frequency of Specific Dysfluency Types					
Dates/setting of follow-up probe	**Percent Stuttering**	**PRO**	**PAU**	**REP**	**INT**	**REV**	**INC**
Follow-up #1 Date:							
Follow-up #2 Date:							
Follow-up #3 Date:							

Offer booster treatment if the follow-up probe dysfluency rates are unacceptable. On completion of the booster treatment, schedule additional follow-up sessions.

Part 3

Treatment of Stuttering in School-Age Children

Treatment of Stuttering in School-Age Children

Treatment Options

Stuttering may be effectively treated in school-age children. As noted in the previous section, treatment of stuttering in preschoolers is efficiently done with fluency reinforcement, reinforcement plus corrective feedback, and response cost. In treating school-age children, fluency shaping and its components are additional procedures the clinicians may use (Guitar, 2006; Shapiro, 1999). Choices for effectively treating stuttering in school-age children include:

- **A Comprehensive Fluency Shaping Procedure.** This includes airflow management, and slower rate of speech achieved through syllable prolongation, and normal prosodic features. Most school-age children can master these fluency skills. This procedure may be needed for children with high dysfluency rate and significant mismanagement of airflow associated with stuttered speech.

- **Slower Rate of Speech.** This procedure uses only one of the skill components of the comprehensive fluency shaping procedure. In this procedure, the clinician targets a slower rate of speech as the single fluency-enhancing skill. Omitting airflow management simplifies treatment. If the child does not exhibit marked mismanagement of airflow during stuttering, the clinician can use this abbreviated fluency shaping with only slower speech as the treatment target. When slower rate of speech is the treatment target, normal prosodic features are targeted toward the end of treatment to induce natural-sounding fluency.

- **Response Cost.** This is a highly effective procedure with both preschool and school-age children. The procedure includes positive reinforcement for fluent productions by presenting tokens and reinforcement withdrawal for stuttering by removing tokens. The procedure does not target such fluency skills as airflow management, gentle phonatory onset, or slower rate of speech. Consequently, the procedure does not induce unnatural-sounding speech. Therefore, it is unnecessary to spend time on restoring normal-sounding fluency. This is an efficient procedure to treat children who stutter.

- **Pause-and-Talk (Time-Out).** Another highly effective procedure is pause-and-talk, also known as (nonexclusion) time-out from positive reinforcement. Because the time-out procedure is much misunderstood and mismanaged in educational settings, the term pause-and-talk is preferred. In this procedure, the clinician continues to socially reinforce the client's fluent speech by maintaining eye contact, smiling, nodding, expressing agreement, and letting the client engage in continuous conversation. However, when the client stutters, the clinician will immediately say "Stop!," avoid eye contact for about 5 seconds, and prevent the client from talking during this period of time-out from positive reinforcement. In essence, a stutter results in a brief pause in talking with no social reinforcement; therefore, the term pause-and-talk aptly describes the procedure.

The protocols that follow describe these procedures for treating school-age children.

Treatment of Stuttering in School-Age Children: I. Comprehensive Fluency Shaping Procedure

Overview

Fluency shaping is a well-established treatment for children and adults who stutter (Cordes & Ingham, 1998; Guitar, 2006; Shapiro, 1999). In treating the school-age children who stutter, fluency shaping may be more effectively used than in the case of preschoolers, although the method has considerable limitations. The most significant limitations include an unnatural-sounding speech and poor maintenance of fluency. By reinstating normal prosodic features, the unnaturalness of speech can be minimized and by periodic booster treatment, maintenance may be enhanced.

Fluency shaping includes a variety of procedures; it is not clear from the evidence whether all of the component procedures are essential to achieve a desirable outcome (Guitar, 2006; Shapiro, 1999). A fluency shaping program may be comprehensive in that it includes all components generally advocated. A comprehensive fluency shaping program, described in this section, includes the following skills taught to children and adults who stutter:

- **Airflow Management:** A proper management of airflow to produce fluent speech includes two component skills: a slightly greater-than-normal inhalation of air, and a prephonatory exhalation of air. Phonation is initiated on a controlled, sustained exhalation. There is replicated evidence that a proper management of airflow will reliably reduce stuttering.

- **Slower Speech Rate with Syllable Prolongation:** Prolonging syllable duration is an effective strategy to reduce or even totally eliminate dysfluencies. There is considerable replicated evidence (some controlled and some uncontrolled) to support its effectiveness. When the vowel following an initial consonant (the syllable nucleus) is prolonged, dysfluencies are almost always eliminated. This prolongation is different from the typical prolongation (a form of dysfluency) of people who stutter. Typically, people who stutter prolong the initial consonant (e.g., *ssss*up); in prolonged speech treatment, they prolong the following vowel (e.g., s*ooo*p).

- **Normal Prosodic Features:** Comprehensive fluency shaping procedure, especially because of syllable prolongation that reduces the speech rate to unusual levels, induces an unnatural quality of speech. Speech will sound excessively slow and monotonous because of absent intonation. Speech may also be too soft. Therefore, to reduce the social consequences of an unnatural-sounding speech, normal prosodic features—including speech rates, intonation, and loudness variations within the normal limits—are targeted as well. If the speech continues to sound unnatural, social acceptance will be extremely limited, and as a consequence, relapse of stuttering will be highly likely.

Clinicians sometimes include **gentle onset of phonation** as another fluency skill. Gentle initiation of phonation when a slight exhalation is already in progress is thought to be essential for fluency. Although generally well accepted, gentle phonatory onset as a means of achieving fluent speech is supported only by scant experimental evidence. Clinical experience suggests that when the child is asked to manage the airflow and speak at a slower rate, abrupt phonatory onsets are diminished to a great extent. Therefore, the protocols do not expand upon this additional target.

The target fluency skills just listed are systematically taught in a sequential manner. The airflow management is taught first. Following this, the syllable prolongation (slower rate), and normal prosodic features are taught in that order.

To begin with, the clinician describes the fluency targets the client needs to learn. The clinician models the skills described (inhalation, slight exhalation, and slow speech). Making modifications as found necessary for a given client, the clinician:

- Establishes baserates of dysfluencies or stuttering as the clinician defines them. To obtain reliable baserates of dysfluencies in a school-age child, the clinician tape-records an extended conversational speech. Showing pictures in storybooks, the clinician evokes extended speech. The clinician also asks the child to talk on a topic (e.g., birthdays, holiday parties, favorite games, friends and family, vacations) to obtain a sample of monologue-like speech. The clinician asks the child to read aloud a suitable printed passage. If practical, the clinician obtains a home speech sample for analysis of dysfluencies or stuttering. After establishing baserates, the clinician initiates treatment; begins with airflow management.

- Describes, models, and asks the client to imitate slightly more-than-the-normal inhalation of air and a slight exhalation of just inhaled air. To begin with, the clinician teaches this as an isolated skill. The clinician discourages excessive exhalation as this would defeat the purpose of having a continuous supply of air for fluent speech production. A few successful trials are sufficient to move on to the next step.

- Describes and models a slower speech rate achieved through syllable prolongation. This, too, is taught as an isolated skill (without airflow management). The clinician teaches the client to extend the duration of vowels following the initial consonants. The optimal duration of prolongation is client-specific; but it should result in stutter-free speech. For each client, the clinician should find a rate that is slow enough to eliminate dysfluencies. A few successful trials at the single word level should be sufficient to move on to the next step.

- Gives a quick overview of the three skills practiced in isolation. The clinician then describes and models integrated productions of all three skills: starting with an inhalation, quickly moving to a slight exhalation, and ending with syllable-prolonged word production. Integrated fluency skills may need to be practiced for a good portion of a treatment session.

- Moves on to the phrase level training when the client successfully produces a number of words integrated with fluency skills. In learning to produce the fluency skills in two-word phrases, the client adds a new word to the already practiced single word. For instance, a boy who has been practicing fluency skills in saying his first name (e.g., *Jhaaan*") may be asked to say his first and the last name (e.g., "*Jhaaan Jeeekəəəb*"). It is not essential to move from single words to two-word phrases in all cases; the number of words in practice phrases will depend on the client. Some clients may succeed at three to four word phrases at the beginning of this stage.

- Manages the behavioral treatment contingencies promptly and strictly. It may be noted that *fluency shaping* specifies the *target skills* the client learns to produce. Technically, fluency shaping does not specify a new treatment procedure; it specifies target fluency skills the client has to learn. A description of how those skills are taught and learned constitutes treatment. In this technical sense, treatment is still the same familiar behavioral procedures that include instructions, demonstrations, modeling, prompting, positive reinforcement for correct production of targeted skills resulting in stutter-free speech, and corrective feedback for errors in managing the skills and for dysfluencies.

- Targets normal prosodic features when the client sustains stutter-free speech (perhaps a 98% fluency, though it may sound unnatural) across a few sessions. The clinician models a slightly faster rate for the client to imitate. As the client learns to sustain stutter-free speech at the initial faster rate, the clinician models progressively faster rates and varied intonational patterns for the client to imitate. Eventually, the clinician may stabilize a speech rate that is slightly slower than the client's habitual rate that still sounds natural.

- Trains family members, teachers, and peers to recognize various forms of dysfluencies and to prompt and reinforce a slightly slower rate to sustain natural-sounding fluency in home, school, and other nonclinical settings. If practical, the parents of a child may be trained to hold informal treatment sessions at home. Such training may begin as soon as the client sustains stutter-free speech in the clinic. These steps are essential for maintenance of fluency.

- Conducts follow-up assessments and arranges for booster treatment when the results of a follow-up warrant additional treatment. The initial follow-up may be scheduled for 3 months following the dismissal. Additional follow-ups may be scheduled at 6 or 12 month intervals. In all follow-up sessions, the clinician takes an extended speech sample without treatment to calculate the percent stuttering or dysfluency rates.

The comprehensive fluency shaping treatment protocols have been written for:

1. Establishing stutter-free conversational speech
2. Establishing stutter-free narrative speech
3. Stabilizing natural-sounding fluency

Treatment of Stuttering in School-Age Children: I. Comprehensive Fluency Shaping Procedure

Establishing Stutter-Free Conversational Speech

Overview

- With school-age children, the **comprehensive fluency shaping procedure** may be initiated at the word and phrase level or the sentence level, depending on the individual child. The strategy is to initiate treatment at the highest level of response topography possible (e.g., shorter or longer sentences), not necessarily at the lowest level (e.g., single words). Because the treatment has to move through the different levels of response complexity, starting treatment at a higher level the client can perform is more efficient than routinely starting at the lowest level. Within a single session of about 30 to 40 minutes, it is possible to move to conversational level involving simple, short sentences. The treatment protocol begins with single words and phrases and moves quickly to conversations in which the child produces phrases and simple, short sentences.

- With older school-age children and adolescents who stutter, short sentences may be the starting point. A low stuttering frequency and severity may be another factor that suggests the possibility of starting treatment at the sentence level.

- The clinician may use games, toys, storybooks, and pictures in storybooks to evoke speech of varied complexity. The clinician may prompt, instruct, or otherwise encourage the child to produce shorter and longer sentences.

- Frequent modeling of the target skill or skills under training is essential in treating most children. Clinicians may also reduce their own speech rates while teaching the fluency skills. Clinicians who talk fast may find it hard to control the speech rates in children they work with.

- If dysfluencies persist, it is typically because the child has missed one or more of the target fluency skills. Missed prephonatory exhalation (resulting in impounded air in the lungs) and insufficient duration of syllable prolongation are the two most frequent reasons why dysfluencies persist under this form of treatment.

- With most children, verbal reinforcement may be effective. A small gift at the end of the session may help sustain the child's interest in the treatment session. Verbal praise may take several forms:
  - ➤ Great job! You breathed in and breathed out correctly!
  - ➤ Wonderful! You stretched your sounds well!
  - ➤ Very good! I like the way you are talking very slowly!
  - ➤ Fantastic! You are doing everything right!
  - ➤ I like your fluent speech!
  - ➤ Good job! Your speech sounds very smooth!

- Positive reinforcement should be prompt, natural, and should follow all correct production of fluency skills in the beginning stage of treatment. For instance, the clinician should promptly praise the child for inhalation, slight prephonatory exhalation, and sufficient prolongation of syllables. Subsequently, reinforcement may be more specifically directed to fluent productions that include all the target skills. The initial continuous reinforcement may be changed to one of intermittent schedule during natural conversational exchanges.

- Verbal corrective feedback should be offered immediately when the child misses any of the target fluency skills. Regardless of whether a target fluency skill was missed, the clinician should promptly give corrective feedback for all dysfluent productions. The feedback should be prompt, clear, and objective in tone. The child should stop when an error is made or a dysfluency is produced; the child should correct the error and then continue. The clinician may use several forms of corrective feedback; each should point out what went wrong:
  - ➢ Stop, you didn't breathe in before starting to talk!
  - ➢ Stop, you didn't breathe out a little!
  - ➢ Stop, that was too fast! Stretch your speech more!
  - ➢ No, you should slow down some more!
- The same stimulus materials used in baserating dysfluencies in sentences may be appropriate for treatment sessions. Familiar stories and pictures may more readily evoke speech from the child.
- If previously used stimuli fail to provoke interest in the child, the clinician may introduce novel stimuli that will sustain the child's interest.
- To evaluate the child's progress in treatment, the clinician may tape-record each session and later calculate the percent dysfluency or stuttering rate.
- If a correctly implemented comprehensive fluency shaping procedure does not produce satisfactory results, the clinician may consider alternative procedures (e.g., response cost or pause-and-talk). Although there will be individual differences, stuttering frequency during treatment should be significantly reduced in a matter of few sessions. If not, the progress may be judged unsatisfactory, leading to a change in the treatment procedure.

Treatment of Stuttering in School-Age Children: I. Comprehensive Fluency Shaping Procedure

Treatment Protocol for Stutter-Free Conversational Speech

Scripts for Establishing Stutter-Free Speech in Conversation		Note
Clinician	"Sometimes we all have problems talking very smoothly. Our words may get stuck. We may repeat what we say, sometimes not realizing it. We prolong our speech sounds. We may say a lot of *ums*. If one does a lot of these, then the person has a stuttering problem or a fluency problem. When someone stutters, it may also be called a dysfluency—not fluency. We all want to talk very smoothly and fluently. When we are not fluent, we stutter. Do you sometimes stutter?"	The clinician introduces the concepts of stuttering, dysfluency, and fluency
Child	"Yeah, sometimes."	Child shows awareness of his fluency problem
Clinician	"The good news is that you can learn to speak more fluently. If you learn to do a few things right, you, too, can be fluent like most other kids. Do you want to learn to speak fluently?"	The clinician reassures the child
Child	"Yes."	
Clinician	"You can do it. You can talk fluently like other kids. I want to help you talk fluently. Is that Okay?"	Reassures the child
Child	"Okay."	
Clinician	"Alright. To speak fluently and smoothly, you should do a few things right. Have you ever tried to speak when you had run out air in your lungs? Like this." [*demonstrates dysfluent speech production when the air is mostly exhausted.*]	Introduces the first fluency skill
Child	"Yes."	
Clinician	"You just can't talk like that, can you? You should always have enough air power to talk smoothly. We always breathe in some air before we talk. We talk only as we breathe out. Have you noticed that?"	Describes airflow

Establishing Stutter-Free Speech in Conversation, continued

Scripts for Establishing Stutter-Free Speech in Conversation		Note
Child	"Yes."	
Clinician	"Sometimes you may breathe in alright, but forget to breathe out a tiny bit of air before starting to talk. If you hold your air in your chest, and try to talk, you may simply get stuck. Words won't come out of your mouth. Like this." [*demonstrates cessation of phonation when air is impounded in the lungs.*] Do you sometimes have this problem?"	Describes and demonstrates the importance of prephonatory exhalation
Child	"Yeah."	
Clinician	"Right. The trick is to breathe in, breathe out only a tiny bit of air, and then start talking. But there is another thing that makes you stutter. It is talking very fast. When you are in a hurry, you want to say something quickly, and you try to talk fast, do you sometimes stutter?"	Summarizes airflow management skills and introduces the concept of rapid speech rate
Child	"Yes."	
Clinician	"That's right! We all stutter a bit when we try to go much faster than we really can. To beat this problem, we just have to talk slowly. Slow talking means stretching your sounds. You should not stretch many of the first sounds in a word, but the second sound. If you stretch and make your sounds longer, you won't stutter. Of course, you also should do the breathing part correctly. Which means that to beat stuttering and speak fluently, you should breathe in air, breathe out a small amount, and begin talking while stretching your sounds. Listen carefully! I am going to quiz you on this. Breathe in, breathe out a little, stretch your sounds, and talk! You will be much more fluent! Tell me what you should do to speak fluently."	Introduces slower speech through syllable prolongation and summarizes the fluency skills for the child; checks the child's understanding
Child	"Breathe in, breathe out a little, stretch my sounds, and talk."	Shows understanding of the target skills

Establishing Stutter-Free Speech in Conversation, continued

Scripts for Establishing Stutter-Free Speech in Conversation		Note
Clinician	"Great! I knew you were a smart kid! You get an *A plus* on my quiz! You breathe in, breathe out a little, stretch your sounds, and talk! Simple, isn't it? Remember, though, that you breathe in just a bit more air than usual, you breathe out only a tiny bit, but you streeeeeetch your sounds a lot. Are you now ready to start?"	Reinforces the child's understanding, summarizes the fluency skills, and discourages excessive amount of inhalation or exhalation of air
Child	"Yes."	
Clinician	"We will first practice the breathing part. Breathe in like this, and breathe out a tiny bit of air like this." [*demonstrates the airflow*]	Teaching begins with airflow management
Child	Performs the action correctly	
Clinician	"Great job! You did it correctly! Remember, you should breathe out only a small amount of air, like you did perfectly! Okay, one more time. Breathe in and breathe out a little."	Verbal praise
Child	Takes a deep breath and holds the air	Mismanagement of airflow
Clinician	"Oops! You forgot to breathe out a little bit. You shouldn't hold the air like that. Remember, you can't talk that way. Try again. Breathe in and breathe out a little. Like this." [*demonstrates the airflow*]	Prompt corrective feedback
Child	Performs the action correctly	Correct airflow management
Clinician	"That a boy! You did it perfectly! "Now that you know how to breathe in and breathe out a little bit of air before talking, we are ready to move on. You now have to add speech to your breathing. It should be smooth and fluent speech. As you begin to breathe out, you should start talking. It should be sloooow and streeeeetched out like that. [*stretches out the two words*] Are you ready to practice slow speech?" [*asks this question at a very slow rate*]	Verbal praise **If judged essential, the clinician may provide additional practice trials on airflow management. Some children do need more trials.**
Child	"Yes."	

Establishing Stutter-Free Speech in Conversation, continued

Scripts for Establishing Stutter-Free Speech in Conversation		Note
Clinician	"Okay, we can talk just about anything and practice fluent speech. I will ask you a lot of questions, even though I may know some of the answers. I do this only to let you practice fluent speech. I will ask a question or ask you to tell me something. I will then right away show you how to answer it or say something. Now for example, what is your first name? You first breathe in and breathe out a bit like this [*demonstrates*] and as you are breathing out, say, Jhaaaan. You heard how I stretched out the aaaaaa in John. You try it."	Sets the stage of slow speech practice
Child	"Jhaaa . . ."	Mismanaged airflow
Clinician	"Stop! You forgot the breathing part. First do the breathing part and then say Jhaaaaan. Like this." [*models airflow and slow speech on the child's name*]	Corrective feedback for mismanaged airflow. Stops the child from speaking; models the target skills
Child	[*correct airflow*] "Jhaaaan."	Correct response
Clinician	"Excellent! That's exactly what I want you to do! You did the breathing part and you said it very slowly! Now tell me your last name. Do the breathing part and say it slowly. Say, Jhaaaanson." [*demonstrates airflow management and slow rate*]	Verbal praise and initiation of the next trial
Child	[*correct airflow*] "Joh . . ."	Failure to stretch
Clinician	"Stop! You did the breathing part right, but you didn't stretch the syllables. Try it again. Like this. Jhaaaanson." [*demonstrates airflow management and slow rate*]	Corrective feedback and modeling
Child	[*correct airflow*] "Jhaaaanson."	Correct response
Clinician	"Excellent! You did everything right! Tell me your Mom's first name. Remember how you should say it."	Verbal praise and the initiation of the next trial
Child	"Jaaa . . ."	Mismanagement of airflow
Clinician	"No! You forgot the breathing part. Try it again."	Corrective feedback

Establishing Stutter-Free Speech in Conversation, continued

Scripts for Establishing Stutter-Free Speech in Conversation		Note
Child	[*correct airflow*] "Jaaaane."	Correct response
Clinician	"Way to go! You did everything right! Now tell me your Dad's first name. Breathe in breathe out, and stretch out!"	Verbal praise; next trial; prompt
Child	[*correct airflow*] "Taaaam."	Correct response
Clinician	"Wonderful! You are doing really well! How many brothers do you have? Just say one word—a number. Say it correctly."	Verbal praise; the next question
Child	[*correct airflow*] "One."	No stretching
Clinician	"Not correct! You forgot to slow down. Try it again. Don't forget any part."	Corrective feedback
Child	[*correct airflow*] "Oooooone."	Correct response
Clinician	"I like that! You did it correctly! What is your brother's name? Remember everything."	Verbal praise
Child	[*correct airflow*] "Mmmm . . ."	Sound prolongation
Clinician	"Stop! You stuttered. You have to quickly open your mouth and prolong the next sound. Try it again."	Corrective feedback; instruction
Child	[*correct airflow*] "Maaaany."	Correct response
Clinician	"Very good! See, you didn't stutter when you quickly started to say the aaaaa part of your brother's name! Do you have a sister?"	Verbal praise; points out the reason for success
Child	"Yes."	No airflow management, no slow speech
Clinician	"Oops! You forgot everything. Say that again. Make it right."	Corrective feedback
Child	[*correct airflow*] "Yeeees."	Correct response
Clinician	"Excellent! You said it right and you didn't stutter! What is your sister's name?"	Verbal praise; next question
Child	[*correct airflow*] "Maaaanica."	Correct response
Clinician	"Very good! Everything correct! How old is Monica?"	Verbal praise; next question

Establishing Stutter-Free Speech in Conversation, continued

Scripts for Establishing Stutter-Free Speech in Conversation		Note
Child	"FFFif . . ."	Sound prolongation; missing fluency skills
Clinician	"Stop! You forgot breathing and stretching. When you forget, you stutter, you see! Is she fifteen? [*the child nods*] Say fiiiifteeeen." [*demonstrates airflow management and syllable stretching.*]	Corrective feedback and modeling
Child	[*correct airflow*] "Fiiiifteeeen."	Correct response
Clinician	"Excellent! That's the way to do it. You know it was smooth. You have been doing well. Now, maybe you can say two or three words at a time. Tell me your full name. Breathe-and-stretch."	Verbal praise **Treatment shifted to the phrase level.** **However, the clinician may give additional trials at the single-word level if necessary.**
Child	[*correct airflow*] "Jhaaaan Jhaaaanson."	Correct response
Clinician	"That was great! You did everything right! Now, tell me your Mom's full name."	Verbal praise
Child	"Jaaaa . . ."	Missed airflow management
Clinician	"Stop! You forgot the breathing part. Try again."	Corrective feedback
Child	[*correct airflow*] "Jaaaane Jhaaaanson."	Correct response
Clinician	"Wonderful! You are doing great! Tell me your Dad's full name."	Verbal praise
Child	[*correct airflow*] "Taaaam Jhaaaanson."	Correct response
Clinician	"Fantastic! You know how to do it! Tell me your brother's full name."	Verbal praise
Child	[*correct airflow*] "Maaaany Jhaaaanson."	Correct response
Clinician	"Very good! You are breathing and stretching correctly! Now, tell me your sister's full name."	Verbal praise
Child	"Mmm . . ."	Mismanages airflow; sound prolongation
Clinician	"Stop! Did you forget something?"	Corrective feedback. Prompts self-evaluation
Child	"Yeah. Breathing part."	Correct self-evaluation

Establishing Stutter-Free Speech in Conversation, continued

Scripts for Establishing Stutter-Free Speech in Conversation		Note
Clinician	"That's very good! You know what went wrong. Now try that again. Your sister's full name."	Reinforces self-evaluation
Child	[*correct airflow*] "Maaaanica Jhaaaanson."	Correct response
Clinician	"Excellent! Now, try your brother's full name again."	Verbal praise; a second attempt on brother's full name
Child	[*correct airflow*] "Maaaany Jhaaaanson."	Correct response
Clinician	"Good job! I like the way you are talking. Maybe you can now try to say more words each time. For example, if I ask you *where are you now*, you say, *in the school.* Try that."	Verbal praise **Treatment shifted to longer phrases and sentences** **However, the clinician may give additional trials at the two-word phrase level if necessary**
Child	[*correct airflow*] "Iiiiin theee schooool."	Correct response
Clinician	"Excellent! You said three words, all correctly! Where do you live? Say, [*modeling the correct response*] *I live in Fresno.*"	Verbal praise; **from now on, for ease of reading, syllable stretching is not shown orthographically**
Child	[*correct airflow and stretching*] "I live in Fresno."	Correct response
Clinician	"Excellent! You are saying more words correctly! What grade are you in? Say [*modeling the correct response*], *in the fourth grade.*"	Verbal praise
Child	[*correct airflow*] "In the fff . . . "	Sound prolongation
Clinician	"No, you didn't stretch it enough. That's why you stuttered. Try that again like this [*modeling the correct response*], *in the fourth grade.*"	Corrective feedback
Child	[*correct airflow and stretching*] "In the fourth grade."	Correct response
Clinician	"Excellent! That's the way to do it! How many brothers do you have? Say [*modeling the correct response*], *I have one brother.*"	Verbal praise
Child	[*correct airflow and stretching*] "I have one brother."	Correct response
Clinician	"Excellent! You are getting a good hang of it! How many sisters do you have? Remember to say it right."	Verbal praise No modeling; an evoking question
Child	[*correct airflow and stretching*] "I have one sister."	Correct response
Clinician	"Great job! How old is your sister? Start with, *my sister . . .* "	Verbal praise Prompts a longer utterance

Establishing Stutter-Free Speech in Conversation, continued

Scripts for Establishing Stutter-Free Speech in Conversation		Note
Child	[*correct airflow and stretching*] "My sister is fifteen."	Correct response
Clinician	"Very nice! I like the way you are doing the breathing part and stretching your speech. You are not stuttering at all! Now, I think you are ready to try some longer sentences. But you shouldn't forget how to say them. What does your Mom do? Start with, *My mom . . .* "	Verbal praise **Treatment shifted to longer sentences** **However, the clinician may give additional trials at the shorter sentence levels** Prompts a longer sentence
Child	"Mmmm . . ."	No airflow, no stretching
Clinician	"Stop! What happened? But say what happened correctly!"	Corrective feedback Prompted self-evaluation
Child	[*correct airflow and stretching*] "I forgot!"	Correct self-evaluation
Clinician	"Okay, but it's good that you know when things go wrong! You stutter when you forget the breathing and the stretching parts. Now try that again. What does your Mom do?"	Reinforces self-evaluation
Child	[*correct airflow and stretching*] "My mom teaches in a school."	Correct response
Clinician	"That was very nice! That was a long sentence, too! See, you can do it! Tell me what does your Dad do?"	Verbal praise
Child	[*correct airflow and stretching*] "My dad is a musician."	Correct response
Clinician	"Fantastic! You can say long sentences correctly! What kind of musical instrument does your Dad play?"	Verbal praise
Child	[*correct airflow and stretching*] "He plays the piano."	Correct response
Clinician	"Great job! Where does he play?"	Verbal praise
Child	[*correct airflow and stretching until the dysfluent production*] "He plays with the Fresno Ph-ph- . . ."	Partially correct response; sound prolongation
Clinician	"Stop! You stuttered. Move quickly to the next sound and stretch it. Like this. Phiiiilhaaarmooooniiic. Say the whole sentence."	Corrective feedback Models syllable stretching
Child	[*correct airflow and stretching*] "He plays with the Fresno Philharmonic."	Correct response

Establishing Stutter-Free Speech in Conversation, continued

Scripts for Establishing Stutter-Free Speech in Conversation		Note
Clinician	"Very nice! Have you been to your Dad's concerts? Say it in a complete sentence."	Verbal praise Prompts sentence productions
Child	[*correct airflow and stretching*] "Yes, I have gone to many concerts."	Correct response
Clinician	"Good job! You know what, you are very lucky! Those concerts are great, aren't they?"	Verbal praise
Child	[*correct airflow and stretching*] "Yes."	Correct response
Clinician	"Very good! What does your brother Manny do? Say it in a long sentence."	Verbal praise
Child	[*correct airflow and stretching*] "He goes to Fresno city college."	Correct response
Clinician	"Wonderful! See how you can avoid all that stuttering by breathing and stretching correctly! Now, do you have a lot of friends? Sentence, please!"	Verbal praise
Child	[*correct airflow and stretching*] "I have a lot of friends."	Correct response
Clinician	"Fine job of breathing and stretching! Tell me the name of your best friend. Start with, *my best friend's name is . . .*"	Verbal praise Prompts a longer sentence
Child	[*correct airflow and stretching until the dysfluent production*] "My best friend's name is T-t-t-t . . ."	Part-word repetition
Clinician	"Stop! You stuttered because you didn't stretch. Try that again. Stretch really well."	Corrective feedback
Child	[*correct airflow and stretching*] "My best friend's name is Tommy."	Correct response
Clinician	"I like your smooth speech! How old is your best friend Tommy? Start with, *my best friend . . .*"	Verbal praise
Child	[*correct airflow and stretching*] "My best friend Tommy is eleven."	Correct response
Clinician	"Very good! Nice breathing and stretching! Is Tommy a student in this school? A long sentence, please!"	Verbal praise

Establishing Stutter-Free Speech in Conversation, continued

Scripts for Establishing Stutter-Free Speech in Conversation		Note
Child	[*correct airflow and stretching*] "My best friend Tommy is not a student in this school."	Correct response
Clinician	"Wonderful! Really long, smooth sentence! So which school does he attend? Start with *he attends* . . . and tell me where the school is."	Verbal praise
Child	[*correct airflow and stretching*] "He attends Freedom Intermediate School in Sanger."	Correct response
Clinician	"Great job! Does Tommy live in your neighborhood? *Yes, he* . . ."	Verbal praise Prompts a longer sentence
Child	[*correct airflow and stretching*] "Yes, he lives in our neighborhood."	Correct response
Clinician	"Excellent! Your speech is very smooth. Do you get to play with him almost every day? *Yes I* . . ."	Verbal praise
Child	[*correct airflow and stretching*] "Yes, I play with him almost every day."	Correct response
Clinician	"You are doing really well!"	Verbal praise

The clinician continues to teach the fluency skills in the manner described in the protocols. The number of sessions in the establishment phase will be child-specific. When the child has sustained fluency skills as well as stutter-free speech in conversational speech across three or four sessions, the clinician shifts training to the next phase, which involves narrative speech.

The following protocols may be used to establish stutter-free speech in narrative speech.

Treatment of Stuttering in School-Age Children:
I. Comprehensive Fluency Shaping Procedure

Establishing Stutter-Free Narrative Speech

Overview

- With school-age children, the **comprehensive fluency shaping procedure** initiated at the conversational speech level should be shifted to narrative speech level as soon as possible. In the narrative speech level, the clinician tells stories to the child and asks the child to retell the stories using the airflow management and syllable prolongation.

- The clinician selects stories that are appropriate for the child under treatment. Stories from the child's grade level may be especially useful. The child may be asked to bring a storybook he or she reads at home or in the classroom. In all cases, the stories selected should be relevant to the child's ethnocultural background, although stories of universal appeal may be especially useful with a variety of children.

- Frequent modeling of the target skill or skills under training should not be essential at this level of training. Nonetheless, clinicians may reduce their own speech rates while narrating stories to the child. Clinical experience suggests that slower and more deliberate narration tends to initiate slower rate of speech as the child begins to narrate the story back to the clinician. Clinicians who narrate stories at a fast speech rate may find it hard to control the speech rates in children who retell the stories.

- If dysfluencies persist, it is typically because the child has missed one or more of the target fluency skills. Regardless of the level of treatment, missed prephonatory exhalation (resulting in impounded air in the lungs) and insufficient duration of syllable prolongation are the two most frequent reasons why dysfluencies persist under this form of treatment.

- Verbal reinforcement for accurate management of fluency skills and corrective feedback for stuttering or mismanaged fluency skills may be continued as in the previous level of treatment.

Treatment of Stuttering in School-Age Children:
I. Comprehensive Fluency Shaping Procedure

Treatment Protocol for Stutter-Free Narrative Speech

Scripts for Establishing Stutter-Free Speech in Narration		Note
Clinician	"You have been doing really well in learning to breathe correctly for speech and slowing down. Your speech has been very smooth for several sessions. I am now going to tell you a story. I want you to listen carefully, because when I am finished with it, I want you to tell me the whole story. You should tell me the story with correct breathing and very slow speech. Okay?"	Introduces the new narrative task
Child	"Okay."	
Clinician	"Now listen carefully. I want you to tell me everything I tell you in this story. "This is the story of a clever crow. One hot summer day, the crow got very thirsty. He was looking for some water. He flew here. He flew there, looking for water. Then he saw a pot with a little bit of water in it. He sat on the top of the pot and put his head into it to drink the water. But he couldn't reach the water. The water was way down in the bottom of that pot. He stretched his neck and he bent his body to reach the water. No matter how hard he tried, he couldn't reach the water. Sight of the water made him even more thirsty. He then looked around and saw some pebbles on the ground. He thought of a clever idea. He picked up one pebble and dropped it into the pot. He picked up another pebble and dropped it into the pot. He saw the water was rising, but he still couldn't reach it. He dropped many more pebbles into the pot. He saw the water coming up fast! He put a lot more pebbles into the pot. Then the water came all the way up! He then sat on the top of the pot and drank all the water in it. That's the end of the story. "Now you tell me the story. Remember the breathing part and the slow speech."	Tells the story of the clever and thirsty crow

Establishing Stutter-Free Speech in Narration, continued

Scripts for Establishing Stutter-Free Speech in Narration		Note
Child	[*begins with correct airflow and slow speech*] "It was a hot summer day. There was a crow. He got very thirsty. He was looking for some water. He flew here. He flew there. Then he saw a pot with a little bit of water in it. He sat on the top of the pot [*speeds up the rate; the clinician says "slow down;" the child slows down*] and tried to drink the water. But he couldn't drink it. The water was in the bottom of that pot. He stretched his neck and he bent his body. But he couldn't drink the water. He became more thirsty because he saw water in the pot. He then saw some pebbles on the ground. He thought of a clever idea. He picked up one pebble [*speeds up the rate; the clinician says "slow down;" the child slows down*] and dropped it into the pot. He picked up another pebble and dropped it into the pot. Water was coming up, but he still couldn't reach it. He dropped many more pebbles into the pot. Then the water came all the way up! He drank all the water in it. That's the end of the story."	Narrates the story in stutter-free speech Receives prompts to slow down when the speech rate increases
Clinician	"That was a great story! Your speech was very smooth, too! I had to remind you only twice to go slow! "Are you ready for another story?"	Verbal praise During the child's narration, gave prompts to speak slowly
Child	"Oh yeah! I like your stories!"	
Clinician	"Again, listen carefully! You have to tell me the whole story. "Once upon a time, there was a farmer. He owned a lot of land. The farmer loved to eat chocolate cakes and ride on his shiny black horse. He had three sons. When the farmer became old, he wanted to retire. He wanted to take it easy, eat good food, and ride his horses. He then decided that he would give his farm to one of his sons who was the smartest of all. He couldn't decide who was the smartest. So he arranged a contest for them. He gave his sons a hundred dollars each and told them to spend it any way they liked. The farmer also told them that he would decide who gets the farm depending on how they spent their money. *(continued)*	Tells another story in two parts

Establishing Stutter-Free Speech in Narration, continued

Scripts for Establishing Stutter-Free Speech in Narration		Note
Clinician *(continues)*	"That is the first part of the story. You tell me the first part and then I will tell you the rest. Don't forget the breathing part and the slow speech."	Asks the child to narrate the first part
Child	"Once upon a time, there was a farmer. He had three sons. He owned a lot of land. The farmer loved to eat chocolate cakes and ride on his black horse. When the farmer became old, he wanted to retire. He wanted to eat good food and ride his horses. He then decided that [*speeds up the rate; the clinician says "slow down;" the child slows down*] he would give his farm to a son who was the smartest of all. He didn't know who was the smartest son. So he arranged a contest for them. He gave each son a hundred dollars. He told them to spend it any way they liked and he will decide who gets the farm depending on how they spent their money."	Stutter-free speech Gets prompted to slow down only once
Clinician	"That was great! Your speech was very smooth. It was slow and nice! You are a good storyteller, too! Now I will tell you the rest of the story. "After three days, the sons came home in the evening. Each son secretly hid what he had bought in a separate room. Each wanted to surprise and impress his Dad to get the farm. When the night fell, the sons went to their Dad and said they were ready to show how they spent their money. The first son took the father to a room and opened the doors. To his delight, the farmer saw two dozen huge chocolate cakes, all decorated beautifully! The farmer's mouth was watering like crazy! The second son then took him to another room. When he opened the door, the farmer saw a huge shiny, black horse! He was so thrilled that he was ready to ride the horses right then. But the third son said, 'Dad, I want to show you how I spent the money,' so the farmer followed him to the third room. When the third son opened the door, the farmer stepped in and saw a large table on which there were two dozen huge candles burning beautifully! The son then told his father, 'Dad, I spent two dollars and forty cents on the candles and ten cents on a box of matches. I spent a total of two dollars and fifty cents. Here is your ninety-seven dollars and fifty cents. Please take it back.'" *(continued)*	Verbal praise Tells the rest of the story

Establishing Stutter-Free Speech in Narration, continued

Scripts for Establishing Stutter-Free Speech in Narration		Note
Clinician *(continues)*	"You tell me this story and also guess who got the farm. Don't forget how you should to talk."	
Child	"After spending their money, the sons came home. It was evening. Each son went to a room and secretly hid the thing he bought. Each wanted to surprise and impress his Dad. Each wanted the farm for himself. When it was nighttime, the sons told their Dad they were ready to show what they bought. The first son took the father to a room and showed two dozen huge chocolate cakes. They were nicely decorated. The farmer's mouth was watering like crazy! The second son then took him to another room. And showed the farmer a huge and shiny black horse! Dad was thrilled. He wanted to ride that horse. But the . . . [*the clinician prompts: "third son"*] third son wanted to show what he bought. The farmer followed him. When the third son opened the door, the farmer saw a large table. He saw . . . [*the clinician prompts: "two dozen"*] two dozen huge candles burning beautifully! The son then told his father, 'Dad, I spent two dollars and some cents? [*the clinician prompts: "forty cents"*] yes, forty cents on the candles and how many? [*the clinician prompts: "ten cents"*] yes, ten cents on a box of matches.' He said, I totally spent . . . how much was it? [*the clinician prompts: "two dollars and fifty cents"*] yes, two dollars and fifty cents. Here is your ninety-seven dollars and some cents. Please take it back.'"	Narrates with stutter-free speech
Clinician	"That was fantastic! You did not stutter once! You did everything right! Now guess who got the farm?"	Verbal praise
Child	"I think the third son got the farm."	A stutter-free production
Clinician	"Good talking, and correct guess! But why do you think the third son got the farm?"	Verbal praise
Child	"The candles were nice! He saved a lot of money for his Dad!"	A stutter-free production
Clinician	"Smooth speech. And, you are right! The third son got the farm because he was wise in spending Dad's money. The farmer decided that his smartest third son will take good care of the farm."	Verbal praise

If the child could not maintain at least a 97 to 98% stutter-free speech in story narration, the clinician may tell additional stories and have the child repeat them. When a child retells a story, the clinician should:

• Verbally praise the child at the end of the narration
• Stop the child and give corrective feedback if there is evidence of mismanagement of fluency skills and remind the child about the fluency skills to be maintained
• Pay greater attention to slower rate than to airflow management
• Prompt story elements when the child is unsure of any aspects of a story being retold

When the child has maintained stutter-free speech in narratives across two or three sessions, the clinician may shift training to the next level in which normal prosodic features are re-established.

Following protocols help establish prosodic features essential for normal-sounding speech.

Treatment of Stuttering in School-Age Children: I. Comprehensive Fluency Shaping Procedure

Stabilizing Natural-Sounding Fluency

Overview

* The immediate effects of fluency shaping is not normal fluency; it is *stutter-free speech*, as it may indeed, almost completely, be free of stuttering. Unfortunately, the stutter-free speech generated by fluency shaping is an unnatural-sounding speech. The stutter-free speech is too slow, sometimes too soft, and always too monotonous to be socially acceptable.

* Children who are treated with fluency shaping may be reluctant to talk in a slow and monotonous manner in the classroom or with their friends. They may sense a negative reaction from certain listeners who do not understand why the child is speaking so slowly. Children themselves may think that their speech is unacceptable. They may find the constant monitoring of speech rate and airflow required to reduce stuttering a tiring exercise. Some children may think that they would rather stutter and speak naturally than adopt an unnatural manner of speaking to reduce their stuttering.

* Because of those problems associated with fluency shaping, it is essential to shape natural-sounding speech before the child is dismissed. Natural-sounding speech is most effectively reinstated with a rate that approximates the child's typical, pretreatment rate. Most listeners do not quantitatively measure a speaker's rate of speech. They make global judgments as to whether the speech sounds natural or not. Therefore, clinicians, too can make judgments of speech naturalness. This judgment may include not only the rate but also the intonational patterns (pitch and loudness variations). Clinicians in the schools may invite comments about a child's speech naturalness from teachers, peers, and others. Family members are always among the best judges of speech naturalness.

* Natural-sounding fluency is induced essentially in a shaping program. In this procedure, the client may be asked to:
  ➢ gradually increase the rate of speech
  ➢ increase and vary the loudness of voice
  ➢ vary the vocal pitch throughout an utterance

* In instating natural-sounding speech, the clinician will:
  ➢ frequently model faster rate and improved intonation
  ➢ systematically reinforce any movement toward more natural-sounding speech
  ➢ give prompt corrective feedback when the client exhibit slower and monotonous speech

The protocols to follow are written to achieve these goals of natural-sounding speech.

Treatment of Stuttering in School-Age Children:
I. Comprehensive Fluency Shaping Procedure
Treatment Protocol for Natural-Sounding Speech

Scripts for Stabilizing Natural-Sounding Speech		Note
Clinician	"You have been doing really well in learning to breathe correctly for speech and slowing down. Your speech has been very smooth for several sessions. You have hardly stuttered in the last few sessions. But to avoid stuttering, you have been speaking very slowly. It is a bit too slow for most situations, isn't it? You wouldn't like to talk this slowly, even though it helps you not stutter, in the classroom or when you are with friends. Even at home, you may want to talk a little faster. Right?"	Explains the need for the next stage of treatment
Child	"Right."	
Clinician	"When people talk very slowly, their speech is kind of flat, isn't it? It may also be very soft. You don't have ups and downs in your voice like this [*demonstrates pitch variations*]. You want to talk not too slowly, loudly enough, and speak with a voice that shows ups and downs, like I am doing now. You should also speak without stuttering. That's the natural way of talking. The natural way of talking means that you sound like kids who don't stutter. We now have to practice the trick of not stuttering while speaking more naturally. Do you understand what I mean by natural way of talking? Do you want to talk more naturally and yet without stuttering?"	Describes the problems associated with slow speech
Child	"Yes. I want to talk more naturally. I don't want to stutter."	Shows understanding
Clinician	"Very good. That's what we will practice now. No stuttering, but faster, more natural speech. Like most people talk. [*models a rate slightly faster than the child's clinical rate*] Now let us start with a slightly faster speech. You can talk, maybe more like this, and see what happens. Remember, your goal is not to stutter when you speed up. Therefore, you have to increase the speed of your speech gradually. If you suddenly go too fast, you may lose control of your smooth speech. It's like driving too fast and losing control of the car. Do you understand?"	Models a slightly faster rate for the child to imitate

Stabilizing Natural-Sounding Speech, continued

Scripts for Stabilizing Natural-Sounding Speech		Note
Child	"Yes I do."	
Clinician	[*still speaking at only a slightly higher rate than the child's clinical rate*] "To practice more natural speech, we can have a conversation about anything. Now, tell me what you did this last weekend. Talk slightly faster like this, but without stuttering."	Initiates treatment
Child	"I don't remember."	Slightly increased speech rate
Clinician	[*modeling the target rate*] "You spoke slightly faster as I wanted! Very good. Try to remember what you did. What did you do Saturday morning? Speak slightly faster like this."	Verbal praise
Child	"Saturday morning I watched some cartoons."	Increased speech rate
Clinician	[*modeling the target rate*] "Very good! You are talking a little bit faster, but you are not stuttering! That's what we want. Well, what kind of cartoons did you watch? Were they funny? Scary?"	Verbal praise; maintains conversation
Child	"They were funny. One was scary."	Increased speech rate
Clinician	[*modeling the target rate*] "Can you tell me about the funny cartoons you saw? Who were the characters? What happens in the cartoon?"	Evoking speech
Child	[*Talks about specific cartoons watched*]	Maintains the target speech rate
Clinician	[*Helps maintain conversation; asks questions, prompts details, periodically reinforces the increased speech rate, and stops when the child's rate increases too fast or when the child stutters.*] [*modeling the target rate*] "Okay we can talk about something else now. Tell me about your grandma and grandpa. Do they live in town?"	Provides verbal praise and corrective feedback Introduces a new topic of conversation
Child	"Yes, they live in town."	Maintains the target speech rate
Clinician	[*modeling the target rate*] "Good speech! You are doing well in talking slightly faster. Do they live near your home or are they far away? How often do you see them?"	Verbal praise
Child	"They live nearby. [*excessive rate increase*] We see them . . ."	Inappropriate target speech rate

Stabilizing Natural-Sounding Speech, continued

Scripts for Stabilizing Natural-Sounding Speech		Note
Clinician	[*modeling the target rate*] "Oops! You are going too fast. Slow down a bit and tell me about your recent trip to your grandparents' house."	Corrective feedback for excessively fast speech rate
Child	"Okay, I will talk this fast. We see them almost every Sunday. We meet in our church on Sunday mornings. Then sometimes we go to their house for lunch. Sometimes they come to our house for lunch. Sometimes we go to a restaurant for lunch. Last Sunday we all went to a restaurant and had lunch."	Maintains the target speech rate
Clinician	[*modeling the target rate*] "That was fantastic! You said a lot with good speed. You didn't stutter either! Do you remember what restaurant you went to last Sunday? Is that your favorite restaurant?"	Verbal praise
Child	"Yeah, it is my favorite restaurant. It is called the Big Town Waffles. [*slows down too much*] We went . . . "	Reverts to the clinical rate
Clinician	[*models the target rate and intonation*] "Stop! That is too slow. Did you notice, your speech became [*models the slower rate with flat intonation*] too flat, like this, as you slowed down! No ups and downs in your voice? [*models the target rate and intonation*] Talk a little bit faster like this, and keep those ups and downs in your voice, like this. Alright, did you go to the Big Town Waffles last Sunday for lunch? What did you eat there?"	Corrective feedback; models both the inappropriate and appropriate speech patterns
Child	"Yes, we went to the Big Town Waffles for lunch last Sunday. I had waffles with strawberries, banana, whipped cream, and ice cream."	Maintains the slightly increased target rate
Clinician	"Very nice speed! You are not stuttering either! Maybe now you can increase the speed just a tiny bit. [*modeling a slightly increased, new target speech rate*] Maybe you can talk more like this. Do you have another favorite restaurant?"	Verbal praise
Child	"We sometimes go to Mama Mia Pizza. I love pizza. [*excessive increase in speech rate*] My Mmmmom . . . "	Too fast a rate and a sound prolongation
Clinician	"Oh No! Stop, you are going too fast. See what happens when you go too fast? You stutter! [*modeling the target rate*] Talk more like this. You were saying, *my Mom . . .* "	Corrective feedback; modeling

Stabilizing Natural-Sounding Speech, continued

Scripts for Stabilizing Natural-Sounding Speech		Note
Child	"Yeah. My Mom and Dad don't like pizza. They never take us to pizza places. But my grandparents like pizza. They take my sister and me to Mama Mia."	Maintains the target rate
Clinician	[*modeling the target rate*] "That was great! You are slowly speeding up but not stuttering! What kind of pizza do you like? Does your sister like the same kind?"	Verbal praise
Child	"We like different kinds of pizza. I like only cheese and sausage pizza. My sister likes only cheese and pepperoni pizza. My grandma and grandpa like only vegetarian pizza. Yuck! Every time we go there, my grandparents have to order three kinds of pizza!"	Maintains the target rate
Clinician	"You are doing really well. Your voice is also going up and down as you talk. But you can still practice that a little bit more as you talk. This time, I want you to ask me a few questions. I will model them for you with voice going up and down. Okay?" [*the child nods*] Okay. Ask me, *how are* **you** *today?*" [*models a target rate and higher pitch on the bolded word*]	Describes pitch variations as the explicit target **Bold** type face suggests increased vocal pitch on that word
Child	"How are **you** today?"	Higher pitch on *you*
Clinician	"I am fine, thank you! That was good speech! You kept a good speed and your voice went up on the word *you*. Now ask me, *how* **are** *you today?*"	Verbal praise and modeling
Child	"How **are** you today?"	Correct imitation
Clinician	"Very good. Ask me, *how are you* **today**?"	Verbal praise; modeling
Child	"How are you **today**?"	Correct imitation
Clinician	"That was good! You know how to vary your voice."	May continue this type of treatment for additional time

The number of sessions in which the clinician stabilizes natural-sounding speech will be child-specific. The child is ready for dismissal only when probes in which reinforcement and corrective feedback are kept to a minimum and yet the child maintains a desirable rate and natural-sounding speech with few or no dysfluencies.

If necessary, the clinician may reuse the protocols given for narrative speech. The child may be asked to retell the same stories with progressively faster rate and desirable patterns of intonation.

Treatment of Stuttering in School-Age Children:
I. Comprehensive Fluency Shaping Procedure

Treatment Recording Sheet

Personalize and print this page from the CD.

Name of the child:	DOB:
Name of the parents:	Phone:
Diagnosis: Stuttering	Session date(s):
Clinician:	Comments:

Chart the child's progress for each session with your preferred method. You may calculate a percent dysfluency or stuttering rate based on the number of words spoken. If more detailed data are warranted, score the individual dysfluency types and add them up to calculate the dysfluency rate.

Essential Measures		Optional Measures: Frequency of Specific Dysfluency Types					
Dates of Service	Percent Stuttering	Prolongations	Pauses	Repetitions	Interjections	Revisions	Incomplete Phrases

Treatment of Stuttering in School-Age Children: I. Comprehensive Fluency Shaping Procedure

Probe Protocol

Probe Procedure

- Record two conversational speech samples, each 5 to 7 minutes in duration
- Record a 3-minute monologue; ask the child to talk about a topic such as:
  - ➢ Birthday parties
  - ➢ Vacations
  - ➢ Visit to a zoo or a theme park
  - ➢ Favorite games or TV shows
  - ➢ Weekend activities
  - ➢ Family and friends
  - ➢ Teachers and friends at school
  - ➢ Any other child-specific topic
- Obtain a 5-minute home speech sample
- Record one or more extraclinic speech samples in such places as the child's classroom, cafeteria, and the playground
- Analyze the percent dysfluency or stuttering rate
- Personalize the *Probe Recording Sheet* and record the dysfluency or stuttering rates; print the sheet for child's clinical file

Treatment of Stuttering in School-Age Children:
I. Comprehensive Fluency Shaping Procedure

Probe Recording Sheet

Personalize and print this page from the CD.

Name of the child:	DOB:
Name of the parents:	Phone:
Diagnosis: Stuttering	Session date(s):
Clinician:	Comments:

Analyze the probe speech samples with your preferred method. You may calculate a percent dysfluency or stuttering rate based on the number of words spoken. If more detailed data are warranted, score the individual dysfluency types and add them up to calculate the dysfluency rate.

Take at least three clinic probe samples. If possible, obtain three extraclinic probe samples.

Essential Measures		Optional Measures: Frequency of Specific Dysfluency Types					
Dates/Setting of Probe	Percent Stuttering	PRO	PAU	REP	INT	REV	INC
1. /mm/dd/yy/ Clinic							
2. /mm/dd/yy/ Clinic							
3. /mm/dd/yy/ Clinic							
1. /mm/dd/yy/ Home							
2. /mm/dd/yy/ Classroom							
3. /mm/dd/yy/ Playground							

PRO (Prolongations); PAU (Pauses); REP (Repetitions); INT (Interjections); REV (Revisions); INC (Incomplete phrases).

Dismiss the child from current services when the child's stuttering or dysfluency rate stays below the target percentage in conversational probes. Schedule follow-ups and booster treatments as needed.

Treatment of Stuttering in School-Age Children: II. Prolonged Speech

Overview

In treating school-age children who stutter, prolonged speech may be an exclusive treatment program. Unlike the fluency shaping procedure described in the previous section, an exclusive prolonged speech procedure omits the airflow management and does not specifically target gentle phonatory onset. There are only two fluency skills to master: prolonged speech (initially) and natural-sounding speech (later). Therefore, an exclusive prolonged speech procedure is a simplified fluency shaping technique, although it retains the limitations of the latter (Cordes & Ingham, 1998; Guitar, 2006; Shapiro, 1999). The most significant limitations include an unnatural-sounding speech and poor maintenance of fluency. Although no controlled data are available, clinical impression is that children who are treated with prolonged speech maintain fluency better than adults who are treated with the same technique. In fact, children who are effectively treated with any procedure maintain fluency better than adults treated with any procedure.

An exclusive prolonged speech technique includes the following:

- **Slower Speech Rate with Syllable Prolongation.** Prolonging syllable duration to reduce the speech rate is an effective strategy to control or even totally eliminate dysfluencies. There is considerable replicated evidence (some controlled and some uncontrolled) to support its application (Cordes & Ingham, 1998). When the vowel following an initial consonant (the syllable nucleus) is prolonged, dysfluencies are almost always eliminated. This prolongation is different from the typical prolongation (a form of dysfluency) of people who stutter. Typically, people who stutter prolong the initial consonant (e.g., *ssss*up); in prolonged speech treatment, they prolong the following vowel (e.g., s*ooo*p).

- **Normal Prosodic Features.** Syllable prolongation that reduces the speech rate to unusual levels induces an unnatural quality to speech. Speech will sound excessively slow and monotonous because of absent intonation. Speech may also be too soft. Therefore, to reduce the social consequences of an unnatural-sounding speech, normal prosodic features—including speech rates, intonation, and loudness variations within the normal limits—are targeted as well. If the speech continues to sound unnatural, social acceptance will be extremely limited, and as a consequence, relapse of stuttering will be highly likely.

Initially, the clinician teaches the child to prolong the syllables and blend words into each other. When stutter-free speech is well established across a few sessions, the clinician allows the child to speak progressively faster to reshape the normal prosodic features and natural-sounding fluent speech. Making modifications as found necessary for a given client, the clinician:

- Establishes baserates of dysfluencies or stuttering as the clinician defines them. To obtain reliable baserates of dysfluencies in a school-age child, the clinician tape-records an extended conversational speech. Showing pictures in storybooks, the clinician evokes extended speech. The clinician also asks the child to talk on a topic (e.g., birthdays, holiday parties, favorite games, vacations) to obtain a sample of monologue-like speech. The clinician asks the child to read aloud a suitable printed passage. If practical, the clinician obtains a home speech sample for analysis of dysfluencies or stuttering. After establishing baserates, the clinician initiates treatment.

- Describes and models a slower speech rate achieved through syllable prolongation. The clinician teaches the client to extend the duration of vowels following the initial consonants. The optimal duration of prolongation is client-specific; but it should result in stutter-free speech. For each client, the clinician should find a rate that is slow enough to eliminate dysfluencies. A few successful trials at the single word level should be sufficient to move on to the next step.

- Moves on to the phrase level training when the client successfully produces a number of words with syllable stretching. In learning to produce the fluency skills in two-word phrases, the client adds a new word to the already practiced single word. For instance, a boy who has been practicing fluency skills in saying his first name (e.g., *Jhaaan*") may be asked to say his first and the last name (e.g., "*Jhaaan Jeeekɔɔɔb*"). It is not essential to move from single words to two-word phrases in all cases; the number of words in practice phrases will depend on the client. Some clients may succeed at three to four word phrases at the beginning of this stage.

- Manages the behavioral treatment contingencies promptly and strictly. It may be noted that syllable prolongation is a target skill the client learns to produce. Technically, *prolonged speech* does not specify a new treatment procedure; it specifies a target fluency skill the client has to learn. A description of how the skill is taught and learned constitutes treatment. In this technical sense, treatment is still the same familiar behavioral procedures that include instructions, demonstrations, modeling, prompting, positive reinforcement for correct production of the targeted skill and the resulting stutter-free speech, and corrective feedback for errors in managing the skills and for dysfluencies.

- Targets normal prosodic features when the client sustains stutter-free speech (perhaps a 98% fluency, though it may sound unnatural) across a few sessions. The clinician models a slightly faster rate for the client to imitate. As the client learns to sustain stutter-free speech at the initial faster rate, the clinician models progressively faster rates and varied intonational patterns for the client to imitate. Eventually, the clinician may stabilize a speech rate that is slightly slower than the client's habitual rate that still sounds natural.

- Trains family members, teachers, and peers to recognize various forms of dysfluencies and to prompt and reinforce a slightly slower rate to sustain natural-sounding fluency in home, school, and other nonclinical settings. If practical, the parents of a child may be trained to hold informal treatment sessions at home. Such training may begin as soon as the client sustains stutter-free speech in the clinic. These steps are essential for maintenance of fluency.

- Conducts follow-up assessments and arranges for booster treatment when the results of a follow-up warrant additional treatment. The initial follow-up may be scheduled for 3 months following the dismissal. Additional follow-ups may be scheduled at 6 or 12 month intervals. In all follow-up sessions, the clinician takes an extended speech sample without treatment to calculate the percent stuttering or dysfluency rates.

Three treatment protocols have been written for an exclusive prolonged speech procedure:

1. Establishing stutter-free conversational speech
2. Establishing stutter-free narrative speech
3. Stabilizing natural-sounding fluency

Treatment of Stuttering in School-Age Children: II. Prolonged Speech

Establishing Stutter-Free Conversational Speech

Overview

- With school-age children, the **prolonged speech procedure** may be initiated at the word and phrase level or the sentence level, depending on the individual child. The strategy is to initiate treatment at the highest level of response topography possible (e.g., shorter or longer sentences), not necessarily at the lowest level (e.g., single words). Because the treatment has to move through the different levels of response complexity, starting treatment at a higher level the client can perform is more efficient than routinely starting at the lowest level.

- Even when the lowest level of single words seems to be needed for a given child, the clinician should swiftly move on to phrases and sentences. Lingering for too long at the single word level is both inefficient and suggestive of potential misapplication of the treatment procedure.

- With older school-age children and adolescents who stutter, short sentences may be the starting point. A low stuttering frequency and severity may be another factor that suggests the possibility of starting treatment at the sentence level.

- The clinician may use games, toys, storybooks, and pictures in storybooks to evoke speech of varied complexity. The clinician may prompt, instruct, or otherwise encourage the child to produce shorter and longer sentences.

- Frequent modeling of prolonged speech is essential in treating most children. Clinicians may also reduce their own speech rates while teaching prolonged speech. Clinicians who talk fast may find it hard to control the speech rates in children they work with.

- If dysfluencies persist, it is typically because the child has failed to sufficiently prolong the syllables.

- With most children, verbal reinforcement may be effective. A small gift at the end of the session may help sustain the child's interest in the treatment session. Verbal praise may take several forms:
  - ➤ Wonderful! You stretched your sounds well!
  - ➤ Very good! I like the way you are talking very slowly!
  - ➤ Fantastic! You are doing everything right!
  - ➤ I like your fluent speech!
  - ➤ Good job! Your speech sounds very smooth!

- Positive reinforcement should be prompt, natural, and should follow prolongation of syllables in the former stages of treatment and normal prosodic features in the latter. The initial continuous reinforcement may be changed to one of intermittent schedule during natural conversational exchanges.

- Verbal corrective feedback should be offered immediately when the child fails to prolong syllables or produces a dysfluency. The feedback should be prompt, clear, and objective in tone. The child should stop when an error is made (failure to prolong) or a dysfluency is produced; the child should correct the error and then continue. The clinician may use several forms of corrective feedback; each should point out what went wrong:

> ➤ Stop, that was too fast! Stretch your speech more!
> ➤ No, you should slow down some more!
> ➤ Stop, you stuttered there! Slow down some more and say it!

• The same stimulus materials used in baserating dysfluencies in sentences may be appropriate for treatment sessions. Familiar stories and pictures may more readily evoke speech from the child.

• If previously used stimuli fail to provoke interest in the child, the clinician may introduce novel stimuli that will sustain the child's interest.

• To evaluate the child's progress in treatment, the clinician may tape-record each session and later calculate the percent dysfluency or stuttering rate.

• If a correctly implemented prolonged speech approach does not produce satisfactory results, the clinician may consider alternative procedures (e.g., response cost or pause-and-talk). Although there will be individual differences, stuttering frequency should be significantly reduced in a matter of few sessions. If not, the progress may be judged unsatisfactory, leading to a change in the treatment procedure.

Treatment of Stuttering in School-Age Children: II. Prolonged Speech

Treatment Protocol for Conversational Speech

Scripts for Establishing Stutter-Free Speech in Conversation		Note
Clinician	"Sometimes we all have problems talking very smoothly. Our words may get stuck. We may repeat what we say, sometimes not realizing it. We prolong our speech sounds. We may say a lot of *ums*. If one does a lot of these, then the person has a stuttering problem or a fluency problem. When someone stutters, it may also be called a dysfluency—not fluency. We all want to talk very smoothly and fluently. When we are not fluent, we stutter. Do you sometimes stutter?"	The clinician introduces the concepts of stuttering, dysfluency, and fluency
Child	"Yeah, sometimes."	Child shows awareness of his fluency problem
Clinician	"The good news is that you can learn to speak more fluently. If you learn to do a few things right, you, too, can be fluent like most other kids. Do you want to learn to speak fluently?"	The clinician reassures the child
Child	"Yeah."	
Clinician	"Good, I can help you speak more fluently, smoothly. Have you noticed that when you are in a hurry, you want to say something quickly, and you try to talk fast, do you sometimes stutter?"	Summarizes airflow management skills and introduces the concept of rapid speech rate
Child	"Yes."	
Clinician	"That's right! We all stutter a bit when we try to go much faster than we really can. To beat this problem, we just have to talk slowly. Slow talking means stretching your speech sounds. You should not stretch the first sound in a word, but the second sound. If you stretch and make your sounds longer, you won't stutter. Now I am going to give you a quiz. Now tell me what you should do to speak fluently."	Introduces slower speech through syllable prolongation; checks the child's understanding
Child	"I should stretch my sounds and talk."	Shows understanding of the target skill

Establishing Stutter-Free Speech in Conversation, continued

Scripts for Establishing Stutter-Free Speech in Conversation		Note
Clinician	"Great! I knew you are a smart kid! You get an *A plus* on my quiz! You stretch or prolong your sounds, and talk! [*Demonstrates syllable stretching*] When you talk slowly like this, you eliminate most of your stuttering. Are you now ready to start?"	Reinforces the child's understanding and emphasizes prolonged speech
Child	"Yes."	
Clinician	"Very good! [*models syllable stretching*] Slooow and streeeetched out speeeech sounds like this [*stretches out the syllables and blends the words*]. Are you ready to practice slow speech?" [*asks this question at a very slow rate*]	Verbal praise Models slow speech
Child	"Yes."	
Clinician	"Okay, we can talk just about anything and practice slow and fluent speech. I will ask you a lot of questions, even though I may know some of the answers. I do this only to let you practice slow speech. I will ask a question or ask you to tell me something. I will then right away show you how to answer it or say something. Now for example, what is your first name? Say, Jhaaaan. You heard how I stretched out the aaaaaa in John. You try it."	Sets the stage of slow speech practice Begins treatment
Child	"John"	
Clinician	"Oops! You forgot to stretch the syllables. Say, Jhaaaaan." [*models slow speech on the child's name*]	Corrective feedback; stops the child from speaking; models the target skill
Child	[*correct stretching*] "Jhaaaan."	Stutter-free speech
Clinician	"Excellent! That's exactly what I want you to do! You said it very slowly! Now tell me your last name. Say, Jhaaaanson." [*models slow rate*]	Verbal praise and initiation of the next trial
Child	"Joh . . ."	Fails to stretch
Clinician	"Stop! You didn't prolong the syllables. Try it again. Like this. Jhaaaanson." [*models slow rate*]	Corrective feedback and modeling
Child	[*correct stretching*] "Jhaaaanson."	Stutter-free speech
Clinician	"That was good stretching! Tell me your Mom's first name. Remember how you should say it."	Verbal praise and the initiation of the next trial
Child	"Jaaane."	Correct syllable stretching

Establishing Stutter-Free Speech in Conversation, continued

Scripts for Establishing Stutter-Free Speech in Conversation		Note
Clinician	"Way to go! You stretched your syllables! Now tell me your Dad's first name. Stretch it out!"	Verbal praise; next trial; prompt
Child	[*prolongation*] "Taaaam."	Stutter-free speech
Clinician	"Wonderful! How many brothers do you have? Just say one word—a number. Stretch and say."	Verbal praise; the next question
Child	"One."	No stretching
Clinician	"Not correct! You forgot to prolong the sounds. Try it again. Don't forget any part."	Corrective feedback
Child	[*prolongation*] "Oooooone."	Correct prolongation; stutter-free
Clinician	"I like that! You did it correctly! What is your brother's name? Don't forget prolongation."	Verbal praise; a prompt
Child	[*failed to prolong*] "Mmmm . . ."	Sound prolongation
Clinician	"Stop! You stuttered. Quickly open your mouth and prolong the next sound. Try it again."	Corrective feedback; instruction
Child	[*correct stretching*] "Maaaany."	Correctly prolonged response
Clinician	"Very good! See, you didn't stutter when you quickly started to say the aaaaa part of your brother's name! Do you have a sister?"	Verbal praise; points out the reason for success
Child	"Yes."	No syllable stretching
Clinician	"Oops! You forgot to stretch. Say that again. Make it right."	Corrective feedback
Child	[*correct prolongation*] "Yeeees."	Stutter-free speech
Clinician	"Excellent! You said it right and you didn't stutter! What is your sister's name?"	Verbal praise; next question
Child	[*correct prolongation*] "Maaaanica."	Stutter-free speech
Clinician	"Very good! You are doing well in stretching your syllables. How old is Monica?"	Verbal praise; next question
Child	[*failed to prolong*] "FFFif . . ."	Sound prolongation; no syllable stretching
Clinician	"Stop! You forgot to stretch. When you forget, you stutter, you see! Is she fifteen? [*the child nods*] Say *fiiiifteeeen*." [*demonstrates syllable stretching*]	Corrective feedback and modeling

Establishing Stutter-Free Speech in Conversation, continued

Scripts for Establishing Stutter-Free Speech in Conversation		Note
Child	[*correct stretching*] "Fiiiifteeeen."	Stutter-free speech
Clinician	"Excellent! That's the way to do it. You know it was smooth. Now, may be you can say two or three words at a time. Tell me your full name. Prolong the syllables."	Verbal praise **Treatment shifted to the phrase level. However, the clinician may give additional trials at the single-word level if necessary**
Child	[*correct stretching*] "Jhaaaan Jhaaaanson."	Stutter-free speech
Clinician	"That was great! Very good stretching! Now, tell me your Mom's full name."	Verbal praise
Child	[*correct stretching*] "Jaaaane Jhaaaanson."	Stutter-free speech
Clinician	"Wonderful! You are doing great! Tell me your Dad's full name."	Verbal praise
Child	[*correct stretching*] "Taaaam Jhaaaanson."	Stutter-free speech
Clinician	"Fantastic! You know how to do it! Tell me your brother's full name."	Verbal praise
Child	[*correct stretching*] "Maaaany Jhaaaanson."	Stutter-free speech
Clinician	"Very good! You are stretching your syllables correctly! Now, tell me your sister's full name."	Verbal praise
Child	[*lack of stretching*] "Mmm . . ."	Sound prolongation
Clinician	"Stop! Did you forget something?"	Corrective feedback. Prompts self-evaluation
Child	"Yeah. I forgot to stretch."	Correct self-evaluation
Clinician	"That's very good! You know what went wrong. Now try that again. Your sister's full name."	Reinforces self-evaluation
Child	[*correct stretching*] "Maaaanica Jhaaaanson."	Stutter-free speech
Clinician	"Excellent! Now, try your brother's full name again."	Verbal praise; a second attempt on brother's full name
Child	[*correct stretching*] "Maaaany Jhaaaanson."	Stutter-free speech
Clinician	"Good job! I like the way you are talking. Maybe you can now try to say more words each time. For example, if I ask you *where are you now*, you say, *in the school*. Try that."	Verbal praise **Treatment shifted to longer phrases and sentences** **However, the clinician may give additional trials at the two-word phrase level if necessary**
Child	[*correct airflow*] "Iiiiin theee [*in the*] schooool."	Stutter-free speech

Establishing Stutter-Free Speech in Conversation, continued

Scripts for Establishing Stutter-Free Speech in Conversation		Note
Clinician	"Excellent! You said three words, all correctly! Where do you live? Say, [*modeling syllable stretching*] *I live in Fresno.*"	Verbal praise; **from now on, for ease of reading, syllable stretching is not shown orthographically**
Child	[*correct stretching*] "I live in Fresno."	Stutter-free speech
Clinician	"Excellent! You are saying more words correctly! What grade are you in? Say [*modeling syllable stretching*], *in the fourth grade.*"	Verbal praise
Child	[*failure to stretch*] "In the fff . . ."	Syllable prolongation
Clinician	"No, you didn't stretch it enough. That's why you stuttered. Try that again like this [*modeling syllable stretching*] *in the fourth grade.*"	Corrective feedback
Child	[*correct stretching*] "In the fourth grade."	Stutter-free speech
Clinician	"Excellent! That's the way to do it! How many brothers do you have? Say, [*modeling the correct response*] *I have one brother.*"	Verbal praise
Child	[*correct stretching*] "I have one brother."	Stutter-free speech
Clinician	"Excellent! You are getting a good hang of stretching your sounds. How many sisters do you have? Remember to say it right."	Verbal praise No modeling; an evoking question
Child	[*correct stretching*] "I have one sister."	Stutter-free speech
Clinician	"Great job! How old is your sister? Start with, *my sister . . .*"	Verbal praise Prompts a longer utterance
Child	[*correct stretching*] "My sister is fifteen."	Stutter-free speech
Clinician	"Very nice! I like the way you are prolonging your speech. You are not stuttering at all! Now, I think you are ready to try some longer sentences. But you shouldn't forget how to say them. What does your Mom do? Start with, *My mom . . .*"	Verbal praise **Treatment shifted to longer sentences** **However, the clinician may give additional trials at the phrase or shorter sentence levels** Prompts a longer sentence
Child	[*failure to stretch*] "Mmmm . . ."	Sound prolongation
Clinician	"Stop! What happened? But say what happened correctly!"	Corrective feedback Prompted self-evaluation
Child	[*correct stretching*] "I forgot to stretch!"	Correct self-evaluation

Establishing Stutter-Free Speech in Conversation, continued

Scripts for Establishing Stutter-Free Speech in Conversation		Note
Clinician	"I am glad you understand why you stutter! When you don't stretch, you stutter. Now try that again. What does your Mom do?"	Reinforces self-evaluation
Child	[*correct stretching*] "My mom teaches in a school."	Stutter-free speech
Clinician	"That was very nice! That was a long sentence, too! See, you can do it! Tell me what does your Dad do?"	Verbal praise
Child	[*stretching*] "My dad is a musician."	Stutter-free speech
Clinician	"Fantastic! You can say long sentences with syllable stretching! What kind of musical instrument does your Dad play?"	Verbal praise
Child	[*correct stretching*] "He plays the piano."	Stutter-free speech
Clinician	"Great job! Where does he play?"	Verbal praise
Child	[*correct stretching until the dysfluent production*] "He plays with the Fresno Ph-ph- . . ."	Partially correct response; sound prolongation
Clinician	"Stop! You stuttered. Move quickly to the next sound and stretch it. Like this. Phiiiilhaaarmooooniiic. Say the whole sentence."	Corrective feedback Models syllable stretching
Child	[*correct stretching*] "He plays with the Fresno Philharmonic."	Stutter-free speech
Clinician	"Very nice! Have you been to your Dad's concerts? Say it in a complete sentence."	Verbal praise Prompts sentence productions
Child	[*correct stretching*] "Yes, I have gone to many concerts."	Stutter-free speech
Clinician	"Good job! You know what, you are very lucky! Those concerts are great, aren't they?"	Verbal praise
Child	[*correct stretching*] "Yes."	Stutter-free speech
Clinician	"Very good! What does your brother Manny do? Say it in a long sentence."	Verbal praise
Child	[*correct stretching*] "He goes to Fresno city college."	Stutter-free speech
Clinician	"Wonderful! See how you can avoid all that stuttering by stretching correctly! Now, do you have a lot of friends? Sentence, please!"	Verbal praise
Child	[*correct stretching*] "I have a lot of friends."	Stutter-free speech

Establishing Stutter-Free Speech in Conversation, continued

Scripts for Establishing Stutter-Free Speech in Conversation		Note
Clinician	"Fine job of syllable stretching! Tell me the name of your best friend. Start with, *my best friend's name is . . .*"	Verbal praise Prompts a longer sentence
Child	[*correct stretching until the dysfluent production*] "My best friend's name is T-t-t-t . . ."	Part-word repetition
Clinician	"Stop! You stuttered because you didn't stretch. Try that again. Stretch really well."	Corrective feedback
Child	[*correct stretching*] "My best friend's name is Tommy."	Stutter-free speech
Clinician	"I like your smooth speech! How old is your best friend Tommy? Start with, *my best friend . . .*"	Verbal praise
Child	[*correct stretching*] "My best friend Tommy is eleven."	Stutter-free speech
Clinician	"Very good! Nice stretching! Is Tommy a student in this school? A long sentence, please!"	Verbal praise
Child	[*correct stretching*] "No, my best friend Tommy is not a student in this school."	Stutter-free speech
Clinician	"Wonderful! Really long, smooth sentence! You stretched all the syllables. So which school does he attend? Start with *he attends . . .* and tell me where the school is."	Verbal praise
Child	[*correct stretching*] "He attends Freedom Intermediate School in Sanger."	Stutter-free speech
Clinician	"Great job! Does Tommy live in your neighborhood? *Yes, he . . .*"	Verbal praise Prompts a longer sentence
Child	[*correct stretching*] "Yes, he lives in our neighborhood."	Stutter-free speech
Clinician	"Excellent! Your speech is very smooth. Do you get to play with him everyday? *Yes I . . .*"	Verbal praise
Child	[*correct stretching*] "Yes, I play with him almost everyday."	Stutter-free speech
Clinician	"You are doing really well!"	Verbal praise

The clinician continues to teach prolonged speech skill in the manner described in the protocols. The number of sessions in the establishment phase will be child-specific. When the child has sustained stutter-free conversational speech across three or four sessions, the clinician shifts training to the next phase, which involves narrative speech.

The following protocols may be used to establish stutter-free narrative speech.

Treatment of Stuttering in School-Age Children: II. Prolonged Speech

Establishing Stutter-Free Narrative Speech

Overview

- With school-age children, the **prolonged speech procedure** initiated at the conversational speech level should be shifted to narrative speech level as soon as possible. At the narrative speech level, the clinician tells stories to the child and asks the child to retell the stories with prolonged syllables.

- The clinician selects stories that are appropriate for the child under treatment. Stories from the child's grade level may be especially useful. The child may be asked to bring a storybook he or she reads at home or in the classroom. In all cases, the stories selected should be relevant to the child's ethnocultural background, although stories of universal appeal may be especially useful with a variety of children.

- Frequent modeling of prolonged syllables should not be essential at this level of training. Nonetheless, clinicians may reduce their own speech rates while narrating stories to the child. Clinical experience suggests that slower and more deliberate narration tends to initiate slower rate of speech as the child begins to narrate the story back to the clinician. Clinicians who narrate stories at a fast speech rate may find it hard to control the speech rates in children who retell the stories.

- If dysfluencies persist, it is typically because the child did not prolong the syllable to an extent to eliminate dysfluencies. Regardless of the level of treatment, insufficient duration of syllable prolongation is the dominant reason why dysfluencies persist under this form of treatment.

- Verbal reinforcement for prolonged speech and corrective feedback for stuttering or insufficient syllable prolongation may be continued as in the previous level of treatment.

Treatment of Stuttering in School-Age Children:
II. Prolonged Speech

Treatment Protocol for Narrative Speech

Scripts for Establishing Stutter-Free Speech in Narration		Note
Clinician	"You have been doing really well in learning to speak slowly, by stretching the syllables. Your speech has been very smooth for several sessions. I am now going to tell you a story. I want you to listen carefully, because when I am finished with it, I want you to tell me the whole story. You should tell me the story with very slow speech. Okay?"	Introduces the new narrative task
Child	"Okay."	
Clinician	"Now listen carefully. I want you to tell me everything I tell you in this story. "This is the story of a clever crow. One hot summer day, the crow got very thirsty. He was looking for some water. He flew here. He flew there, looking for water. Then he saw a pot with a little bit of water in it. He sat on the top of the pot and put his head into it to drink the water. But he couldn't reach the water. The water was way down in the bottom of that pot. He stretched his neck and he bent his body to reach the water. No matter how hard he tried, he couldn't reach the water. Sight of the water made him even more thirsty. He then looked around and saw some pebbles on the ground. He thought of a clever idea. He picked up one pebble and dropped it into the pot. He picked up another pebble and dropped it into the pot. He saw the water was rising, but he still couldn't reach it. He dropped many more pebbles into the pot. He saw the water coming up fast! He put a lot more pebbles into the pot. Then the water came all the way up! He then sat on the top of the pot and drank all the water in it. That's the end of the story. "Now you tell me the story. Remember to stretch your syllables."	Tells the story of the clever and thirsty crow

Establishing Stutter-Free Speech in Narration, continued

Scripts for Establishing Stutter-Free Speech in Narration	Note
Child	[*begins with correct syllable stretch*] "It was a hot summer day. There was crow. He got very thirsty. He was looking for some water. He flew here. He flew there. Then he saw a pot with a little bit of water in it. He sat on the top of the pot [*speeds up the rate; the clinician says, "slow down;" the child slows down*] and tried to drink the water. But he couldn't drink it. The water was in the bottom of that pot. He stretched his neck and he bent his body. But he couldn't drink the water. He became more thirsty because he saw water in the pot. He then saw some pebbles on the ground. He thought of a clever idea. He picked up one pebble [*speeds up the rate; the clinician says, "slow down;" the child slows down*] and dropped it into the pot. He picked up another pebble and dropped it into the pot. Water was coming up, but he still couldn't reach it. He dropped many more pebbles into the pot. Then the water came all the way up! He drank all the water in it. That's the end of the story."	Narrates the story with syllable stretching and stutter-free speech

Receives prompts to slow down when the speech rate increases

Second prompt to slow down |
| Clinician | "Great story! Your speech was very smooth, too! I reminded you only twice to go slow!

"Are you ready for another story?" | Verbal praise

During the child's narration, gave prompts to speak slowly |
| Child | "Oh yeah! I like your stories!" | |
| Clinician | "Again, listen carefully! You have to tell me the whole story.

"Once upon a time, there was a farmer. He owned a lot of land. The farmer loved to eat chocolate cakes and ride on his shiny black horse. He had three sons. When the farmer became old, he decided it was time for him to retire. He wanted to take it easy, eat good food, and ride his horses. He then decided that he would give his farm to one of his sons who was the smartest of all. He couldn't decide who was the smartest. So he arranged a contest for them. He gave his sons a hundred dollars each and told them to spend it any way they liked. The farmer also told them that he would decide who gets the farm depending on how they spent their money. *(continued)* | Tells another story in two parts |

Establishing Stutter-Free Speech in Narration, continued

Scripts for Establishing Stutter-Free Speech in Narration	Note
Clinician *(continues)*	"That is the first part of the story. You tell me the first part and then I will tell you the rest. Don't forget the breathing part and the slow speech."	Asks the child to narrate the first part
Child	"Okay. "Once upon a time, there was a farmer. He had three sons. He owned a lot of land. The farmer loved to eat chocolate cakes and ride on his black horse. When the farmer became old, he wanted to retire. He wanted to eat good food and ride his horses. He then decided that [*speeds up the rate; the clinician says, "slow down;" the child slows down*] he would give his farm to a son who was the smartest of all. He didn't know who was the smartest son. So he arranged a contest for them. He gave each son a hundred dollars. He told them to spend it any way they liked and he would decide who gets the farm depending on how they spent their money."	Narrates the second story with syllable stretching and stutter-free speech Receives a single prompt to slow down
Clinician	"That was great! Your speech was slow and smooth! You are a good storyteller, too! Now I will tell you the rest of the story. "After three days, the sons came home in the evening. In a separate room, each son secretly hid what he had bought for his Dad. Each wanted to surprise and impress his Dad to get the farm. When the night fell, the sons went to their Dad and said they were ready to show how they spent their money. The first son said, 'first I want to show you what I bought for you' and took the father to a room. He then opened the doors for his Dad to see. To his delight, the farmer saw two dozen huge chocolate cakes, all decorated beautifully! The farmer's mouth was watering like crazy! He wanted to eat them right away. But the second son said, 'Dad, you should see what I bought for you' and took him to another room. When he opened the door, the farmer saw a huge shiny, black horse! He was so thrilled that he didn't want to wait to ride the horse. But the third son said, 'Dad, I want to show you how I spent the money,' so the farmer followed him to the third room. When the third son opened the door, the farmer stepped in and saw a large table on which *(continued)*	Verbal praise Tells the rest of the story

Establishing Stutter-Free Speech in Narration, continued

Scripts for Establishing Stutter-Free Speech in Narration		Note
Clinician *(continues)*	there were two dozen huge candles burning beautifully! The son then told his father, 'Dad, I spent two dollars and forty cents on the candles and ten cents on a box of matches. I spent a total of two dollars and fifty cents. Here is your ninety-seven dollars and fifty cents. Please take it back.' You tell me this story and also guess who got the farm. Don't forget how you need to talk."	
Child	"After spending their money, the sons came home. It was evening. Each son went to a room and secretly hid the thing he bought. Each wanted to surprise and impress his Dad. Each wanted the farm for himself. When it was nighttime, the sons told their Dad they were ready to show what they bought. The first son took the father to a room and showed two dozen huge chocolate cakes. They were nicely decorated. The farmer's mouth was watering like crazy! He wanted to eat them right then. But the second son took him to another room. And showed the farmer a huge and shiny black horse! Dad was thrilled. He wanted to ride that horse. But the third son wanted to show what he bought. The farmer followed him. When the third son opened the door, the farmer saw a large table. He saw two dozen huge candles burning beautifully! The son then told his father, 'Dad, I spent two dollars and some cents? [*the clinician prompts: "forty cents"*] yes, forty cents on the candles and how many? [*the clinician prompts: "ten cents"*] yes, ten cents on a box of matches.' He said, I totally spent . . . how much was it? [*the clinician prompts: "two dollars and fifty cents"*] yes, two dollars and fifty cents. Here is your ninety-seven dollars and some cents. Please take it back.'"	Narrates with syllable stretching and stutter-free speech
Clinician	"That was fantastic! You did not stutter once! You did everything right! Now guess who got the farm?"	Verbal praise
Child	"I think the third son got the farm."	A stutter-free production
Clinician	"Good talking, but why do you think the third son got the farm?"	Verbal praise
Child	"The candles were nice! He saved a lot of money for his Dad!"	A stutter-free production

Establishing Stutter-Free Speech in Narration, continued

Scripts for Establishing Stutter-Free Speech in Narration		Note
Clinician	"I like your smooth speech. And, you are right! The third son got the farm because he was wise in spending Dad's money. The farmer decided that his smartest third son will take good care of the farm."	Verbal praise

If the child could not maintain at least a 97 to 98% stutter-free speech in story narration, the clinician may tell additional stories and have the child repeat them. When a child retells a story, the clinician should:

- Verbally praise the child at the end of the narration
- Stop the child and give corrective feedback for excessively fast rate or dysfluencies and remind the child to slow down
- Prompt story elements when the child is unsure of any aspects of a story being retold

When the child has maintained stutter-free speech in narratives across two or three sessions, the clinician may shift training to the next level in which normal prosodic features are re-established.

Following protocols help establish the prosodic features essential for normal-sounding speech.

Treatment of Stuttering in School-Age Children: II. Prolonged Speech

Stabilizing Natural-Sounding Speech

Overview

- The immediate effects of syllable prolongation is not described as *(normal) fluency*; it is always described as *stutter-free speech*, as it may indeed, almost completely, be free of stuttering. Unfortunately, the stutter-free speech generated by stretching the syllables is an unnatural-sounding speech. The stutter-free speech is too slow, sometimes too soft, and always too monotonous to be socially acceptable.

- Children who are treated with fluency shaping may be reluctant to talk in a slow and monotonous manner in the classroom or with their friends. They may sense a negative reaction from certain listeners who do not understand why the child is speaking so slowly. Children themselves may think that their speech is unacceptable. They may find the constant monitoring of speech rate required to reduce stuttering a tiring exercise. Some children may think that they would rather stutter and speak naturally than adopt an unnatural manner of speaking to reduce their stuttering.

- Because of those problems associated with syllable stretching, it is essential to shape natural-sounding speech before the child is dismissed. Natural-sounding speech is most effectively reinstated with a rate that approximates the child's typical, pretreatment rate. Most listeners do not quantitatively measure a speaker's rate of speech. They make global judgments as to whether the speech sounds natural or not. Therefore, clinicians, too can make judgments of speech naturalness. This judgment may include not only the rate but also the intonational patterns (pitch and loudness variations). Clinicians in the schools may invite comments about a child's speech naturalness from teachers, peers, and others. Family members are always among the best judges of speech naturalness.

- Natural-sounding fluency is induced essentially in a shaping program. In this procedure, the client may be asked to:
  - ➢ gradually increase the rate of speech
  - ➢ increase and vary the loudness of voice
  - ➢ vary the vocal pitch throughout an utterance

- In instating natural-sounding speech, the clinician will:
  - ➢ frequently model faster rate and improved intonation
  - ➢ systematically reinforce any movement toward more natural-sounding speech
  - ➢ give prompt corrective feedback when the client exhibit slower and monotonous speech

The protocols to follow are written to achieve these goals of natural-sounding speech.

Treatment of Stuttering in School-Age Children:
II. Prolonged Speech

Treatment Protocol for Natural-Sounding Speech

Scripts for Stabilizing Natural-Sounding Speech		Note
Clinician	"You have been doing really well in learning to speak slowly and avoid stuttering. Your speech has been very smooth for several sessions. You have hardly stuttered in the last few sessions. But to avoid stuttering, you have been speaking very slowly. It is a bit too slow for most situations, isn't it? You wouldn't like to talk this slowly, even though you don't stutter when you talk like that. You may not like to talk like that in the classroom or when you are with friends. Even at home, you may want to talk a little faster. Right?"	Explains the need for the next stage of treatment
Child	"Right."	
Clinician	"When people talk very slowly, their speech is kind of flat, isn't it? It may also be very soft. You don't have ups and downs in your voice like this. [*demonstrates pitch variations*] You want to talk not too slowly, loudly enough, and speak with a voice that shows ups and downs, like I am doing now. You should also speak without stuttering. That's the natural way of talking. The natural way of talking means that you sound like kids who don't stutter. We now have to practice the trick of not stuttering while speaking more naturally. Do you understand what I mean by natural way of talking? Do you want to talk more naturally and yet without stuttering?"	Describes the problems associated with slow speech
Child	"Yes. I want to talk more naturally. I don't want to stutter."	Show understanding
Clinician	"Very good. That's what we will practice now. No stuttering, but faster, more natural speech. Like most people talk. Now let us start with a slightly faster speech. You can talk, may be more like this [*models a rate slightly faster than the child's clinical rate*], and try what happens. Remember, your goal is not to stutter when you speed up. Therefore, you have to increase the speed of your speech gradually. If you suddenly go too fast, you may lose control of your smooth speech. It's like driving too fast and losing control of the car. Do you understand?"	Models a slightly faster rate for the child to imitate

Stabilizing Natural-Sounding Speech, continued

Scripts for Stabilizing Natural-Sounding Speech		Note
Child	"Yes I do."	
Clinician	[*still speaking at only a slightly higher rate than the child's clinical rate*] "To practice more natural speech, we can have a conversation about anything. Now, tell me what you did this last weekend. Talk slightly faster like this, but without stuttering."	Initiates treatment
Child	"I don't remember."	Slightly increased speech rate
Clinician	[*modeling the target rate*] "You spoke slightly faster as I wanted! Very good. Try to remember what you did. What did you do Saturday morning? Speak slightly faster like this."	Verbal praise
Child	"Saturday morning I watched some cartoons."	Increased speech rate
Clinician	[*modeling the target rate*] "Very good! You are talking a little bit faster, but you are not stuttering! That's what we want. Well, what kind of cartoons did you watch? Were they funny? Scary?"	Verbal praise; maintains conversation
Child	"They were funny. One was scary."	Increased speech rate
Clinician	[*modeling the target rate*] "Can you tell me about the funny cartoons you saw? Who were the characters? What happens in the cartoon?"	Evoking speech
Child	[*Talks about specific cartoons watched*]	Maintains the target speech rate
Clinician	[*Helps maintain conversation; asks questions, prompts details, periodically reinforces the increased speech rate, and stops when the child's rate increases too fast or when the child stutters.*]	Provides verbal praise and corrective feedback
	[*modeling the target rate*] "Okay we can talk about something else now. Tell me about your grandma and grandpa. Do they live in town?"	Introduces a new topic of conversation
Child	"Yes, they live in town."	Maintains the target speech rate
Clinician	[*modeling the target rate*] "Good speech! You are doing well in talking slightly faster. Do they live near your home or are they far away? How often do you see them?"	Verbal praise
Child	"They live nearby. [*excessive rate increase*] We see them . . ."	Inappropriate target speech rate

Stabilizing Natural-Sounding Speech, continued

Scripts for Stabilizing Natural-Sounding Speech		Note
Clinician	[*modeling the target rate*] "Oops! You are going too fast. Slow down a bit and tell me about your recent trip to your grandparents' house."	Corrective feedback for excessively fast speech rate
Child	"Okay, I will talk this fast. We see them almost every Sunday. We meet in our church on Sunday mornings. Then sometimes we go to their house for lunch. Sometimes they come to our house for lunch. Sometimes we go to a restaurant for lunch. Last Sunday we all went to a restaurant and had lunch."	Maintains the target speech rate
Clinician	[*modeling the target rate*] "That was fantastic! You said a lot with good speed. You didn't stutter either! Do you remember what restaurant you went to last Sunday? Is that your favorite restaurant?"	Verbal praise
Child	"Yeah, it is my favorite restaurant. It is called the Big Town Waffles. [*slows down too much*] We went . . ."	Reverts to the clinical rate
Clinician	[*models the target rate and intonation*] "Stop! That is too slow. Did you notice, your speech became [*models the slower rate with flat intonation*] too flat, like this, as you slowed down! No ups and downs in your voice? [*models the target rate and intonation*] Talk a little bit faster like this, and keep those ups and downs in your voice, like this. Alright, did you go to the Big Town Waffles last Sunday for lunch? What did you eat there?"	Corrective feedback; models both the inappropriate and appropriate speech patterns
Child	"Yes, we went to the Big Town Waffles for lunch last Sunday. I had waffles with strawberries, banana, whipped cream, and ice cream."	Maintains the slightly increased target rate
Clinician	"Very nice speed! You are not stuttering either! Maybe now you can increase the speed just a tiny bit. [*modeling a slightly increased, new target speech rate*] May be you can talk more like this. Do you have another favorite restaurant?"	Verbal praise
Child	"We sometimes go to Mama Mia Pizza. I love pizza. [*excessive increase in speech rate*] My Mmmmom . . ."	Too fast a rate and a sound prolongation
Clinician	"Oh No! Stop, you are going too fast. See what happens when you go too fast? You stutter! [*modeling the target rate*] Talk more like this. You were saying, *my Mom . . .*"	Corrective feedback; modeling

Stabilizing Natural-Sounding Speech, continued

Scripts for Stabilizing Natural-Sounding Speech		Note
Child	"Yeah. My Mom and Dad don't like pizza. They never take us to pizza places. But my grandparents like pizza. They take my sister and me to Mama Mia."	Maintains the target rate
Clinician	[*modeling the target rate*] "That was great! You are slowly speeding up but not stuttering! What kind of pizza do you like? Does your sister like the same kind?"	Verbal praise
Child	"We like different kinds of pizza. I like only cheese and sausage pizza. My sister likes only cheese and pepperoni pizza. My grandma and grandpa like only vegetarian pizza. Very bad! My grandparents have to order three kinds of pizza!"	Maintains the target rate
Clinician	"You are doing really well. Your voice is also going up and down as you talk. But you can still practice that a little bit more as you talk. This time, I want you to ask me a few questions. I will model them for you with voice going up and down. Okay?" [*the child nods*] Okay. Ask me, *how are **you** today?*" [*models a target rate and higher pitch on the bolded word*]	Describes pitch variations as the explicit target **Bold** type face suggests increased vocal pitch on that word
Child	"How are **you** today?"	Higher pitch on *you*
Clinician	"I am fine, thank you! That was good speech! You kept a good speed and your voice went up on the word *you*. Now ask me, *how **are** you today?*"	Verbal praise and modeling
Child	"How **are** you today?"	Correct imitation
Clinician	"Very good. Ask me, *how are you **today**?*"	Verbal praise; modeling
Child	"How are you **today**?"	Correct imitation
Clinician	"That was good! You know how to vary your voice."	May continue this type of treatment for additional time

The number of sessions in which the clinician stabilizes natural-sounding speech will be child-specific. The child is ready for dismissal only when probes in which reinforcement and corrective feedback are kept to a minimum and yet the child maintains a desirable rate and natural-sounding speech with few or no dysfluencies.

If necessary, the clinician may reuse the protocols given for narrative speech. The child may be asked to retell the same stories with progressively faster rate and desirable patterns of intonation.

Treatment of Stuttering in School-Age Children: II. Prolonged Speech

Treatment Recording Sheet

Personalize and print this page from the CD.

Name of the child:	DOB:
Name of the parents:	Phone:
Diagnosis: Stuttering	Session date(s):
Clinician:	Comments:

Chart the child's progress for each session with your preferred method. You may calculate a percent dysfluency or stuttering rate based on the number of words spoken. If more detailed data are warranted, score the individual dysfluency types and add them up to calculate the dysfluency rate.

Essential Measures		Optional Measures: Frequency of Specific Dysfluency Types						
Dates of Service	Percent Stuttering	Prolongations	Pauses	Repetitions	Interjections	Revisions	Incomplete Phrases

Treatment of Stuttering in School-Age Children:
II. Prolonged Speech

Probe Protocol

Probe Procedure

* Record two conversational speech samples, each 5 to 7 minutes in duration
* Record a 3-minute monologue; ask the child to talk about a topic such as:
  * Birthday parties
  * Vacations
  * Visit to a zoo or a theme park
  * Favorite games or TV shows
  * Weekend activities
  * Family and friends
  * Teachers and friends at school
  * Any other child-specific topic
* Obtain a 5-minute home speech sample
* Record one or more extraclinic speech samples in such places as the child's classroom, cafeteria, and the playground
* Analyze the percent dysfluency or stuttering rate
* Personalize the *Probe Recording Sheet* on the CD and record the dysfluency or stuttering rates; print the sheet for child's clinical file

Treatment of Stuttering in School-Age Children: II. Prolonged Speech

Probe Recording Sheet

Personalize and print this page from the CD.

Name of the child:	DOB:
Name of the parents:	Phone:
Diagnosis: Stuttering	Session date(s):
Clinician:	Comments:

Analyze the probe speech samples with your preferred method. You may calculate a percent dysfluency or stuttering rate based on the number of words spoken. If more detailed data are warranted, score the individual dysfluency types and add them up to calculate the dysfluency rate.

Take at least three clinic probe samples. If possible, obtain three extraclinic probe samples.

Essential Measures		Optional Measures: Frequency of Specific Dysfluency Types					
Dates/Setting of Probe	Percent Stuttering	PRO	PAU	REP	INT	REV	INC
1. /mm/dd/yy/ Clinic							
2. /mm/dd/yy/ Clinic							
3. /mm/dd/yy/ Clinic							
1. /mm/dd/yy/ Home							
2. /mm/dd/yy/ Classroom							
3. /mm/dd/yy/ Playground							

PRO (Prolongations); PAU (Pauses); REP (Repetitions); INT (Interjections); REV (Revisions); INC (Incomplete phrases).

Dismiss the child from current services when the child's stuttering or dysfluency rate stays below the target percentage in conversational probes. Schedule follow-ups and booster treatments as needed.

Treatment of Stuttering in School-Age Children:
III. Pause-and-Talk (Time-Out)

Overview

In addition to fluency shaping and prolonged speech, pause-and-talk, also known as time-out from positive reinforcement (TO), is effective in treating school-age children who stutter. Pause-and-talk has been researched in a number of studies and has been found to be remarkably effective in eliminating stuttering in older children and adults. It is one of the most effective methods available for treating stuttering.

Pause-and-talk includes reinforcement for fluency and reinforcer withdrawal for stuttering. Throughout the administration of this procedure, the clinician offers attention as reinforcer for fluency. Every time the child stutters, the clinician withdraws this attention for a brief period of 5 seconds. In essence, the clinician places contingencies on fluent as well as dysfluent productions.

It is important to note that in pause-and-talk, the clinician does not explicitly and specifically reinforce fluent productions. The client receives attention two conversational partners pay to each other in normal discourse. Even though this attention is contingent on fluent speech, it is not explicitly stated, nor is it accompanied by verbal reinforcement that points out fluency. Sudden and prompt withdrawal of attention is specifically contingent on each stuttering or dysfluency.

Before starting treatment with pause-and-talk, the clinician should establish the baserates of dysfluencies in sentences, conversational speech, and narratives as described in a previous section. Regardless of the treatment procedures used, the baserate protocols remain the same for preschool children. After establishing the baserates, the clinician may chose either the fluency shaping procedure, pause-and-talk, or response cost, described in section 4. In this section, protocols for the pause-and-talk method are described.

Student clinicians and parents can be relatively easily trained to administer the pause-and-talk procedure. An experimental single-subject design study has demonstrated the feasibility of training parents to exclusively administer treatment at home (Carter-Wagner & Hegde, 1998). Most parents who receive pause-and-talk treatment in the clinic may be trained to hold brief informal treatment sessions in which they pay attention to fluent speech and withhold it for dysfluencies. The parents may eventually stop formally, systematically, and abruptly withholding attention from dysfluent productions (that may be produced at low and acceptable limits) but continue to pay keenly interested attention to fluent speech. Continued attention for fluency without its abrupt withdrawal for greatly reduced stuttering may be sufficient to maintain fluency across time and situations.

Appropriate for Older Students and Adolescents

Pause-and-talk may be effectively used to treat stuttering in older students and adolescents as well. Pause-and-talk, however, may be inappropriate for preschoolers. Treating preschoolers requires toys, picture cards, storybooks, and so forth to keep them talking. When speech is evoked with such stimulus materials, the eye contact between the child and the clinician is not constant. Furthermore, contingent on stuttering, it is difficult to stop a 3-year-old child from talking because the child is also engrossed in stimulus manipulations. For older children and adolescents who can be engaged in conversational speech, pause-and-talk will work as well as it does with adults. Several studies have shown effectiveness of pause-and-talk with older students and adolescents (e.g., Ahlander & Hegde, 2000; Hegde & Parson, 1989; Onslow et al., 1997). Therefore, although the protocols that follow are more specifically written for school-age children, they may be used with adolescents with modifications in conversational topics to suit the child.

Protocols for pause-and-talk have been written for:

1. Treatment at the conversational speech level
2. Treatment at the narrative speech level

Because pause-and-talk is typically initiated at the conversational speech level, the treatment with this procedure may be completed with fewer levels of training than some of the other procedures, especially fluency shaping procedures.

Treatment of Stuttering in School-Age Children: III. Pause-and-Talk

Treatment at the Conversational Speech Level

Overview

- With school-age children, the **pause-and-talk** method may be initiated at the conversational speech level; the method may be less efficient when the child has to look at pictures and describe what is seen. The method requires eye contact between the clinician and the child; therefore, conversational speech is essential for this method to work effectively. In fact, this is the reason why pause-and-talk is not offered as one of the most effective alternatives in treating preschoolers who need extensive stimulus materials to evoke speech.

- Frequent modeling of fluent productions for the client to imitate—a common characteristic of most stuttering treatment procedures—is not a typical part of pause-and-talk. The clients are rarely asked to imitatively produce fluent speech in pause-and-talk procedure.

- Pause-and-talk has two components: Reinforcement for fluency and reinforcement withdrawal for stuttering.

- **To reinforce fluency**, the clinician:
  - Maintains eye contact as the client talks fluently
  - Pays attention to what the client is saying
  - Maintains a pleasant facial expression, including smiling
  - Makes comments typical of everyday conversation, including expressions of agreement and disagreement; nods and shakes head as found appropriate
  - Asks questions, prompts responses, suggests topics of conversation, and uses any device that keeps the client talking
  - Minimizes his or her own speech to what is necessary to stimulate speech in the client

- **To withdraw reinforcement for stuttering**, the clinician:
  - Says "Stop" to the client at the earliest sign of a dysfluency or stutter [*makes sure the client stops talking*]
  - Terminates the eye contact
  - Looks at his or her watch to count five seconds
  - Alternatively, looks elsewhere and estimates the five seconds of time-out duration
  - Remains still for the duration of time-out
  - Maintains a neutral facial expression
  - Reestablishes the eye contact at the end of the time-out duration
  - Says something that will prompt the client to resume talking (e.g., "You were saying," "Please continue," "Go ahead," "You can talk now," etc.)
  - Alternatively, gestures the client to continue talking, especially in the later stages of treatment (e.g., a hand gesture that suggests *please continue*)

- The time-out duration should never be too long. A 5-second time-out is effective.

- To evaluate the child's progress in treatment, the clinician may tape-record each session and later calculate the percentages of dysfluency or stuttering.

- If a correctly implemented pause-and-talk procedure does not produce satisfactory results, the clinician may consider alternative procedures (e.g., the response cost procedure described later or the fluency shaping procedure, described earlier). Although there will be individual differences, stuttering frequency should be significantly reduced in a matter of few sessions. If not, the progress may be judged unsatisfactory, leading to a change in the treatment procedure.

- As with any behavioral treatment, attention should be contingent strictly on fluent speech. The clinician should not continue to pay attention when a dysfluent production is in progress. As soon as some earliest sign of a dysfluent speech production is noticed, the clinician should say "Stop" and make sure the client stops talking. Some of the early signs of stuttering include the following:
  - ➤ Quivering or puckering of the lips
  - ➤ Knitting of the eyebrows
  - ➤ Suddenly increased tension in the facial, shoulder, or chest muscles
  - ➤ A slight hesitation that may mushroom into a full-fledged stutter
  - ➤ An attempt to avoid eye contact
  - ➤ Tensed movements of hand or feet

- The time-out duration should never follow a fluent production because of a slowness in recognizing a dysfluent production.

- The clinician should take note that in the pause-and-talk procedure, such fluency shaping skills as gentle phonatory onset, airflow management, and slower rate of speech are not targeted. A common error to be avoided is to inadvertently induce slower speech. Modeling of fluent speech is not frequently used in the pause-and-talk method, but if it ever becomes necessary, it should be done at a normal rate of speech. Strictly implemented pause-and-talk procedure does not negatively alter speech prosody, including rate of speech. In fact, the speech rate may, within the normal range, slightly increase when the method reduces dysfluencies.

- If the child begins to speak slowly to increase fluency and thus avoid the time-out periods, the clinician may instruct the child to speak faster. A normally fast rate may be modeled for the child to imitate.

Treatment of Stuttering in School-Age Children:
III. Pause-and-Talk

Treatment Protocol for Conversational Speech

Scripts for Pause-and-Talk in Conversation		Note
Clinician	"Sometimes we all have problem talking very smoothly. Our words may get stuck. We may repeat what we say, sometimes not realizing it. We prolong our speech sounds. We may say a lot of ums. If one does a lot of these, then the person has a stuttering problem or a fluency problem. When someone stutters, it may also be called a dysfluency—not fluency. We all want to talk very smoothly and fluently. When we are not fluent, we stutter. Do you sometimes stutter?"	The clinician introduces the concepts of stuttering, dysfluency, and fluency
Child	"Yeah, sometimes."	Child shows awareness of one's own fluency problem
Clinician	"The good news is that you can learn to speak more fluently. If you learn to do a few things right, you, too, can be fluent like most other kids. Do you want to learn to speak fluently."	The clinician reassures the child
Child	"Yes."	
Clinician	"You can do it. You can talk fluently like other kids. I want to help you talk fluently. Is that Okay?"	Reassures the child
Child	"Okay."	
Clinician	"All right. To speak fluently and smoothly, you should eliminate all those stutterings. There is a simple way to eliminate them. If you stop talking when you stutter and remain silent for 5 seconds, your stuttering will decrease. It is hard for you to stop when you stutter, and that's where I come in! I will help you stop and remain silent for 5 seconds every time you stutter. Whenever you stutter or even begin to stutter, I will say, "Stop." You then *(continued)*	Introduces the pause-and-talk

Pause-and-Talk in Conversational Speech, continued

Scripts for Pause-and-Talk in Conversation		Note
Clinician *(continues)*	stop talking immediately, and I will stop looking at you, just to show that it is not talking time. I may be looking at my watch or the floor or the ceiling, or anything other than your face. When I say "Stop" you simply should completely stop talking, even if you are in the middle of a word. You should be absolutely silent until I look at you again. When I look at you again, you can start talking—continue what you were saying. I call this the pause-and-talk method. You simply pause when you stutter for 5 seconds, and then talk. Simple enough? [*the child nods*] So let me see if you understand this. Whenever you even begin to stutter, what do I do?"	Describes pause-and-talk
Child	"You say, *Stop.*"	Understands
Clinician	"Very good! When I say, 'Stop,' what do you do?"	Checks the child's understanding
Child	"I should stop talking for 5 seconds."	Understands
Clinician	"Good. What will I be doing during those 5 seconds when you remain silent? And why do I do that?"	Checks the child's understanding
Child	"You will looking at something else, not my face. You do that to show that we cannot talk."	Understands
Clinician	"Very good! You understand what we should do and why. Are you ready to do this pause-and-talk?"	Verbal praise for the child's understanding
Child	"Yes."	
Clinician	"Okay, we can start talking about anything. You should look at my face and talk continuously. Tell me all about your family. I want to know how many brothers and sisters you have, their names, ages, and what they do. Your Mom's and Dad's names, what they do. How many friends you have and the names of your friends. Any pets you have. The idea is for you to talk a lot. Okay, you can start telling me about your family. Start with your Dad's name."	Instructs on the need to talk continuously

Pause-and-Talk in Conversational Speech, continued

Scripts for Pause-and-Talk in Conversation		Note
Child	"My Dad's name is B-b . . . "	Dysfluency; cessation of eye contact
Clinician	"Stop." [*Avoids eye contact; sits motionless.*] "Okay, your Dad's name."	5-sec time-out Re-establishes eye contact
Child	"My Dad's name is Benjamin. My Mom's name is Carlota. [*the clinician asks, "What does your Dad do? And your Mom?"*] My Dad sells insurance. My Mom teaches at the Mariposa Academy. I have t-t . . . "	Eye contact with the clinician Gets prompted from the clinician Dysfluency; cessation of eye contact
Clinician	"Stop." [*Avoids eye contact; sits motionless.*] "You have . . . "	5-sec time-out Re-establishes eye contact
Child	"I have two sisters and one brother. My sisters are all older than me. [*the clinician asks, "How old are they? What are their names?"*] One sister is e-e . . . "	Eye contact with the clinician Dysfluency; cessation of eye contact
Clinician	"Stop." [*Avoids eye contact; sits motionless.*] "Please continue. Tell me all about your two sisters and one brother."	5-sec time-out Re-establishes eye contact
Child	"My oldest sister is twenty and her name is Erika. My second sister is sixteen and her name is Marlow. [*the clinician asks, "What do they do?"*] Erika goes to college. [*the clinician asks, "Where? What college?"*] She goes to Fresno State. Marlow g-g-g . . . "	Eye contact with the clinician Gets prompted Dysfluency; cessation of eye contact
Clinician	"Stop." [*Avoids eye contact; sits motionless.*] "Okay, Marlow goes . . . "	5-sec time-out Re-establishes eye contact
Child	"Marlow goes to Mariposa High. She is a freshman . . . [*the clinician prompts: "Your brother?"*] Oh yeah. My brother is fourteen. He is in the eighth grade. He goes to Bush Intermediate School. [*the clinician prompts: "Yourself?"*] I am twelve. I am in the sixth grade. I come to this school. [*the clinician asks, "What is the name?"*] You know! This is the King Elementary School."	Fluent speech; no time-out

Pause-and-Talk in Conversational Speech, continued

Scripts for Pause-and-Talk in Conversation		Note
Clinician	"Good talking! Do you live close to school? How do you get here everyday?"	Initiates a new topic of conversation
Child	"I-I . . . "	Dysfluency; cessation of eye contact
Clinician	"Stop." [*Avoids eye contact; sits motionless.*] "Yes, continue."	5-sec time-out Re-establishes eye contact
Child	"I live far from here. My Dad drops me off here every day. [*the clinician asks, "No school bus?"*] Yes, there is school bus. It comes too early. I am not ready. My Mom tried to put me on the bus many times. I just can't get up that early to get ready for the bus. My Dad gives me a ride every day."	Fluent speech; no time-out
Clinician	"How does your brother get to school? Is his school also far from your home? Also, tell me how your sisters get to their school or college."	Continues conversation Maintains eye contact
Child	"My brother's school is also far from our home. He takes a bus to his school. He somehow mmm . . . "	Dysfluency; cessation of eye contact
Clinician	"Stop." [*Avoids eye contact; sits motionless.*] "Yes, *your brother somehow . . . *"	5-sec time-out Re-establishes eye contact
Child	"He somehow manages to get up early to catch his bus. Mom wakes him up, though. Sometimes she shakes him up. She has to do it two three times! [*the clinician prompts: "Your sisters . . . "*] Yeah. My oldest sister Erika drives her car to her college. Marlow just walks to her school. Her school is just around the corner from our house."	Fluent speech; no time-out
Clinician	"Great talking! Now you tell me all about your friends. Your friends in the neighborhood, your friends in the school, who is your best friend, and everything. Do you have many friends?"	Initiates a new topic of conversation
Child	"Yeah, I have a lot. [*the clinician prompts: "name your friends at school and your neighborhood."*] Gee, I have ssss . . . "	Dysfluency; cessation of eye contact
Clinician	"Stop." [*Avoids eye contact; sits motionless.*] "Okay, you may talk now."	5-sec time-out Re-establishes eye contact

Pause-and-Talk in Conversational Speech, continued

Scripts for Pause-and-Talk in Conversation		Note
Child	"I have so many friends it's hard to remember all the names! I will try. I have at least 6 or 7 friends in the school. They are all in my class. One of them is Carlos. Then I have Samantha, Belinda, Sam, Joe, and Ethan. Oh I forgot! Noah. Noah is my newest friend. I like him a lot. He is my best friend now. [*the clinician asks: "Who was before?"*] Ethan was my best friend. We had a fight in cafeteria. I still like him, but Noah is my best friend in school."	Fluent speech; no time-out
Clinician	"In your neighborhood?"	
Child	"I have some. I have Ch-ch . . . "	Dysfluency; cessation of eye contact
Clinician	"Stop." "You have . . . "	5-sec time-out Re-establishes eye contact
Child	"I have Chad. Chad is older than me. He is thirteen or fourteen. We sometimes go skateboarding in our neighborhood. Then I have Danny. Danny is only 9, but he is good at computer games. He comes to my place and we play games on my computer. He always wins, though!"	Fluent speech; no time-out
Clinician	"Who else?"	
Child	"I have Antonio. He is t-t- . . . "	Dysfluency; cessation of eye contact
Clinician	"Stop." [*gestures to continue*]	5-sec time-out Re-establishes eye contact
Child	"Antonio. He is ten. He is new in our neighborhood. I don't know him well, but he is very nice. He has a lot of books in his room. I like to read his storybooks. He lets me borrow his books."	Fluent speech; no time-out
Clinician	"That sounds like a nice friend!"	

Continue to administer pause-and-talk in this manner until the child's stuttering is reduced significantly. When the dysfluency rate is well under 5%, initiate pause-and-talk treatment at the level of narrative speech. Use the story protocols that follow in having the child retell stories.

Treatment of Stuttering in School-Age Children: III. Pause-and-Talk

Treatment at the Narrative Speech Level

Overview

- With school-age children, the **pause-and-talk** procedure initiated at the conversational speech level should be shifted to narrative speech level as soon as possible. At the narrative speech level, the clinician tells stories to the child and asks the child to retell the stories as fluently as possible.

- The clinician selects stories that are appropriate for the child under treatment. Stories from the child's grade level may be especially useful. The child may be asked to bring a storybook he or she reads at home or in the classroom. In all cases, the stories selected should be relevant to the child's ethnocultural background, although stories of universal appeal may be especially useful with a variety of children.

- A need to impose pause-and-talk contingent on stuttering should be minimal at this stage of treatment.

- If a high rate of dysfluencies persist when fluency in narrative speech is targeted, the clinician may revert to the previous level of treatment.

- After some time at the simpler level of treatment, the clinician may once again shift treatment to the more complex narrative speech level.

- Prompt stopping of the client at the earliest sign of a stutter and interested attention paid to all fluent segments of speech will continue as before.

Treatment of Stuttering in School-Age Children:
III. Pause-and-Talk

Treatment Protocol for Narrative Speech

Scripts for Pause-and-Talk in Narration		Note
Clinician	"You have been doing really well in learning to speak fluently. Have you noticed your stuttering is way down? Your speech has been very smooth for several sessions. "I think it is time for you to tell some long stories without stuttering. I will tell you a story. I want **you** to listen carefully, because when I am finished with it, I want you to tell me the whole story. The goal is for you to retell the story with little or no stuttering. Okay?"	Introduces the new narrative task
Child	"Okay."	
Clinician	Now listen carefully. I want you to tell me everything I tell you in this story. "This is the story of a clever crow. Once upon a time, there lived a very clever crow. On one hot summer day, the crow got very thirsty. He began looking for some water. He flew here. He flew there, looking for water. As he was flying, high above, he saw a pot on the ground with a little bit of water in it. He flew down and sat on the top of the pot. He put his head into it to drink the water. But he couldn't reach the water. The water was way down in the bottom of that pot. He stretched his neck and he bent his body to reach the water. No matter how hard he tried, he couldn't reach the water. The sight of the water made him even more thirsty. He then looked around and saw some pebbles on the ground. He thought of a clever idea. He picked up one pebble and dropped it into the pot. He picked up another pebble and dropped it into the pot. He saw the water was rising, but he still couldn't reach it. He dropped many more pebbles into the pot. He saw the water coming up fast! He put a lot more pebbles into the pot. With all the pebbles at the bottom of the pot, the water came all the way up! He then sat on the top of the pot and drank all the water in it. That's the end of the story. *(continued)*	Tells the story of the clever and thirsty crow

Pause-and-Talk in Narrative Speech, continued

Scripts for Pause-and-Talk in Narration		Note
Clinician *(continues)*	Now you tell me the story. Remember to be as fluent as possible. Look at me when you tell the story."	
Child	"It was a hot summer day. There was a clever crow. He got very thirsty. He began looking for some water. He flew here. He flew there. When he was flying high, he saw a pot with a little bit of water in it. He ffffl . . ."	Narrates the story Dysfluency; cessation of eye contact
Clinician	"Stop." [*Avoids eye contact; sits motionless.*] "Yeah, tell me."	5-sec time-out Re-establishes eye contact
Child	"He flew down and sat on the top of the pot and tried to drink the water. But he couldn't drink it. The water was in the bottom of that pot. He stretched his neck and he bent his body. But he couldn't drink the water. Seeing all that water inside the pot made him even more thirsty. He then saw some pebbles on the ground. He thought of a clever idea. He picked up one pebble and dropped it into the pot. He picked up another pebble and dropped it into the pot. Water was coming up, but he still couldn't reach it. He dropped many more pebbles into the pot. Then the water came all the way up! He drank all the water in it. That's the end of the story."	Fluent speech; no time-out
Clinician	"That was a great story! Your speech was very fluent, too! Keep up the good work. "Are you ready for another story?"	Verbal praise for storytelling
Child	"Oh yes! I like stories!"	
Clinician	"Again, listen carefully! You have to tell me the whole story. "Once upon a time, there was a farmer. He owned a lot of land. The farmer loved to eat chocolate cakes and ride on his shiny black horse. He had three sons. When the farmer became old, he decided it was time for him to retire. He wanted to take it easy, eat good food, and ride his horses. He then decided that he would give his farm to one of his sons who was the smartest of all. He couldn't decide who was the smartest. So he arranged a contest for them. He gave his sons a hundred dollars each and told them to spend *(continued)*	Tells another story in two parts

Pause-and-Talk in Narrative Speech, continued

Scripts for Pause-and-Talk in Narration		Note
Clinician *(continues)*	it any way they liked. The farmer also told them that he would decide who gets the farm depending on how they spent their money. "That is the first part of the story. You tell me the first part and then I will tell you the rest. Don't forget to speak as fluently as possible."	Asks the child to narrate the first part
Child	"Okay. "Once upon a time, there was a farmer. He had three sons. He owned a lot of land. The farmer loved to eat chocolate cakes and ride on his black horse. Um-um . . . "	Dysfluency; cessation of eye contact.
Clinician	"Stop." [*Avoids eye contact; sits motionless.*] "Alright. Tell me now."	5-sec time-out Re-establishes eye contact
Child	"When the farmer became old, he wanted to retire. He wanted to eat good food and ride his horses. He then decided that he would give his farm to a son who was the smartest of all. He didn't know who was the smartest son. So he arranged a contest for them. He gave each son a hundred dollars. He told them to spend it any way they liked and he would decide who gets the farm depending on how they spent their money."	
Clinician	"You are doing a great job of telling me that story. Now I will tell you the rest of it. Listen carefully. "After three days, the sons came home in the evening. Each son secretly hid what he had bought in a separate room. Each wanted to surprise and impress his Dad to get the farm. When the night fell, the sons went to their Dad and said they were ready to show how they spent their money. The first son took the father to a room and opened the doors. To his delight, the farmer saw two dozen huge chocolate cakes, all decorated beautifully! The farmer's mouth was watering like crazy! The second son then took him to another room. When he opened the door, the farmer saw a huge shiny, black horse! He was so thrilled that he was ready to take ride that horse right then. But the third son said, 'Dad, I want to show you how I spent the money,' so the *(continued)*	Tells the rest of the story

Pause-and-Talk in Narrative Speech, continued

Scripts for Pause-and-Talk in Narration		Note
Clinician *(continues)*	farmer followed him to the third room. When the third son opened the door, the farmer stepped in and saw a large table on which there were two dozen huge candles burning beautifully! The son then told his father, 'Dad, I spent two dollars and forty cents on the candles and ten cents on a box of matches. I spent a total of two dollars and fifty cents. Here is your ninety-seven dollars and fifty cents. Please take it back.' "You tell me this story and also guess who got the farm."	
Child	"After spending their money, the sons came home. It was evening. Each son went to a room and secretly hid the thing he had bought. Each wanted to surprise and impress his Dad. Each wanted the farm for himself. When it was nighttime, the sons told their Dad they were ready to show what they bought. The first son took the father to a room and showed two dozen huge chocolate cakes. They were nicely decorated. The farmer's mouth was watering like crazy! The second son then took him to another room. And showed the farmer a huge and shiny black horse! Dad was thrilled. He wanted to ride that horse. But the third son said, 'I want to show you what I bought for you.' The farmer followed him to the room. When the third son opened the door, the farmer saw a large table. He saw two dozen huge candles burning beautifully! The son then told his father, 'Dad, I spent two dollars and some cents? [*the clinician prompts: "forty cents"*] yes, forty cents on the candles and how many? [*the clinician prompts: "ten cents"*] Yes, ten cents on a box of matches.' He said, I totally spent . . . how much was it? [*the clinician prompts: "two dollars and fifty cents"*] yes, two dollars and fifty cents. Here is your ninety-seven dollars and some cents. Please take it back.' "	Narrates fluently
Clinician	"That was fantastic! You told me the story so fluently! Now guess who got the farm?"	Verbal praise for story telling

Pause-and-Talk in Narrative Speech, continued

Scripts for Pause-and-Talk in Narration		Note
Child	"I think the third son got the farm."	Fluent production
Clinician	"Why do you think the third son got the farm?"	
Child	"He saved a lot of money for his Dad!"	Fluent production
Clinician	"You are right! The third son got the farm because he was wise in spending Dad's money. The farmer decided that his smartest third son would take good care of the farm. "Are you ready for another story?"	
Child	"Sure!"	
Clinician	"This is the story of a small ant and a big bird. Once upon a time, there was a small ant. One day the ant was creeping along in the forest. It was a hot day. The ant was very thirsty. Remember the thirsty crow? The ant had the same problem. While moving along, he saw a little pond. The ant was very happy to see the pond full of water! But when he crawled to the edge of the pond to reach for water, his tiny legs slipped and he fell into the pond. The poor ant was drowning! He was going to die! He cried out 'help, help!' But who is there to help? Well, there was a big bird sitting on a tree. She was watching the sad ant struggling in the water. The bird quickly thought of a clever plan to save the ant. She plucked a huge leaf from the tree and dropped it into the pond! The struggling ant somehow managed to climb on to the leaf. The leaf slowly floated to the shore and the ant climbed out of the pond. The story is not finished, but you tell me what I just told you. I will tell you the rest after I hear this much from you."	Tells a new, longer story, but stops in the middle to have the child tell the first part
Child	"This is a story of a tiny ant and a big bird. The ant was thirsty like the crow in the other story. He was creeping in the forest. It was a hot day. He then saw a little pond. He wanted to drink water. When he got close to the water, his tiny legs slipped and he fell into the pond. The poor little ant was drowning! He was going to die! So he cried, 'help! help!' There was no one there to help. But a bird was sitting in a tree. She saw the ant, almost drowning. The bird quickly thought of *(continued)*	Child retells the first part of the story; fluent productions

Pause-and-Talk in Narrative Speech, continued

Scripts for Pause-and-Talk in Narration		Note
Child *(continues)*	something. She wanted to save the ant. There was a big leaf on the tree. She plucked it and dropped it to the pond. The ant climbed on to the leaf and came out of the pond!"	
Clinician	"That was excellent! You remembered everything! Now I will tell you the rest of the story.	Verbal praise for story telling
	"The ant was tired from his adventure in the pond. He wanted to go home. When he was going home, he saw a hunter. The hunter was trying to catch the big bird that had saved the ant. The bird did not see the hunter, so he was still happily sitting there! Just when the hunter was ready to throw a net to catch the bird, the ant bit him hard on his toe! What did the hunter do? He just screamed 'Ouch!' The bird heard the scream and quickly flew away! The big bird saved the small ant first and the small ant saved the big bird! The end.	Tells the rest of the story
	"Now you tell me the rest of the story I just told you."	
Child	"The ant was tired. He was going home. He then sss-saw . . . "	A sound prolongation
Clinician	"Stop." [*Avoids eye contact; sits motionless.*] "Tell me."	5-sec time-out Re-establishes eye contact
Child	"He then saw a hunter. Hunter was trying to catch the bird that saved the ant. He was trying to catch the bird with a net. The bird did not see the hunter. He was happily sitting on the tree. When the hunter was about to throw a net on the bird to catch it, the ant bit his toe! The hunter screamed 'Ouch!' The bird heard it. He quickly flew away. The big bird saved the little ant. Then, the little ant saved the big bird."	Fluent narrative
Clinician	"That was great! Again you remembered the story! I liked your fluent speech, too!"	Verbal praise for story telling and fluency

To stabilize fluency, continue to treat the child in the manner described. Revert to conversational speech if necessary. Offer additional narrative experiences to the child. Probe for fluency and stuttering when the child has maintained fluency at 98% or better across three sessions.

Treatment of Stuttering in School-Age Children:
III. Pause-and-Talk

Treatment Recording Sheet

Personalize and print this page from the CD.

Name of the child:	DOB:
Name of the parents:	Phone:
Diagnosis: Stuttering	Session date(s):
Clinician:	Comments:

Chart the child's progress for each session with your preferred method. You may calculate a percent dysfluency or stuttering rate based on the number of words spoken. If more detailed data are warranted, score the individual dysfluency types and add them up to calculate the dysfluency rate.

Essential Measures		Optional Measures: Frequency of Specific Dysfluency Types						
Dates of Service	Percent Stuttering	Prolongations	Pauses	Repetitions	Interjections	Revisions	Incomplete Phrases

Treatment of Stuttering in School-Age Children: III. Pause-and-Talk

Probe Protocol

Probe Procedure

- Record two conversational speech samples, each 5 to 7 minutes in duration
- Record a 3-minute monologue; ask the child to talk about a topic such as:
  - ➢ Birthday parties
  - ➢ Vacations
  - ➢ Visit to a zoo or a theme park
  - ➢ Favorite games or TV shows
  - ➢ Weekend activities
  - ➢ Friends and the family
  - ➢ Teacher, academic subjects, and the school activities
  - ➢ Any other child-specific topic
- Obtain a 5-minute home speech sample
- Record one or more extraclinic speech samples in such places as the child's classroom, cafeteria, and the playground
- Analyze the percent dysfluency or stuttering rate
- Personalize the *Probe Recording Sheet* and record the dysfluency or stuttering rates; print the sheet for child's clinical file

Treatment of Stuttering in School-Age Children:
III. Pause-and-Talk

Probe Recording Sheet

Personalize and print this page from the CD.

Name of the child:	DOB:
Name of the parents:	Phone:
Diagnosis: Stuttering	Session date(s):
Clinician:	Comments:

Analyze the probe speech samples with your preferred method. You may calculate a percent dysfluency or stuttering rate based on the number of words spoken. If more detailed data are warranted, score the individual dysfluency types and add them up to calculate the dysfluency rate.

Take at least three clinic probe samples. If possible, obtain three extraclinic probe samples.

Essential Measures		Optional Measures: Frequency of Specific Dysfluency Types					
Dates/Setting of Probe	Percent Stuttering	PRO	PAU	REP	INT	REV	INC
1. /mm/dd/yy/ Clinic							
2. /mm/dd/yy/ Clinic							
3. /mm/dd/yy/ Clinic							
1. /mm/dd/yy/ Home							
2. /mm/dd/yy/ Classroom							
3. /mm/dd/yy/ Playground							

PRO (Prolongations); PAU (Pauses); REP (Repetitions); INT (Interjections); REV (Revisions); INC (Incomplete phrases).

Dismiss the child from current services when the child's stuttering or dysfluency rate stays below the target percentage in conversational probes. Suggested criterion is less than 2% dysfluency rate in the clinic and less than 5% in natural settings. Schedule follow-ups and booster treatments as needed.

Treatment of Stuttering in School-Age Children: IV. Response Cost

Overview

In addition to fluency shaping and pause-and-talk, described in the previous sections, response cost is another effective alternative for treating stuttering in school-age (as well as preschool) children. Therefore, the response cost protocols given for preschoolers will be adapted in this section for school-age children who stutter. Response cost has a long history of research. The technique was found to be effective in studies conducted several decades ago. Recently, a relatively large study involving mainly preschoolers included 6 school-age children who stuttered. The results of this study demonstrated that the technique can be extremely effective in treating stuttering in school-age (as well as preschool) children (Hegde, 2004). The school-age children included in the study ranged in age from 6 to 10 years. They participated in an experimental study conducted within the single-subject ABAB design (Hegde, 2004). Following baserates, treatment was offered, withdrawn during semester breaks, and reinstated following the breaks. Treatment resulted in marked reduction in stuttering, and initial treatment withdrawal caused an increase in stuttering. Reinstatement of fluency resulted in systematic and clinically significant reductions in stuttering. Increase in stuttering following treatment withdrawal helped rule out the possibility that the children would have recovered without treatment (spontaneous recovery). All 6 school-age children achieved normal-sounding fluency with a dysfluency rate well under 2% in most cases. Up to four years of follow-up has shown that the children have maintained fluency and that the parents no longer consider their children as stutterers.

Response cost procedure includes reinforcement for fluency and reinforcer withdrawal for stuttering. Tokens are the most commonly used conditioned-generalized reinforcers (Hegde, 1998). In the initial stages of treatment, tokens can be more effective than verbal reinforcers because they may be exchanged for a variety of reinforcers (the small gifts the children exchange the tokes for). Once fluency is stabilized, tokens may be unnecessary.

It is important to note that the response cost includes both verbal praise and corrective verbal feedback. In essence, it includes more than one type of contingency for stuttering and fluency. Each token is presented along with verbal praise. For example, the clinician might say, "That was fluent speech, here is your token!" and present the token to the child. Therefore, fluency is reinforced with verbal praise as well as tokens. Similarly, each token withdrawal is accompanied by verbal corrective feedback. For instance, the clinician might say, "No, that was bumpy speech" and withdraw a token from the child. Therefore, stuttering meets both verbal corrective feedback and token withdrawal.

Eventually, the clinician may fade the token presentation and maintain fluency only with verbal praise. Simultaneously, the token withdrawal is also faded out. An occasional verbal corrective feedback may help keep the stuttering frequency well below the adopted criterion (e.g., less than 4% of the words spoken).

Before starting treatment with response cost, the clinician should establish the baserates of dysfluencies in sentences, conversational speech, and narratives as described in a previous section. Regardless of the treatment procedures used, the baserate protocols remain the same for children. After establishing the baserates, the clinician may select either the comprehensive fluency shaping, slower rate (prolonged speech), pause-and-talk, or response cost to treat school-age children who stutter. In this section, protocols for the response cost procedure are offered.

Student clinicians and parents can be relatively easily trained to administer the response cost procedure. Most parents may be trained to hold brief informal treatment sessions in which they present tokens for fluent productions and withdraw tokens for stuttering. The parents may eventually fade the tokens out and maintain fluency with occasional verbal praise for fluency and verbal corrective feedback for stuttering.

Treatment of Stuttering in School-Age Children:
IV. Response Cost

Treatment at the Sentence Level

Overview

- With school-age children, the **response cost method** may be initiated at the sentence level.

- When the child produces single words and phrases in response to questions about the stimulus materials, the clinician may prompt, instruct, or otherwise encourage the child to produce shorter and longer sentences.

- In contrast to the baserate sessions, however, the clinician may model and immediately ask the child to imitate shorter and longer sentences. Stuttering frequency typically decreases when children immediately imitate a fluent production, which gives an opportunity for the clinician to reinforce fluency. Frequent modeling in the beginning stages of treatment is essential to stabilize fluency at the sentence level.

- Tokens bridge the gap between the desirable fluent productions and the eventual reinforcer the child gets by exchanging the tokens earned in the treatment session.

- As noted, positive verbal reinforcement should accompany all token presentation. In the final stages of treatment, only the verbal praise may be sufficient to sustain fluency.

- The clinician may reinforce fluent productions with a variety of verbal statements plus token presentation. While preschoolers seem to better understand the concepts of smooth speech than *fluent speech*, school-age children understand both *smooth speech* and *fluent speech*. Therefore, the terms *smooth speech* and *fluent speech* may be used in treating school-age children. Initially, tokens may be presented with an announcement, but later such announcements may be skipped (as in the last two examples):
  - ➤ That was great! You said it smoothly, here is your token!
  - ➤ Wonderful! You are such a smooth talker! You get a token!
  - ➤ That was nice fluent speech! Another token for you!
  - ➤ I like your fluent speech! [*presents a token*]
  - ➤ You are doing a great job! [*presents a token*]

- When the child produces a dysfluency, the clinician withdraws a token while offering verbal corrective feedback. The verbal feedback and token withdrawal should be prompt. In addition, the verbal feedback should be clear (unambiguous) and objective in tone. The clinician may use several forms of corrective feedback to accompany token withdrawal; initially, the clinician may announce that a token is being withdrawn, but such announcements are not always necessary, as shown in the following examples:
  - ➤ Stop, that was bumpy! I get one of your tokens!
  - ➤ Oh no! You didn't say it smoothly. I am taking a token back!
  - ➤ That was bumpy! [*withdraws a token*]
  - ➤ Stop, you are having trouble saying it, I get a token from you!
  - ➤ No, that was not smooth! [*withdraws a token*]

- At the beginning of each treatment session, the clinician should present a variety of small gifts and ask the child to select one for the day. The gift should be prominently displayed as the child works during the session. The child may be told that he or she will get a token for talking smoothly and that the tokens received are like money. He or she should have enough money to "buy" the gift at the end of the session. More than the instructions, the actual experience of earning, losing, and retaining enough tokens to "buy" the gift at the end of the session are what informs the child of the essence of treatment.

- Although flat, coin-like, plastic tokens are commonly used, the clinician can select tokens of any kind. Some plastic tokens are colorful and come in different shapes. Children are especially attracted to colorful tokens of unusual shapes.

- In the beginning stages of treatment, the clinician should frequently model fluent production so the child accumulates tokens. The frequency of modeling may be gradually reduced as the child becomes more fluent.

- The clinician should ensure that the child does not run out of tokens at the end of a session (token bankruptcy), resulting in a failure to acquire the selected gift. The child should always get the selected gift, but the tokens earned should also be contingent on fluent productions. Tokens cannot be just given at the end of a session because the child is token-bankrupt. The child cannot be given the gift without tokens, although a set number of tokens is not necessary. Some tokens left is good reason to give the gift.

- The clinician can use a few strategies to avoid token bankruptcy. Obviously, token bankruptcy is likely when the child earns too few tokens and loses too many. To avoid this problem, clinician must increase the frequency of token presentation and decrease the frequency of token withdrawal. In other words, the clinician should increase opportunities for fluent productions and decrease the chances of stuttering. To accomplish this, the clinician may:

  ➢ Model fluent production more often, resulting in increased fluency and higher level of token earning

  ➢ Require single words or phrases, instead of sentences, that also result in increased fluency and higher level of token earning

  ➢ Present two tokens, instead of the typical single token, for longer fluent productions; the clinician in such cases should point out the reason for giving an extra token (e.g., "here is an extra token, because you said a very long sentence fluently")

  ➢ Extend the treatment session by a few minutes to give a few extra tokens for fluency

- On occasion, a child may **react negatively** to the first token withdrawal. In the study described earlier (Hegde, 2004), three of the 35 preschool children reacted negatively when the clinician withdrew the first token. A 3-year-old girl said "I don't want to talk" (a strategy she had used at home before the treatment when the parents gave corrective feedback); a 4-year-old boy declared that he was not going to cry because "he was a big boy" (but the crying seemed imminent); and a 2.6-year-old girl showed reluctance to continue with the treatment. Although these examples are from preschool children, the possibility of a school-age child exhibiting negative reactions cannot be discounted. In all three cases involving preschool children, the negative reaction was eliminated with **role-reversal**. Each child was given an opportunity to give tokens to the clinician for smooth speech and withdraw tokens for bumpy speech. Such a role-reversal, conducted for about 2 to 3 minutes in a session, completely eliminated the negative reaction and the child was enthusiastically ready for continued treatment with response cost. None of the three children ever again exhibited any form of negative reaction. Similar role-reversal might work well with school-age children.

- The same stimulus materials used in baserating dysfluencies in sentences may be appropriate for treatment sessions. Familiar stories and pictures may more readily evoke speech from the child.

- If previously used stimuli fail to provoke interest in the child, the clinician may introduce novel stimuli that will sustain the child's interest.

- To evaluate the child's progress in treatment, the clinician may tape-record each session and later calculate the percent dysfluency or stuttering rate.

- If a correctly implemented response cost procedure does not produce satisfactory results, the clinician may consider alternative procedures (e.g., fluency shaping or pause-and-talk). Although there will be individual differences, stuttering frequency should be significantly reduced in a matter of few sessions. If not, the progress may be judged unsatisfactory, leading to a change in the treatment procedure.

- As with any behavioral contingency-based treatment, token presentation should strictly follow a fluent production and token withdrawal should follow a dysfluent production. The clinician should be careful not to present a token when a dysfluency is imminent or in progress. Similarly, a token withdrawal should not follow when a dysfluency has run its course and the following fluent production is underway. Each type of consequence should be strictly contingent on the specified response topography.

- The clinician should take note that in the response cost procedure, such fluency shaping skills as gentle phonatory onset, airflow management, and slower rate of speech are not targeted. A common error to be avoided is to inadvertently induce slower speech. Fluent productions should be modeled at a normal rate of speech. Strictly implemented response cost procedure does not negatively alter speech prosody, including rate of speech. To the contrary, when the response cost method is successful, the speech rate may slightly increase, although within the normal range.

- If the child begins to speak slowly to increase fluency and thus earn more tokens and to avoid token loss due to stuttering, the clinician may instruct the child to speak faster. A normally fast rate may be modeled for the child to imitate.

Treatment protocols are offered at four levels of training:

1. Treatment at the sentence level
2. Treatment at the continuous speech level
3. Treatment at the narrative speech level
4. Treatment at the conversational speech level

Treatment of Stuttering in School-Age Children:
IV. Response Cost

Treatment Protocol for Sentences

Scripts for Response Cost in Sentences		Note
Clinician	"Sometimes we all have problems talking very smoothly. Our words may get stuck. We may repeat what we say, sometimes not realizing it. We prolong our speech sounds. We may say a lot of *ums*. If one does a lot of these, then the person has a stuttering problem or a fluency problem. When someone stutters, it may also be called a dysfluency—not fluency. We all want to talk very smoothly and fluently. When we are not fluent, we stutter. Do you sometimes stutter?"	The clinician introduces the concepts of stuttering, dysfluency, and fluency
Child	"Yeah, sometimes."	Shows awareness of his fluency problem
Clinician	"You can learn to speak more fluently. With some hard work, you, too, can be fluent like most other kids. Do you want to learn to speak fluently?"	Reassures the child
Child	"Yes."	
Clinician	"You can do it. You can talk fluently like other kids. I want to help you talk fluently. Is that Okay?"	Reassures the child
Child	"Okay."	
Clinician	"Alright. To help you talk more fluently, we will use these tokens. [*showing some tokens*] I will give you a token every time you say something fluently. But every time you stutter, I will take a token away from you. These tokens are like money. At the end of the session, you should have enough tokens—it is like having enough money—to buy your gift from me. [*showing a box of reinforcers*] You can select one of these gifts. Pick one."	Introduces the response cost method
Child	[*selects a gift for the day*]	

Response Cost at the Sentence Level, continued

Scripts for Response Cost in Sentences		Note
Clinician	"Remember, this is a simple game we will be playing. You talk fluently, [*placing a cup in front of the child*] I place a token into this cup. It's your cup. You stutter, I will take a token from your cup and put it into my cup. [*points to another cup*] You should try to keep as many tokens as possible for yourself by talking smoothly. At the end of the session, you can buy that gift [*points to the gift*] with the token money. Now tell me, how do you get the gift?"	Instructs the child about the response cost procedure
Child	"With the token money."	Child understands
Clinician	"You are right! You give me your tokens at the end, I give you your gift. But how do you get the tokens?"	Checks the child's understanding of token earning
Child	"By talking smoothly."	Child understands
Clinician	"What happens when you stutter?"	Checks the child's understanding of token loss
Child	"You take a token from my cup."	Child understands
Clinician	"That's right! You understand everything. Talk smoothly, you get a token. Stutter, you lose a token. At the end, you give me your tokens, you get this gift. Remember, you should work hard to get the gift. Working hard when you are with me means talking fluently. Okay?"	Summarizes the procedure
Child	"Okay."	
Clinician	"Alright, let's begin then! I want you to get that gift today! [*showing the picture of a farm scene*] You know we have talked about this picture before. You can talk about this again, only this time, I want you to talk fluently. What do you see here? Do you see a farm or a home? Tell me in a sentence and make it fluent."	The first treatment trial
Child	"I see a farm."	Fluent production
Clinician	"That's great! You said it fluently! Here is your first token! Now, what do you see here? Say it in a fluent sentence."	**The first token presentation along with verbal praise for fluency**; initiation of the next trial

Response Cost at the Sentence Level, continued

Scripts for Response Cost in Sentences		Note
Child	"I-I-I . . . "	Sound repetition
Clinician	"Oh no! That was a stutter. I am taking your token back. Say, *I see a dog.*"	The **first token removal along with verbal corrective feedback;** models a fluent sentence production at normal rate
Child	"I see a dog."	Fluent imitation of the model
Clinician	"You are excellent! This is your token! Now see this man. What is this man doing here? Say, *he is . . .* "	Token presentation and verbal praise for fluency; initiates the next trial
Child	"He is feeding the cow."	Fluent production
Clinician	"Great! Your speech was fluent. You get another token. Now, what is this calf doing here? Say, *the calf is jumping.*"	Reinforces the child with verbal praise and a token; initiates the next modeled trial
Child	"The calf is jumping."	Fluent imitation of modeled speech
Clinician	"Fantastic! Another token for you! You see, how you are getting more tokens! "Now let's look at this part of the picture here. What is this? Say, *this is hay.*"	Reinforces the child with a token and verbal praise; initiates the next modeled trial
Child	"This is hay."	Fluent imitation of modeled speech
Clinician	"I like how you are talking! Here is a token for your fluent speech! Now let's see. Who likes to eat hay? Say, *the cow likes to eat hay.*"	Token presentation and verbal praise; next modeled trial
Child	"The cow llllikes . . . "	Sound prolongation
Clinician	"No, you stuttered. I get a token back. Say, *the cow likes to eat hay,* and say it fluently."	Token withdrawal, corrective feedback; modeling fluent production
Child	"The cow likes to eat hay."	Fluent imitation
Clinician	"That was wonderful! You get another token! "Now look here. What is she doing here? Say, *she is milking the cow.*"	Verbal and token reinforcement; initiation of next modeled trial
Child	"She is mmmmilking . . . "	Sound prolongation
Clinician	"No, you stuttered. I take a token back. Say, *she is milking the cow.*"	Immediate corrective feedback and token withdrawal; modeling fluent production
Child	"She is mmmmilking . . . "	Second failed attempt at fluent imitation

Response Cost at the Sentence Level, continued

Scripts for Response Cost in Sentences		Note
Clinician	"Oops! I have to take a token back from you. Say, *she is milking the cow.*"	Prompt corrective feedback and token withdrawal; modeling of a fluent production
Child	"She is milking the cow."	Successful third attempt
Clinician	"That was great! Here is a token for that. See, you can talk fluently! Now look here. What is this pig doing here? Say, *the pig is drinking water.*"	Praises the child for the fluent production and models a new sentence on this next trial
Child	"The pig is drinking water."	Fluent imitation
Clinician	"You are super! Nice, fluent, speech! Another token for you! Now let's look here. What is this cat doing? Say, *the cat is sleeping.*"	Reinforces the child with a token and verbal praise; initiates the next modeled trial
Child	"The cat is sleeping."	A fluently imitated production
Clinician	"Wonderful! You are working really hard to say it smoothly! Have this token! Okay, what is this girl doing here? Say, *she is chasing chickens.*"	Reinforces the child with a token and verbal praise and initiates the next modeled trial
Child	"She is chasing chickens."	Fluent imitation
Clinician	"That was fluent again! Another token for you. "Now look at this part here. What are these children doing here? Say, *they are playing with hay.*"	Offers token and verbal reinforcement; initiates the next modeled trial
Child	"They are playing with hay."	Fluently imitated production
Clinician	"Very nice! I like that smooth speech! "You see two men here? What are they doing here? Say, *they are carrying wood.*"	Reinforces the child and initiates the next modeled trial
Child	"They are c-c-c-carry . . . "	Sound repetition
Clinician	"Stop! I have to take one of your tokens. Now, make it smooth, and say, *they are carrying wood,* and you will get your token back."	Gives corrective feedback and withdraws a token; models fluent sentence; promises a token for fluency
Child	"They are c-c-c-carry . . . "	Sound repetition; second failed attempt
Clinician	"No, that was bumpy again. [*withdraws a token without announcement*] Say, *they are carrying wood.*"	Corrective feedback and unannounced token withdrawal; fluent sentence modeling
Child	"They are carrying wood."	A fluent production

Response Cost at the Sentence Level, continued

Scripts for Response Cost in Sentences		Note
Clinician	"Wonderful! A token for that nice speech! Look at this part of the picture now. What are these boys doing here?"	Reinforces and asks an evoking question (no modeling)
Child	"They are riding horses."	A fluent production
Clinician	"Excellent! Another token for you! Now let us look at this picture. See, this picture here shows a fair going on. Have you ever been to a fair?"	Offers verbal praise and a token, moves on to the next stimulus **Injects a brief conversational exchange**
Child	"Yes."	
Clinician	"Who took you to the fair? Tell me in a sentence."	A more open-ended question
Child	"My mom and d-d-da . . ."	A part-word (sound) repetition
Clinician	"Oops! [*takes a token without announcement*] Say, *my mom and dad took me to the fair.*"	Corrective feedback and unannounced token withdrawal; models a fluent production
Child	"My mom and dad took me to the fair."	A fluent sentence production
Clinician	"That's great! A token for your fluent speech! Now look here. What are these kids doing?"	Verbal praise plus token **Reverts to picture description**
Child	"They are taking a ride."	A fluent production
Clinician	"Wonderful! [*presents a token without announcement*] Did you take a ride when you went to the fair?"	Verbal praise plus unannounced token presentation **Another conversational exchange**
Child	"Yes."	A fluent response
Clinician	"Very good! What kind of ride was it? Tell me in a sentence."	Verbal praise, no token for the single-word response; open-ended question
Child	"It was a roller-coaster ride."	A fluent production
Clinician	"You are doing great! [*presents a token*] Who went on the ride with you? Don't forget to say it in a sentence."	Verbal praise plus unannounced token; open-ended question
Child	"My brother went with me."	A fluent production
Clinician	"Nice, fluent speech! Another token, and your cup is filling-up! Thanks for working so hard!"	Verbal praise plus token

Exchange the tokens with the child's preferred gift at the end of each session. Continue to treat in this manner until the child sustains 98% or better fluent speech across three sessions. When this or a similar criterion is met, shift treatment to the next stage in which fluency in narrative speech is targeted.

Treatment of Stuttering in School-Age Children: IV. Response Cost

Treatment at the Continuous Speech Levels

Overview

- With school-age children, the response cost method initiated at the isolated sentence level with frequent modeling may be shifted to more continuous speech levels sooner than it is possible with preschool children. When the response cost method results in significant reduction in stuttering frequency in isolated sentences, the child may be ready to move on to the continuous speech level. If the child's fluency drops significantly when continuous speech is evoked, the clinician should move back to the sentence level for additional training. Continuous speech may be reintroduced after a period of additional training at the level of evoked individual sentences.

- To begin with, the clinician may use the same stimulus materials that were used in baserating fluency at the continuous speech level. The protocols reflect this strategy. Using familiar stimuli may evoke continuous speech more readily than unfamiliar stimuli. Eventually, the clinician may introduce new materials and topics of conversation to evoke and reinforce fluent speech.

- Initially, the clinician encourages the child to produce more continuous speech with such prompts as "Tell me about everything you see here," "Say it in longer sentences," "Talk about all that's happening," "Say more than one sentence at a time," and so forth.

- The clinician should promptly and enthusiastically reinforce fluent productions with verbal praise and tokens. The clinician should equally promptly withdraw tokens and offer corrective feedback in an objective tone. In the beginning stage of continuous speech treatment, the clinician should model fluent sentences as often as found necessary and ask the child to imitate. The clinician should model all fluent productions at normal rate. The effects of the response cost method does not depend on a slower rate, an explicit airflow management, or gentle onset of phonation. Therefore, the clinician should not inadvertently induce any of these fluency shaping targets.

- The duration of treatment at complex levels of response topography (e.g., narration and conversation) will depend on the individual child. The criterion of treatment success and the individual child's progress in treatment will help determine when to shift training to higher levels. A suggested criterion is less than 2% dysfluency or stuttering rate (based on the number of words spoken) in the at least three clinic sessions to initiate treatment in narrative speech and then in conversational speech.

Treatment of Stuttering in School-Age Children:
IV. Response Cost

Treatment Protocol for Continuous Speech

Scripts for Response Cost in Continuous Speech		Note
Clinician	[*showing the picture of a farm scene*] "Remember, we talked about this picture before? You told me stories about this picture. I want you to do the same again. This time, I want you to tell me everything in smooth speech. First tell me what these people are doing here. Remember to talk in long and smooth sentences. You can start with, *these people are working on the farm.*"	The first trial; prompting a sentence production
Child	"These people are working on the farm."	Fluent production
Clinician	"Excellent! That was a long and smooth sentence! You deserve a token for that! Okay, I will point to all these people and you tell me what they are doing. Start with these kids here. Tell me about everything they are doing." [*points to children; continues to point to different parts of the picture to prompt more continuous speech*]	Verbal praise and token presentation; instructions to evoke more continuous speech
Child	"The kids are playing with hay. They are throwing hay everywhere."	Fluent production
Clinician	"Good job! I like that smooth speech! Here is your token."	Gives verbal praise and a token; points to another part of the picture
Child	"They-they-they . . . "	Word repetition
Clinician	"Oh no! That was bumpy. I have to take a token back. Make it smooth this time and make it a long sentence."	Gives prompt corrective feedback and withdraws a token
Child	"The children are climbing on this ladder. But this boy here is about to fall down from the ladder!"	Fluent productions
Clinician	"Excellent! A token for your fluent speech! What about this part here?"	Gives verbal praise and a token; points to another part of the picture
Child	"They are chasing all the ch-ch-ch- . . . "	Part-word repetition
Clinician	"No. [*withdraws a token*] Who are chasing all the chickens? I want you to say the whole thing. Start with *the children* . . . "	Gives corrective feedback and removes a token unannounced; prompts a longer production

Response Cost in Continuous Speech, continued

Scripts for Response Cost in Continuous Speech		Note
Child	"The children are chasing all the chickens."	Fluent production
Clinician	"I like that smooth speech! [*presents a token*] Tell me all about what these big people are doing. Say more sentences this time. I want you to say many long sentences."	Verbal praise and unannounced token presentation; points to different parts of the picture to evoke more continuous speech
Child	"These men are working. They are digging dirt. That woman is milking the cow. This man is feeding the cow. Some more men are carrying wood. These girls are sitting on the grass. They are eating something."	Produced continuous fluent speech as the clinician pointed to different parts of the picture **Such lengthy and fluent responses are opportunities to offer two or more tokens to avoid token bankruptcy**
Clinician	"That was fantastic! You said so many sentences smoothly! [*presents a token*] That's what I want you to do. Now let us look at this new picture here. You have seen this before. It shows a fair, doesn't it? I will point to different parts of the picture. You tell me all you see and everything that is happening in this picture. Remember, you should say a lot of sentences. Now start here. What do you see and what are they doing?"	Verbal praise plus token for fluent and continuous speech; introduction of new picture stimulus (scene at a fair)
Child	"I-I-I . . ."	Begins with a word repetition
Clinician	"No. [*withdraws a token*] Start with, *I* . . ."	Corrective feedback, unannounced token withdrawal, and a prompt
Child	"I see a lot of kids. They are riding on a roller coaster. The roller coaster is very big. People here are eating hot dogs. Some kids here are taking a ride on this big wheel. The girls are sitting on a bench and eating cotton candy."	Continuous fluent speech production
Clinician	"Excellent! You talked smoothly. [*presents a token*] Okay, tell me more about this part here. Like you just did, tell me a lot. Say it in many sentences."	Verbal praise and token presentation; shows another part of the picture
Child	"I see a little zoo here. Kids are petting a lamb. They are looking at the baby cow. The mommy cow is licking the baby cow. A man is brushing that horse. The girls are feeding some chickens. Here the boy is taking a ride on a p-p-p-"	The clinician may prompt a word the child does not know
Clinician	"No. [*withdraws a token*] Make it smooth and say the whole sentence, start with *here the* . . ."	Corrective feedback and token withdrawal; prompts
Child	"Here the boy is taking a ride on a pony."	Fluent production

Response Cost in Continuous Speech, continued

Scripts for Response Cost in Continuous Speech		Note
Clinician	"Wonderful! Token for your smooth speech! Now let's look at this new picture. It shows a birthday party. Tell me what is going on here. First tell me whose birthday is being celebrated."	Verbal praise, token presentation, and drawing attention to a new picture
Child	"This girl's birthday is being celebrated . . . [*the clinician gestures the child to continue*] She is wearing a pink hat. She is opening presents. There are many kids here. They are wearing pink and blue hats. D-d-dad . . . "	Five fluent sentences before a sound repetition
Clinician	"That was a stutter. [*withdraws a token*] Make it smooth and tell me what the Dad is doing."	Token withdrawal and corrective feedback. Continues to point to others in the picture
Child	"Dad is setting the table. Mom is . . . [*the clinician prompts: "pouring"*] pouring juice. These two boys are playing ball. These girls are dancing."	Fluent productions
Clinician	"That was great! [*presents a token*] You said so many sentences smoothly!"	Verbal praise and token presentation

Exchange the tokens with the child's preferred gift at the end of each session. When the adopted criterion of fluency is met,k shift training to the narrative speech level.

Treatment of Stuttering in School-Age Children:
IV. Response Cost

Treatment at the Narrative Speech Level

Overview

- With school-age children, response cost procedure completed at the continuous speech level should be advanced to the narrative speech level as soon as practical. When fluency systematically increases at the continuous speech level across several sessions, the child may be ready to move on to the narrative speech level.

- If the child's fluency drops significantly when narrative speech is evoked, the clinician can move back to the lower level for additional training.

- Narrative speech may be reintroduced after a period of additional training at the lower level.

- At this stage, the clinician tells stories to the child and asks the child to retell them. The clinician selects simple stories for preschoolers. Storybooks written for preschool children may be selected for treatment sessions. In selecting the stories, the clinician should consider the ethnocultural background of the child. The selected stories may be of universal appeal, but the clinician should, in addition, select stories from the child's cultural background.

- The clinician encourages the child to tell the story in all its details and prompts story elements when the child is unsure. Various other strategies to promote good narrative speech are specified in the protocols that follow.

- The clinician promptly and enthusiastically reinforces fluent production with verbal praise and a token presentation. The clinician equally promptly withdraws a token and offers corrective verbal feedback for each stuttering. The need for modeling at this level of treatment should be minimal.

- The clinician should tell the stories at the normal rate to avoid inducing a slow speech by instructions, modeling, or the manner of storytelling.

- The clinician may continue to implement the maintenance strategies introduced in the earlier level. Family members who initially observe the sessions may join the clinician to present a token and verbal reinforcement for each fluent production and withdraw a token while giving corrective feedback for stuttering. Additional information is offered on maintenance strategies in a later section of the protocols.

- The duration of treatment at the narrative speech level will depend on the individual child. The criterion of treatment success and the individual child's progress in treatment will help determine when to dismiss the child from services. A suggested criterion is less than 2% dysfluency or stuttering rate (based on the number of words spoken) in the clinic sessions and well under 5% in natural settings.

Treatment of Stuttering in School-Age Children: IV. Response Cost

Treatment Protocol for Narrative Speech

Scripts for Response Cost in Story Retelling		Note
Clinician	"Now, I will tell you a story and I want you to remember everything I tell you. When I am finished, I want **you** to tell **me** the same story. I want you to talk smoothly as you tell me the stories. Okay?	Introducing the storytelling task
	"Now listen carefully. Once upon a time there was a little boy. Every time he saw a big moon in the sky, he would ask his Mom, 'Mom, can I touch the moon?' Mom would say, 'it is too far! If you are a bird, you can fly to the moon to touch it.' Then one morning, the boy got up from the bed, ran to his Mom, and told, 'Mom, last night I flew to the moon and touched it!' The Mom said, 'yes, I saw you touch the moon. But I didn't see you fly to the moon. How did you fly?' The boy said, 'Mom, it was only in my dream!' The end. Now you tell me the same story. You can start with once upon a time . . . "	Tells a brief story
Child	"Once upon a t-t-time. . . "	Sound repetition
Clinician	"Oops! That was a stutter. [*withdraws a token*] Say, *once upon a time . . .* "	Corrective feedback and token withdrawal; modeled fluent production
Child	"Once upon a time, there was a little boy. When he saw a big moon in the sky, he wanted to touch it. [*the clinician prompts: "He asked Mom . . . "*] He asked, 'Mom, can I touch the moon?' Mom said, 'if you are a bird, you can touch it.' [*the clinician prompts: "Then one morning . . .*] Then one morning, the boy got up from the bed, ran to his Mom, and said, 'Mom, last night I flew to the moon and touched it!' [*the clinician prompts: "and the Mom said . . . "*] The Mom said 'I saw you touch the moon. But I didn't see you fly to the moon. How did you fly?' The boy said, 'Mom, it was only in my dream!' The end."	A fluent narrative Receives prompts from the clinician whenever there is a bit of a hesitation in the flow of speech

Response Cost in Narrative Speech, continued

Scripts for Response Cost in Story Retelling		Note
Clinician	"Nice story telling! [*presents a token*] I liked that smooth speech you had! You are a good storyteller! I will tell you another story. Listen carefully. I want you to tell me the story again.	Verbal praise and token presentation for fluent storytelling
	"This is the story of a clever crow. Once upon a time, there lived a very clever crow. On one hot summer day, the crow got very thirsty. He began looking for some water. He flew here, he flew there, looking for water. As he was flying, high above, he saw a pot on the ground with a little bit of water in it. He flew down and sat on the top of the pot. He put his head into it to drink the water. But he couldn't reach the water. The water was way down in the bottom of that pot. He stretched his neck and he bent his body to reach the water. No matter how hard he tried, he couldn't reach the water. The sight of the water made him even more thirsty. He then looked around and saw some pebbles on the ground. He thought of a clever idea. He picked up one pebble and dropped it into the pot. He picked up another pebble and dropped it into the pot. He saw the water was rising, but he still couldn't reach it. He dropped many more pebbles into the pot. He saw the water coming up fast! He put a lot more pebbles into the pot. With all the pebbles at the bottom of the pot, the water came all the way up! He then sat on the top of the pot and drank all the water in it. That's the end of the story.	Tells a new story to the child
	"Now you tell me the story. Remember to be as fluent as possible."	
Child	"It was a hot summer day. There was a clever crow. He got very thirsty. He began looking for some water. He flew here. He flew there. When he was flying high, he saw a pot with a little bit of water in it. He ffffl . . . "	Narrates the story Dysfluency
Clinician	"Stop, that was a stutter." [*withdraws a token*] Say, *he flew down . . .*"	Corrective feedback and token withdrawal; prompts and models fluent production
Child	He flew down and sat on the top of the pot and tried to drink the water. But he couldn't drink it. The water was in the bottom of that pot. He stretched his neck and he bent his body. But he couldn't drink the water. Seeing *(continued)*	

Response Cost in Narrative Speech, continued

Scripts for Response Cost in Story Retelling		Note
Child *(continues)*	all that water inside the pot made him even more thirsty. He then saw some pebbles on the ground. He thought of a clever idea. He picked up one pebble and dropped it into the pot. He picked up another pebble and dropped it into the pot. The water was coming up, but he still couldn't reach it. He dropped many more pebbles into the pot. Then the water came all the way up! He drank all the water in it. That's the end of the story."	Fluent speech; no token withdrawal
Clinician	"That was a great story! Your speech was very fluent, too! Here is your token. [*presents a token*] Are you ready for another story?"	Verbal praise for storytelling; token presentation at the end
Child	"Yes! I like your stories a lot!"	
Clinician	"Again, listen carefully! You have to tell me the whole story. "Once upon a time, there was a farmer. He owned a lot of land. The farmer loved to eat chocolate cakes and ride on his shiny black horse. He had three sons. When the farmer became old, he decided it was time for him to retire. He wanted to take it easy, eat good food, and ride his horses. He then decided that he would give his farm to one of his sons who was the smartest of all. He couldn't decide who was the smartest. So he arranged a contest for them. He gave his sons a hundred dollars each and told them to spend it any way they liked. The farmer also told them that he would decide who gets the farm depending on how they spent their money. "That is the first part of the story. You tell me the first part and then I will tell you the rest. Don't forget to speak as fluently as possible."	Tells another story in two parts Asks the child to narrate the first part
Child	"Okay. "Once upon a time, there was a farmer. He had three sons. He owned a lot of land. The farmer loved to eat chocolate cakes and ride on his black horse. Um-um . . . "	 Dysfluency
Clinician	"That was a dysfluency." [*withdraws a token*] Okay, tell me now.	Token withdrawal

Response Cost in Narrative Speech, continued

Scripts for Response Cost in Story Retelling		Note
Child	"When the farmer became old, he wanted to retire. He wanted to eat good food and ride his horses. He then decided that he would give his farm to a son who was the smartest of all. He didn't know who was the smartest son. So he arranged a contest for them. He gave each son a hundred dollars. He told them to spend it anyway they liked and he would decide who gets the farm depending on how they spent their money."	
Clinician	"You are doing a great job of telling me that story. [*presents a token*]	Token presentation
	"Now I will tell you the rest of it. Listen carefully.	Tells the rest of the story
	"After three days, the sons came home in the evening. Each son secretly hid what he had bought in a separate room. Each wanted to surprise and impress his Dad so he would get the farm. When the night fell, the sons went to their Dad and said they were ready to show how they spent their money. The first son took the father to a room and opened the doors. To his delight, the farmer saw two dozen huge chocolate cakes, all decorated beautifully! The farmer's mouth was watering like crazy! He wanted to eat them all right away! But the second son wouldn't let his Dad stand there and dig into the chocolate cakes. He wanted to show what he had bought. So he took him to another room. When the second son opened the door, the farmer saw a huge shiny, black horse! He was so thrilled that he was ready to take a ride right then. But the third son said, 'Dad, I want to show you how I spent the money,' so the farmer followed him to the third room. When the third son opened the door, the farmer stepped in and saw a large table on which there were two dozen huge candles burning beautifully! The son then told his father, 'Dad, I spent two dollars and forty cents on the candles and ten cents on a box of matches. I spent a total of two dollars and fifty cents. Here is your ninety-seven dollars and fifty cents. Please take it back.'	
	"You tell me this story and also guess who got the farm."	

Response Cost in Narrative Speech, continued

Scripts for Response Cost in Story Retelling		Note
Child	"After spending their money, the sons came home. It was evening. Each son went to a room and secretly hid the thing he had bought. Each wanted to surprise and impress his Dad. Each wanted the farm for himself. When it was night time, the sons told their Dad they were ready to show what they bought. The first son took the father to a room and showed two dozen huge chocolate cakes. They were nicely decorated. The farmer's mouth was watering like crazy! The second son then took him to another room. And showed the farmer a huge and shiny black horse! Dad was thrilled. He wanted to ride that horse. But the third son said, 'I want to show you what I bought for you.' The farmer followed him to the room. When the third son opened the door, the farmer saw a large table. He saw two dozen huge candles burning beautifully! The son then told his father, 'Dad, I spent two dollars and some cents? [*the clinician prompts: "forty cents"*] Yes, forty cents on the candles and how many? [*the clinician prompts: "ten cents"*] Yes, ten cents on a box of matches.' He said, I totally spent . . . how much was it? [*the clinician prompts: "two dollars and fifty cents"*] yes, two dollars and fifty cents. Here is your ninety-seven dollars and some cents. Please take it back."	Narrates fluently
Clinician	"That was fantastic! You told me the story so fluently! [*gives a token to the child*] "Now guess who got the farm?"	Verbal praise and token presentation for storytelling
Child	"I think the third son got the farm."	Fluent production
Clinician	"Fluent speech." [*gives a token to the child*] "Why do you think the third son got the farm?"	
Child	"He saved a lot of money for his Dad!"	Fluent production
Clinician	"You are right! And fluent speech, too." [*gives a token to the child*] "The third son got the farm because he was wise in spending Dad's money. The farmer decided that his smartest third son will take good care of the farm. "Are you ready for another story?"	

Response Cost in Narrative Speech, continued

Scripts for Response Cost in Story Retelling		Note
Child	"Oh Yes! I love your stories!"	
Clinician	"This is the story of a small ant and a big bird. Once upon a time, there was a small ant. One day the ant was creeping along in the forest. It was a hot day. The ant was very thirsty. Remember the thirsty crow? The ant had the same problem. While moving along, he saw a little pond. The ant was very happy to see the pond full of water! But when he crawled to the edge of the pond to reach for water, his tiny legs slipped and he fell into the pond. The poor ant was drowning! He was going to die! He cried out 'help, help!' But who is there to help? Well, there was a big bird sitting on a tree. She was watching the sad ant struggling in the water. The bird quickly thought of a clever plan to save the ant. She plucked a huge leaf from the tree and dropped it into the pond! The struggling ant somehow managed to climb on to the leaf. The leaf slowly floated to the shore and the ant climbed out of the pond. The story is not finished, but you tell me what I just told you. I will tell you the rest after I hear this much from you."	Tells a new, longer story, but stops in the middle to have the child tell the first part
Child	"This is a story of a tiny ant and a big bird. The ant was thirsty like the crow in the other story. He was creeping in the forest. It was a hot day. He then saw a little pond. He wanted to drink water. When he got close to the water, his tiny legs slipped and he fell into the pond. The poor little ant was drowning! He was going to die! So he cried, 'help! help!' There was no one there to help. But a bird was sitting in a tree. She saw the ant, almost drowning. The bird quickly thought of something. She wanted to save the ant. There was a big leaf on the tree. She plucked it and dropped it to the pond. The ant climbed on to the leaf and came out of the pond!"	Child retells the first part of the story; fluent productions
Clinician	"That was excellent! You remembered everything! [*gives a token to the child*] "Now I will tell you the rest of the story. Are you ready to listen? [*the child nods*] "The ant was tired from his adventure in the pond. He wanted to go home. When he was *(continued)*	Verbal praise for storytelling; token presentation Tells the rest of the story

Response Cost in Narrative Speech, continued

Scripts for Response Cost in Story Retelling		Note
Clinician *(continues)*	going home, he saw a hunter. The hunter was trying to catch the big bird that had saved the ant. The bird did not see the hunter, so he was still happily sitting there! Just when the hunter was ready to throw a net to catch the bird, the ant bit him hard on his toe! What did the hunter do? He just screamed 'Ouch!' The bird heard the scream and quickly flew away! The big bird saved the small ant first and the small ant saved the big bird! The end. "Now you tell me the rest of the story I just told you."	
Child	"The ant was tired. He was going home. He then sss-saw . . . "	A sound prolongation
Clinician	"No, that was a stutter. I take one of your tokens." [*withdraws a token from the child*] "Okay, tell me the rest."	Corrective feedback and token withdrawal
Child	"He then saw a hunter. Hunter was trying to catch the bird that saved the ant. He was trying to catch the bird with a net. The bird did not see the hunter. He was happily sitting on the tree! When the hunter was about to throw a net on the bird to catch it, the ant bit his toe! The hunter screamed 'Ouch!' The bird heard it. He quickly flew away. The big bird saved the little ant. Then, the little ant saved the big bird."	Fluent narrative
Clinician	"That was great! Again you remembered the story! You have earned another token!" [*gives a token to the child*]	Verbal praise and token presentation

To stabilize fluency, continue to treat the child in the manner described. Revert to the continuous speech level if necessary. Offer additional narrative experiences to the child. Probe for fluency and stuttering when the child has maintained fluency at 98% or better across three treatment sessions.

Treatment of Stuttering in School-Age Children: IV. Response Cost

Treatment at the Conversational Speech Level

Overview

- With the school-age children, the response cost method completed at the narrative speech level should be shifted to the conversational speech level as soon as practical. When 98% or better fluency is sustained at the narrative speech level across several sessions, the child may be ready to move on to the conversational speech level.

- At this level of training, the clinician simply talks with the child. The clinician asks questions and encourages longer sentence productions in the conversational format. Initially, the clinician may ask questions about the child's family, names of parents, siblings, and friends, while encouraging complete sentence productions.

- The clinician promptly and enthusiastically offers verbal reinforcement and a token for all fluent productions. For each dysfluent production (stuttering), the clinician offers corrective feedback in an objective tone and simultaneously withdraws a token. The need for modeling fluent productions at this stage of treatment should be minimal.

- The clinician should talk to the child at a normal rate to avoid inadvertently inducing a slower speech rate in the child.

- The clinician may continue to use the maintenance strategies introduced in the previous level of treatment. The child may be taken out of the treatment room to informally monitor fluent conversational speech with only verbal praise for fluency and subtle corrective feedback for stuttering (no token presentation or withdrawal).

The duration of treatment at the conversational speech level will depend on the individual child. The criterion of treatment success and the individual child's progress in treatment will help determine when to dismiss the child from services. A suggested criterion is less than 2% dysfluency or stuttering rate (based on the number of words spoken) in the clinic sessions and well under 5% in natural settings.

Treatment of Stuttering in School-Age Children: IV. Response Cost

Treatment Protocol for Conversational Speech

Scripts for Response Cost in Conversational Speech		Note
Clinician	"You have been doing great! I liked the way you told me some stories last time. You got so many tokens last time! Now we are going to just talk for a while and practice fluent speech. Okay?"	Introduces the conversational speech task
Child	"Okay!"	
Clinician	"What is your Mom's name? You should start with *My Mom's* . . . and tell me in a complete, long sentence."	Asks simple questions, prompts the production of complete sentences
Child	"My Mom's nnnname . . ."	A sound prolongation
Clinician	"That was bumpy. [*withdraws a token*] Try that again."	Corrective feedback plus token removal
Child	"My Mom's name is Lydia."	Fluent production
Clinician	"Excellent! Your speech was very smooth! [*presents a token*] Now tell me, what is your Dad's name?"	Verbal praise and token presentation
Child	"My Dad's name is Carlos."	Fluent production
Clinician	"I like your smooth speech and long sentence! [*presents a token*] How many brothers do you have?"	Verbal praise and token presentation Next question
Child	"Two." [*the clinician prompts "I have. . ."*] "I have two brothers."	Fluent production, prompted longer sentence
Clinician	"Great job! [*presents a token*] Are they both older than you?"	Verbal praise and token presentation
Child	"No. One brother is my baby brother. Another is older."	Verbal praise and token presentation
Clinician	"How nice! smooth speech and good sentences! [*presents a token*] Tell me the name of your baby brother and the name of your older brother. Use complete sentences. You should start, *the name of my* . . ."	Verbal praise and token presentation Next question and a prompt
Child	"The name of my baby brother is Antonio. The name of my older brother is Noah."	Fluent production
Clinician	"That was fantastic. You know your speech was smooth, right? [*presents a token*] You are doing really well!"	Verbal praise and token presentation Continues this line of conversation

Response Cost in Conversational Speech, continued

Scripts for Response Cost in Conversational Speech		Note
Clinician	"Is your birthday coming up?"	Introduces a new topic for conversation
Child	"I already had my birthday."	Fluent production
Clinician	"Oh you did? When was it? Did you have a big party? Tell me all about the party. Tell me how many kids attended, what kind of gifts you got, what kind of cake did you have, and all that."	Prompts more continuous speech; does not present a token
Child	"I had a party yesterday. It was a big party. Many friends came . . . [*the clinician prompts:* "*Tell me some names of your friends.*"] My friend Cindy came. Timmy came also. Jennifer, Erick, and Alicia also came. [*the clinician prompts:* "*Tell me about gifts.*"] I got lots of gifts. I got a toy train, storybooks, some chocolate. [*the clinician prompts:* "*What did you get from your Mom and Dad?*"] I got a T-shirt from Mom and Dad. I also got a computer game. My brother gave me a big puzzle."	Fluent, relatively more spontaneous production
Clinician	"Yes, you did get a lot of nice gifts! [*presents a token*] And your speech was very smooth!" "Now tell me, what did you all eat and drink?"	Verbal praise and token presentation Open-ended question
Child	"We ate chocolate cake. [*the clinician prompts:* "*Is that your favorite kind? What other kinds of cakes do you like?*"] Yeah, I like chocolate cake. I also like cheesecake. [*the clinician prompts:* "*What about drinks?*"] We had lemonade. Cindy wanted milk. Erick wanted coke."	Fluent production
Clinician	"Thank you! [*presents a token*] That was smooth speech!" "Did you guys play any games?"	Verbal praise; token presentation Next question
Child	"I tried to put the puzzle together. But it was hard. My brother helped me with it. I can p-p"	A sound repetition
Clinician	"Oops! You stuttered. [*withdraws a token*] Try that again. Start with *I can* . . ."	Corrective feedback plus token removal; sentence prompt
Child	"I can put it together now. My friends also worked on the puzzle I got. Some played my video game. Timmy and Erick just ran around and drove us all crazy!"	Fluent production

Response Cost in Conversational Speech, continued

Scripts for Response Cost in Conversational Speech		Note
Clinician	"Nice, smooth speech! [*presents a token*] Did you give something to your friends?"	Verbal praise and token presentation Next question
Child	"Yeah. They all got a hat, some balloons, and some candy."	Fluent production
Clinician	"Great talking! [*presents a token*] Looks like you guys had a great time!"	Verbal praise and token presentation
Child	"It was fun!"	Fluent production

Continue to apply the response cost procedure in the manner described until the child sustains fluent speech at 98% or better across three or more sessions. Record the dysfluency rates in treatment session. Personalize and print the treatment recording sheet from the CD for your use in individual treatment sessions. Subsequently, conduct a conversational probe for generalized and maintained fluency. See the probe protocols and probe recording sheets following the treatment recording sheet.

Treatment of Stuttering in School-Age Children: IV. Response Cost

Treatment Recording Sheet

Personalize and print this page from the CD.

Name of the child:	DOB:
Name of the parents:	Phone:
Diagnosis: Stuttering	Session date(s):
Clinician:	Comments:

Chart the child's progress for each session with your preferred method. You may calculate a percent dysfluency or stuttering rate based on the number of words spoken. If more detailed data are warranted, score the individual dysfluency types and add them up to calculate the dysfluency rate.

Essential Measures		Optional Measures: Frequency of Specific Dysfluency Types					
Dates of Service	Percent Stuttering	Prolongations	Pauses	Repetitions	Interjections	Revisions	Incomplete Phrases

Treatment of Stuttering in School-Age Children:
IV. Response Cost

Probe Protocol

Probe Procedure

- Record two conversational speech samples, each 5 to 7 minutes in duration
- Record a 3-minute monologue; ask the child to talk about a topic such as:
  - ➢ Birthday parties
  - ➢ Vacations
  - ➢ Visit to a zoo or a theme park
  - ➢ Favorite games or TV shows
  - ➢ Weekend activities
  - ➢ Family and friends
  - ➢ Teachers and school-related activities
  - ➢ Any other child-specific topic
- Obtain a 5-minute home speech sample
- Record one or more extraclinic speech samples in such places as the child's classroom, cafeteria, and the playground
- Analyze the percent dysfluency or stuttering rate
- Personalize the *Probe Recording Sheet* on the CD and record the dysfluency or stuttering rates; print the sheet for child's clinical file

Treatment of Stuttering in School-Age Children:
IV. Response Cost

Probe Recording Sheet

Personalize and print this page from the CD.

Name of the child:	DOB:
Name of the parents:	Phone:
Diagnosis: Stuttering	Session date(s):
Clinician:	Comments:

Analyze the probe speech samples with your preferred method. You may calculate a percent dysfluency or stuttering rate based on the number of words spoken. If more detailed data are warranted, score the individual dysfluency types and add them up to calculate the dysfluency rate.

Take at least three clinic probe samples. If possible, obtain three extraclinic probe samples.

Essential Measures		Optional Measures: Frequency of Specific Dysfluency Types					
Dates/Setting of Probe	Percent Stuttering	PRO	PAU	REP	INT	REV	INC
1. /mm/dd/yy/ Clinic							
2. /mm/dd/yy/ Clinic							
3. /mm/dd/yy/ Clinic							
1. /mm/dd/yy/ Home							
2. /mm/dd/yy/ Classroom							
3. /mm/dd/yy/ Playground							

PRO (Prolongations); PAU (Pauses); REP (Repetitions); INT (Interjections); REV (Revisions); INC (Incomplete phrases).

Dismiss the child from current services when the child's stuttering or dysfluency rate stays below the target percentage in conversational probes. Suggested criterion is less than 2% dysfluency rate in the clinic and less than 4% in natural settings. Schedule follow-ups and booster treatments as needed.

Treatment of Stuttering in School-Age Children: V. Promoting Maintenance of Fluency

Maintenance Strategies

Maintenance of fluency in school-age children who have been treated for their stuttering is less complicated than that in adults. Generally, if stuttering is reduced to less than 1% and sustained across several treatment sessions, chances of maintenance in preschoolers are better than in they are in the case of adults. Nonetheless, chances of relapse of stuttering are still there. Therefore, the clinician should implement procedures designed to promote maintenance of fluency across situations and over time. The general strategies are common to most clients and applicable to all treatment procedures.

To promote maintenance of fluency, the clinician:

- Always selects the most effective procedure for the child; to improve chances of maintenance, the resulting fluency must be strong and the stuttering frequency should be well below 3%; preferably, it should be below 1% at the time of dismissal.

- Gives sufficient treatment at the level of conversational speech and narrative speech; fluency not strengthened at these levels of complex speech is unlikely to be maintained.

- Teaches self-monitoring skills to the child. Instead of saying, "Oh that was bumpy!" asks the child "Oops! What happened?" to promote self-evaluation. Uses similar strategies when the child is fluent so the child can evaluate fluent productions as well. In using response cost, encourages the child to give up a token when he or she stutters. Lets the child take a token when speech is fluent.

- Initially, has the parents observe the treatment sessions and understand how it is implemented; responds fully to their questions about the treatment procedure.

- Later, invites parents into the treatment sessions; points out what the important aspects of treatment to the parents. In subsequent sessions, trains the parents in the administration of the treatment procedure that has worked well for the child. Teaches parents to:
  - ➤ Model fluent productions for the child
  - ➤ Praise the child for fluent productions
  - ➤ Offer gentle corrective feedback for stutterings
  - ➤ Prompt fluent productions before the child begins to talk
  - ➤ Conduct home treatment at least twice a week; perhaps three times after dismissal

- Moves treatment to less structured, more naturalistic settings; takes the child out for a walk, and monitors the child's fluency by offering verbal reinforcement and corrective feedback in a subtle manner.

- Asks parents to contact the clinic if there is an increase in stuttering rate; lets them know that a few sessions of booster treatment at a later date may help sustain fluency.

- Follows-up the client and takes a brief conversational probe sample to assess maintenance of fluency.

- Calculates the percent dysfluency or stuttering rate; if the rate is unacceptable, offers booster treatment.

- Encourages parents to resume treatment sessions at home.

- Schedules further follow-ups.

Treatment of Stuttering in School-Age Children:
V. Maintenance of Fluency
Maintenance Probe Recording Sheet

Personalize and print this page from the CD.

Name of the child:	DOB:
Name of the parents:	Phone:
Diagnosis: Stuttering	Session date(s):
Clinician:	Comments:

Analyze the follow-up speech samples with your preferred method. You may calculate a percent dysfluency or stuttering rate based on the number of words spoken. If more detailed data are warranted, score the individual dysfluency types and add them up to calculate the dysfluency rate.

Essential Measures		Optional Measures: Frequency of Specific Dysfluency Types					
Dates/setting of follow-up probe	Percent Stuttering	PRO	PAU	REP	INT	REV	INC
Follow-up #1 Date:							
Follow-up #2 Date:							
Follow-up #3 Date							

Offer booster treatment if the follow-up probe dysfluency rates are unacceptable. On completion of the booster treatment, schedule additional follow-up sessions.

Part 4

Baserating Stuttering in Adults

Baserating Stuttering in Adults
The Need for Baserates in Conversational Speech

Even though an assessment will have been done on the client, it is essential to establish the pretreatment baserates of dysfluencies or stuttering, as defined by the clinician. A single assessment result may or may not be reliable. Furthermore, an assessment may have been made weeks or months prior to the initiation of treatment. Stuttering (dysfluency) frequency may have changed since the assessment. Therefore, it is essential to baserate stuttering before starting treatment.

Clinic Baserate Procedures for Conversational Speech

The protocols for establishing baserates of stuttering include the following steps:

* **Session 1:** During the first session following assessment, clinician may tape-record a 15- to 20-minute speech sample to measure the dysfluency rates. The remainder of the session may be used to discuss treatment options, expectations regarding treatment, and to get generally get more familiarized with the client, the family, or both.

* **Session 2:** At the beginning of the second session, the clinician may tape-record another 10-minute conversational speech sample, followed by an introduction to treatment. The clinician may describe the planned treatment for the client, justify the treatment in terms of evidence, ask questions the client and his or her companions may have about the offered and alternative treatments, and discuss any other matter that concerns the client and family members.

* **Session 3:** At the beginning of the third session, the clinician may tape-record a third, 5- to 7-minute speech sample before starting treatment. The remainder of the session may be devoted to treatment.

If the first three baserates are divergent by a defined criterion (e.g., more than 3 or 5% variation across three measures), the clinician may take another baserate at the beginning of the next session.

Home Baserate Speech Samples

Whenever practical, the clinician may request the client to tape three speech samples at home, each 5 to 7 minutes in duration and submit them for analysis.

In most cases, it is useful to baserate stuttering in oral reading. Guidelines on recording an oral reading sample are offered in a section that follows baserate protocols for conversational speech.

Baserating Stuttering in Adults

Baserate Protocol for Conversational Speech

Scripts for Baserating Stuttering in Conversation		Note
Clinician	"If you have no objection, I will tape-record our conversation today. I will use the taped speech sample to baserate your stuttering before we start treatment. I will ask a series of questions about you and your family and your work. I know you have filled out our case history form, but I would like to go over some of the questions with you. Our conversation helps me understand you and your speech difficulty in some detail. At the same time, the tape-recorded sample of your conversational speech gives me a chance to later analyze the amount of your stuttering. I may repeat this kind of conversation in the next two sessions, although they will be briefer than this. The amount of stuttering I measure in your speech samples will serve as the baserate. As you progress in treatment, these baserates will help us evaluate the degree of change in your stuttering. We will know whether you are making good progress or not. Okay?"	The clinician engages the client in conversational speech to establish the baserates of stuttering
Client	"Okay."	
Clinician	"For how long have you had your stuttering problem?"	
Client	"S-s-s-since my early childhood days. Mmmmy parents have told me that I began to um . . . um st-st-stutter when I was 3 or so."	A part-word repetition, a sound prolongation, an interjection, and a syllable repetition
Clinician	"Has your stuttering changed over the years? If so, in what ways?"	
Client	"Mmmmy stuttering has had a lot of ups and downs over the years. My Mom told me-told me-told me that it was very bad throughout my elementary school years. I-I-I don't remember much about it. It was much [*a long pause*] b-b-b-better in high school years. Either that or I didn't care that much for my stuttering problem. Then it got worse when I started college. It-it-it improved a little bit as I got used to my college and made friends and felt more c-c-c-comfortable in my new surroundings. Then it got worse again when I started looking for a job after graduation. *(continued)*	A phrase repetition Word repetition and a pause Part-word repetition Word repetition Part-word repetition

Baserating Stuttering in Conversational Speech, continued

Scripts for Baserating Stuttering in Conversation		Note
Client *(continues)*	J-j-j-job interviews were a nightmare for me. Then again, [*a long pause*] once I got settled into my position, it improved somewhat. But for the last few years, it has stayed roughly the same. Nnnnot too bad, not too good."	Sound repetition A pause Sound prolongation
Clinician	"Do you remember anything your parents did or said to help you when you began to stutter?"	
Client	"The earliest thing I rrrremember is that my parents wanted me to t-t-t-take a deep breath and talk. Maybe I was in elementary school when they told me that."	Sound prolongation Part-word repetition
Clinician	"What other kinds of suggestions did your parents, teachers, or friends offer you to control your stuttering?"	
Client	"Llllet me think. S-s-s-some friends would tell me to speak slowly. Oh, yes! My pa-pa-parents also told me to think before I talk. My teachers also told me to-to-to [*a long pause*] take a deep breath before talking."	Sound prolongation; sound repetition; syllable repetition Word repetition A pause
Clinician	"Did you try what others suggested? Did any of those suggestions help?"	
Client	"I don't th-th-think any of them helped. Although I can't swear I tried them all seriously. When I took a deep breath, I usually got stuck. Nnnothing would come out of my mouth. I-I-I couldn't under . . . um under . . . um understand what I was supposed to think. Like when I just wanted to say Mommy, but couldn't get the word out. What was I supposed to think? Llllike I don't know the word Mommy?"	Part-word repetition Sound prolongation Word repetition; part-word repetition and interjections Sound prolongation
Clinician	"Did you get any therapy in your preschool or school years? Assuming your parents have told you about it."	
Client	"I d-d-don't think I received any therapy until I was 7 or 8. I rrrremember going to my therapist when I was eight. Therapy was off and on during my-my-my [*a long pause*] elementary school years. I-I-I attended a few sessions in my high school freshman year. I then st-st-stopped going for therapy. It wasn't important to me."	Part-word repetition Sound prolongation Word repetition and a pause Word repetition Part-word repetition
Clinician	"Do you remember anything about the kinds of therapy you had before?"	

Baserating Stuttering in Conversational Speech, continued

	Scripts for Baserating Stuttering in Conversation	Note
Client	"um . . . um . . . Not much. I think I just played with my therapist in elementary school. My high school therapist tried to make me speak slower, I think. I-I-I am afraid I wasn't too thrilled to do that."	Interjection Word repetition
Clinician	"I see. What about your college years? Did you have any therapy?"	
Client	"Yes, my stu-stu-stuttering was quite noticeable in college, especially during freshman year. Maybe even during my sophomore year. I was t-t-t-errified about making presentations in front of the class. When I had to take that mandatory speech class, I-I-I went to my professor to see iiiif there was a way to avoid that dreaded speech to the class. I confessed to the p-p-professor my fear of speaking in front of the class due to my stuttering problem. My professor bluntly told me there was no way to-no way to- avoid the speech. It's a speech class!—he reminded me. He then told me there is a speech clinic on campus where I can get help. I k-k-kind of considered going to the speech clinic on campus, but never really felt comfortable seeking help. I can't explain it. It's-it's-it's almost 10 years since I graduated from college. Now I think I should have gotten help then. May be it would have been more effective than my previous therapies in schools."	Syllable repetition Sound repetition Word repetition Sound prolongation Part-word repetition Phrase repetition Part-word repetition Word repetition
Clinician	"Have you ever tried, on your own, to speak a bit slowly to control your stuttering?"	
Client	"Well . . . well . . . I have t-t-t-tried that."	Initial word repetition; may be counted as an interjection; a part-word repetition
Clinician	"Did it help? Do you still use that strategy?"	
Client	"On occasion I do. It helps when I do slow down. Ssssometimes I have to slow down a lot to say it better. Then I don't like it."	Sound prolongation
Clinician	"Do you often have difficulty saying your name when someone asks you?"	

Baserating Stuttering in Conversational Speech, continued

Scripts for Baserating Stuttering in Conversation		Note
Client	"Yes, I do. Mmmmy name is often the most difficult to say. It is harder to say when ssssomeone asks for my name. In my school and college years, answering the [*a long pause*] teacher's roll call has been a dreaded thing for me. In my-my grade school classes, I was just terrified when the teacher's roll call approached my name. I knew the previous four or five names! It was a terrible count-down for me! Nnnno matter how I answered— sometimes I would attempt a *yes* and at other times I would try to say *here*—I almost always stuttered. I preferred to raise my hand, but ssssome of my teachers wouldn't look at the class when they called the names out."	Sound prolongation Sound prolongation A pause Word repetition Sound prolongation Sound prolongation
Clinician	"Now let me ask you this. What was your major in college? Why did you choose what you did?"	
Client	"I-I-I majored in ssspsychology. I always wanted to be a psychologist. Mmmmy parents thought I should go to law school. My d-d-d-ad is a lawyer. But law didn't interest me."	Word repetition; sound prolongation; another sound prolongation; a part-word repetition
Clinician	"Did you go to grad school? What kind of psychology did you study in grad school?"	
Client	"I majored in psychology and g-g-g-got my bachelor's degree. But for my grad school, I went to the counseling and family therapy program. Iiiit was a part of-part-of-part of ed department. I wa-wa-wanted to be a family therapist."	Part-word repetition Sound prolongation Phrase repetition; a part-word repetition
Clinician	"Is that what you do now? Counsel families and offer family therapy?"	
Client	"Yes. I am a family therapist with the K-k-k-kern county mental health department."	Part-word repetition

Record two more briefer speech samples on subsequent occasions. Count the number of words or syllables (as you prefer) and count the number of stutterings or dysfluencies (as you define them). Calculate the percent stuttering or dysfluency rate separately for the three samples.

Baserating Stuttering in Adults
The Need for Baserates in Oral Reading

Recording an Oral Reading Sample

In most adults, stuttering (dysfluency) frequency in conversational speech may be different than that in oral reading. Clients who successfully avoid stuttering by word substitutions may stutter less in conversational speech. The same clients will be unable to avoid reading aloud printed words, therefore, their stuttering rate may be higher. Higher stuttering rate in oral reading helps assess specific sounds and words on which the client consistently stutters. Therefore, it is useful to baserate stuttering in an oral reading sample.

Procedures for Baserating Stuttering in Oral Reading

The clinician may consider the following in establishing baserates of stuttering in oral reading:

- **Select appropriate reading materials.** The reading material should match the client's educational and ethnocultural background. The printed passages selected should neither be too difficult nor too easy. In addition, the material should be of interest to the client. The clinician may ask the client to suggest reading material. Perhaps the client will suggest an article in a newspaper, a favorite magazine, or a particular book. If the client regularly reads from a source (such as a specific magazine), the clinician may be sure that the material is appropriate for assessing stuttering in oral reading.

- **Record the oral reading sample in the second or third session.** During the first baserate session, the clinician may ask the client to bring a book, copy of his newspaper, or a magazine to the following session. The oral reading sample may then be recorded with client-selected reading material. In most cases, a 5-minute oral reading sample may be adequate.

- **Calculate the percent stuttering or dysfluency rate.** The clinician may count the number of words read and the number of dysfluencies to calculate the percent dysfluency or stuttering rate.

- **Compare the stuttering or dysfluency rates.** The clinician may compare the stuttering rate in oral reading versus that in conversational speech to identify potential differences and to understand particular sounds or words on which stuttering occurs consistently.

Baserating Stuttering in Adults

Baserate Recording Sheet

Personalize and print this page from the CD.

Name of the child:	DOB:
Name of the parents:	Phone:
Diagnosis: Stuttering	Session date(s):
Clinician:	Comments:

Types of Dysfluencies	Frequency	
	Conversational Speech	Oral Reading
Prolongations		
Sound or syllable prolongations		
Silent prolongations		
Broken words		
Pauses		
Silent pauses		
Repetitions		
Sound or syllable repetitions		
Word repetitions		
Phrase repetitions		
Interjections		
Schwa or *um* interjections		
Word interjections		
Phrase interjections		
Revisions		
Incomplete phrases		
Total number of dysfluencies		
Total number of words spoken		
Percent dysfluency/stuttering rate		

Clinician's comments:

Part 5

Treatment of Stuttering in Adults

Treatment of Stuttering in Adults

Treatment Options

There are various options to effectively treat stuttering in adults (Curlee, 1999a; Conture, 2001; Gregory, 2003; Guitar, 2006; Shapiro, 1999). The techniques that are described in this section also may be used with adolescents and young adults by making slight modifications to the content of conversation; the basic procedures and the contingencies would not change. The protocols described in this section are essentially the same as those offered to treat stuttering in school-age children. The protocols make suitable modifications in their administration to adults. In treating adolescents, young adults, and adults who stutter, the clinician may use one of the following techniques:

- **A Comprehensive Fluency Shaping Procedure.** This includes airflow management, and slower rate of speech achieved through syllable prolongation, and normal prosodic features. Most adults master these fluency skills with relative ease. This procedure may be especially effective with adults with high dysfluency rate and significant mismanagement of airflow associated with stuttered speech.

- **Prolonged Speech.** This procedure uses only one of the skill components of the comprehensive fluency shaping procedure. In this procedure, the clinician targets a slower rate of speech achieved through syllable prolongation as the single fluency-enhancing skill. Omitting airflow management simplifies treatment to a significant extent. If the client does not exhibit marked mismanagement of airflow during stuttering, the clinician can use this abbreviated fluency shaping with only slower speech as the treatment target. With this procedure, normal prosodic features should be targeted toward the end of treatment to induce normal-sounding fluency.

- **Pause-and-Talk (Time-Out).** Another highly effective procedure is pause-and-talk, also known as (nonexclusion) time-out. Because the time-out procedure is much misunderstood and mismanaged in educational settings, the term pause-and-talk is preferred. In this procedure, the clinician continues to socially reinforce the client's fluent speech by maintaining eye contact, smiling, nodding, expressing agreement, and letting the client engage in continuous conversation. However, when the client stutters, the clinician will immediately say "Stop!," avoid eye contact for about 5 seconds, and prevent the client from talking during this period of time-out from positive reinforcement. In essence, a stutter results in a brief pause in talking with no social reinforcement; therefore, the term pause-and-talk aptly describes the procedure.

- **Minimal Prolongation plus Pause-and-Talk.** A fourth option for treating stuttering in adults is a combination of a slight prolongation of syllables in the initial words of utterances, combined with pause-and-talk. This procedure, though still experimental, may be appropriate for clients with a high dysfluency rate. Those who stutter severely often are not the best candidates for pause-and-talk; the procedure results in excessive corrective feedback and very little positive reinforcement. In such cases, a very slight prolongation of the initial syllables in the first word of each utterance may reduce the dysfluency rate to such a low level, that pause-and-talk can then be effectively applied. Protocols are provided for this combination of two techniques.

Response Cost, a highly effective procedure with both preschool and school-age children, is not offered as an option to treat adults who stutter. This is because of clinical experience that suggests that it is difficult to find backup reinforcers for adults. The procedure requires that the clinician not only give tokens for fluency (and withdraw tokens for stuttering), but offer a powerful back-up reinforcer at the end of a session. While small gifts can help reinforce a child, such gifts are obviously inappropriate for adults. The reinforcing back-up event or object has to be of significant value; it is impractical for the clinician to provide them.

It is possible, however, to use response cost with older clients if the family members can be recruited to provide the back-up reinforcers to the client. In such cases, the clinician may:

*   write a behavioral contract the family members (e.g., the client's spouse) and the client signs
*   specify the role of the family member in enforcing the contract; generally, he or she will keep track of the points the client earns in treatment and offers the chosen reinforcer when a sufficient number of points have been earned
*   award not tokens, but points during treatment; a log will be kept of the points earned in each session and cumulatively across sessions
*   get the client's agreement to forgo the back-up reinforcer until a mutually-agreed upon number of points are earned in the treatment sessions
*   give the go ahead to the client and the family member to gain access to the back-up reinforcer when the required number of points are earned
*   arrange to have such back-up reinforcers as:
    *   a gift the family member would have bought anyway, but has now been made contingent on points earned in treatment sessions (e.g., books, CDs and DVDs, personal items)
    *   an activity the client typically enjoys and engages in (ski trips, visits to favorite restaurants, watching movies either at home or in theaters, sports activities, lunch or an evening with friends)

The response cost protocols given in previous sections may be used with suitable content-modification. While the basic technique will remain the same as that described in protocols for school-age children, the content of conversation between an adult client and the clinician will be different.

As noted in the section on school-age client, the response cost procedure does not target such fluency skills as airflow management or slower rate of speech. Consequently, the procedure does not induce unnatural-sounding speech. Therefore, it is unnecessary to spend time on restoring normal-sounding fluency. This is an efficient procedure to treat clients who stutter.

Treatment of Stuttering in Adults:
I. Comprehensive Fluency Shaping Procedure

Overview

Fluency shaping is a well-established treatment for adults who stutter (Cordes & Ingham, 1998; Curlee, 1999a; Conture, 2001; Gregory, 2003; Guitar, 2006; Shapiro, 1999). For several decades, fluency shaping has been used around the world as a standard treatment for adults who stutter. Although pause-and-talk (time-out) is a better alternative to fluency shaping, the latter technique has been popular with clinicians. Its origin is in Goldiamond's 1965 study on inducing stutter-free speech with delayed auditory feedback (DAF) through slower rate of speech effected by syllable prolongations. It soon became evident that delayed auditory feedback is not necessary to induce a slower and prolonged speech in people who stutter. Instructions and modeling are just as effective and are attractive because they do not cost anything to the client or the clinician.

Fluency shaping has several limitations. The most significant limitations include an unnatural-sounding speech and poor maintenance of fluency. Essentially, fluency shaping does not immediately result in normal fluency; it generates stutter-free speech. Clients who have learned to avoid stuttering by this method feel that they need to constantly monitor their speech rate, instead of what they want to say. They believe that their slow and monotonous speech is socially unacceptable. Consequently, they begin to speak at rates that are not conducive to maintaining their stutter-free speech; the result is a relapse of stuttering.

Because the procedure induces unnatural-sounding speech, normal prosodic features are also a treatment target when fluency shaping is used. By reinstating normal prosodic features, the unnaturalness of speech can be minimized and by periodic booster treatment, maintenance may be enhanced.

Fluency shaping includes a variety of procedures; it is not clear from the evidence whether all of the component procedures are essential to achieve a desirable outcome. A fluency shaping program may be **comprehensive** in that it includes all components generally advocated. A comprehensive fluency shaping program, described in this section, includes the following skills taught to adults who stutter:

- **Airflow Management:** A proper management of airflow to produce fluent speech includes two component skills: a slightly greater-than-normal inhalation of air and a prephonatory exhalation of air. The client then initiates phonation on a controlled, sustained exhalation. There is replicated evidence that a proper management of airflow will reliably reduce stuttering.

- **Slower Speech Rate with Syllable Prolongation:** Prolonging syllable duration is an effective strategy to reduce or even totally eliminate dysfluencies. There is considerable replicated evidence (some controlled and some uncontrolled) to support its effectiveness. When the vowel following an initial consonant (the syllable nucleus) is prolonged, dysfluencies are almost always eliminated. This prolongation is different from the typical prolongation (a form of dysfluency) of people who stutter. Typically, people who stutter prolong the initial consonant (e.g., *ssss*up); in prolonged speech treatment, they prolong the following vowel (e.g., s*ooo*p).

- **Normal Prosodic Features:** Comprehensive fluency shaping procedure, especially the syllable prolongation component of it that reduces the speech rate to unusual levels, induces an unnatural quality of speech. Speech will sound excessively slow and monotonous. Speech may also be too soft. Therefore, to reduce the social consequences of an unnatural-sounding speech, normal prosodic features—including normal speech rates, intonation, and loudness variations—are targeted as well. If the speech continues to sound unnatural, social acceptance will be extremely limited, and as a consequence, stuttering may relapse.

Clinicians sometime include **gentle onset of phonation** as another fluency skill. Gentle initiation of phonation when a slight exhalation is already in progress is thought to be essential for fluency. Although generally well accepted, gentle phonatory onset as a means of achieving fluent speech is supported only by scant experimental evidence. Clinical experience suggests that when the client is asked to manage the airflow and speak at a slower rate, abrupt phonatory onsets are diminished to a great extent. Therefore, the protocols do not expand upon this additional target.

The target fluency skills just listed are systematically taught in a sequential manner. The airflow management is taught first. Following this, the syllable prolongation (slower rate), and normal prosodic features are taught in that order.

To begin with, the clinician describes the fluency targets the client needs to learn and models the skills described (inhalation, slight exhalation, and slow speech). Making modifications as found necessary for a given client, the clinician:

- Establishes baserates of dysfluencies or stuttering as the clinician defines them. To obtain reliable baserates of dysfluencies in adults, the clinician tape-records an extended conversational speech. Topic cards, which suggest various topics of conversation (e.g., *favorite games and sports, vacations, current social and political issues, work-related experiences, hobbies, movies, TV shows*), may be useful with most older students and adults. An oral reading sample also may be obtained to assess the differential dysfluency rates in oral reading versus conversational speech. A 3- to 5-minute monologue on a topic of interest also may be recorded. If practical, the clinician may also obtain a home speech sample for analysis of dysfluencies or stuttering. After establishing baserates, the clinician initiates treatment; begins with airflow management.

- Describes, models, and asks the client to imitate slightly more-than-the-normal inhalation of air and a slight exhalation of just inhaled air. To begin with, the clinician teaches this as an isolated skill. The clinician discourages excessive exhalation as this would defeat the purpose of having a continuous supply of air for fluent speech production. A few successful trials are sufficient to move on to the next step.

- Describes and models a slower speech rate achieved through syllable prolongation. This, too, is taught as an isolated skill (without the airflow management). The clinician teaches the client to extend the duration of vowels following the initial consonants. The optimal duration of prolongation is client-specific; but it should result in stutter-free speech. For each client, the clinician should find a rate that is slow enough to eliminate dysfluencies. A few successful trials at the single word level should be sufficient to move on to the next step.

- Gives a quick overview of the three skills practiced in isolation. The clinician then describes and models integrated productions of all three skills: starting with an inhalation, quickly moving to an slight exhalation, and ending with syllable-prolonged word production. Integrated fluency skills may need to be practiced for a good portion of a treatment session.

- Moves on to the phrase level training when the client successfully produces a number of words integrated with fluency skills. In learning to produce the fluency skills in two-word phrases, the client adds a new word to the already practiced single word. For instance, an adult man who has been practicing fluency skills in saying his first name (e.g., *Jhaaan*") may be asked to say his first and the last name (e.g., "*Jhaaan Jeeekəəəb*"). It is not essential to move from single words to two-word phrases in all cases; the number of words in practice phrases will depend on the client. Some clients may succeed at three to four word phrases at the beginning of this stage.

- Manages the behavioral treatment contingencies promptly and strictly. It may be noted that fluency shaping does not specify a new treatment procedure; it specifies the target skills the client has to learn. A description of how those skills are taught and learned constitutes treatment. In this technical sense, treatment is still the same familiar behavioral procedures that include instructions, demonstrations, modeling, prompting, positive reinforcement for correct production of targeted skills resulting in fluency, and corrective feedback for errors in managing the skills and for dysfluencies.

- Targets normal prosodic features when the client sustains stutter-free speech (perhaps a 98% fluency, though it may sound unnatural) across a few sessions. The clinician models a slightly faster rate for the client to imitate. As the client learns to sustain stutter-free speech at the initial faster rate, the clinician models progressively faster rates and varied intonational patterns for the client to imitate. Eventually, the clinician may stabilize a slightly slower than the client's habitual speech rate that still sounds natural.

- Trains family members, friends, and client-selected colleagues to recognize various forms of dysfluencies and to prompt and reinforce slower rate to sustain natural-sounding fluency in home, office, and other nonclinical settings. If practical, spouses or other family members may be trained to hold informal treatment sessions at home. Such training may begin as soon as the client sustains stutter-free speech in the clinic. These steps are essential for maintenance of fluency.

- Conducts follow-up assessments and arranges for booster treatment when the results of a follow-up warrant additional treatment. The initial follow-up may be scheduled for 3 months following the dismissal. Additional follow-ups may be scheduled at 6 or 12 month intervals. In all follow-up sessions, the clinician takes an extended speech sample without treatment to calculate the percent stuttering or dysfluency rates.

The comprehensive fluency shaping protocols have been written for establishing stutter-free speech and for stabilizing natural-sounding fluency.

Treatment protocols are offered to:

1. Establish stutter-free speech in conversation
2. Establish stutter-free speech in narration
3. Stabilize natural-sounding fluency

Treatment of Stuttering in Adults:
I. Comprehensive Fluency Shaping Procedure

Establishing Stutter-Free Conversational Speech

Overview

- With adult clients, the **comprehensive fluency shaping procedure** may be initiated at the word and phrase level or the sentence level, depending on the individual client. The strategy is to initiate treatment at the highest level of response topography possible (e.g., shorter or longer sentences), not necessarily at the lowest level (e.g., single words). Because the treatment has to move through the different levels of response complexity, starting treatment at a higher level the client can perform is more efficient than routinely starting at the lowest level.

- Even when the lowest level of single words seems to be needed for a given client, the clinician should swiftly move on to phrases and sentences. Lingering for too long at the single word level is both inefficient and suggestive of potential misapplication of the treatment procedure. Most older students, adolescents, and adults who stutter may manage the skill at the short sentence level at the very beginning. A low stuttering frequency and severity may be another factor that suggests the possibility of starting treatment at the sentence level.

- The clinician may use various topic cards the client brings to the clinic to evoke sustained monologues or conversational speech. The clinician may prompt, instruct, or otherwise encourage the client to produce shorter and longer sentences.

- Frequent modeling of the target skill or skills under training is essential in treating most clients, including otherwise verbally competent adults. Clinicians may also reduce their own speech rates while teaching the fluency skills. Clinicians who talk fast may find it hard to control the speech rates in clients they work with.

- If dysfluencies persist, it is typically because the client has missed one or more of the target fluency skills. Missed prephonatory exhalation (resulting in impounded air in the lungs) and insufficient duration of syllable prolongation are the two most frequent reasons why dysfluencies persist under this form of treatment.

- With most adolescents and adults, verbal reinforcement is effective. An informative feedback at the end of the session that summarizes the client's progress in comparison with progress in previous sessions may be additionally useful. Verbal praise may take several forms:
  - Great job! You breathed in and breathed out correctly!
  - Wonderful! You stretched your sounds well!
  - Very good! I like the way you are talking very slowly!
  - Fantastic! You are doing everything right!
  - I like your speech with no stuttering in it!
  - Good job! Your speech is completely stutter-free!

- Positive reinforcement should be prompt, natural, and should follow all correct production of fluency skills in the beginning stage of treatment. For instance, the clinician should promptly praise the client for inhalation, slight prephonatory exhalation, and sufficient prolongation of syllables. Subsequently, reinforcement may be more specifically directed to fluent productions that include all the target skills. The initial continuous reinforcement may be changed to one of intermittent schedule during natural conversational exchanges.

- Verbal corrective feedback should be offered immediately when the client misses any of the target fluency skills. Regardless of whether a target fluency skill was missed, the clinician should promptly give corrective feedback for all dysfluent productions. The feedback should be prompt, clear, and objective in tone. The client should stop when an error is made or a dysfluency is produced; the client should correct the error and then continue. The clinician may use several forms of corrective feedback; each should point out what went wrong:
  - ➤ Stop, you didn't breathe-in before starting to talk!
  - ➤ Stop, you didn't breathe-out a little before you started to say something!
  - ➤ Stop, that was too fast! Stretch your speech more!
  - ➤ No, you should slow down some more!

- The same stimulus materials used in baserating dysfluencies in sentences may be appropriate for treatment sessions. Topics of interest to the client may more readily evoke speech from an adult. Therefore, conversations and discussion of topics should be client-selected.

- To evaluate the client's progress in treatment, the clinician may tape-record each session and later calculate the percent dysfluency or stuttering rate.

- If a correctly implemented comprehensive fluency shaping procedure does not produce satisfactory results, the clinician may consider alternative procedures (e.g., pause-and-talk). Although there will be individual differences, speech should be mostly stutter-free in a matter of few sessions. If not, the progress may be judged unsatisfactory, leading to a change in the treatment procedure.

Treatment of Stuttering in Adults:
I. Comprehensive Fluency Shaping Procedure

Treatment Protocol for Conversational Speech

Scripts for Establishing Stutter-Free Conversation		Note
Clinician	"There are a few options for you to speak more fluently than you do now. In the treatment procedure I have selected, you master certain skills that help you speak more fluently. In fact, the skills that you will practice in these sessions will be incompatible with stuttering. This means that you can't stutter and perform these skills simultaneously. The skills are opposites of what happens when someone stutters. For instance, you may fail to breathe in sufficient amount of air before talking. You may fail to breathe out a small amount of air before starting to speak. You may try to speak when you have exhausted your air supply. All of these problems may increase your stuttering. I have noticed that you sometime breathe in and hold the air in your chest. Sometimes you try to continue to talk when you have run out of air. Do you agree that these add to your fluency problems?"	The clinician introduces the concepts of stuttering, dysfluency, and fluency
Client	"Yes. I breathe in, but I don't start talking because the air is stuck there. It is not flowing out. Toward the end of a sentence, I often run out of steam and I find myself stuttering."	Client shows awareness of his airflow problem
Clinician	"If you manage your airflow correctly, many of your dysfluencies will be reduced. You should breathe in, let a small amount of air through your mouth, and then start speaking. Another sure way of reducing your stuttering is to slow down your speech. Have you sometimes used this technique of slowing down to speak more fluently?"	Introduces the concept of slow speech
Client	"Yes. I sometimes deliberately speak slowly to avoid stuttering."	
Clinician	"Has it worked?"	
Client	"Yes, it has. But the problem is to remember to slow down."	

Establishing Stutter-Free Conversation, continued

Scripts for Establishing Stutter-Free Conversation		Note
Clinician	"That's right. Even a simple task like that needs to be systematically practiced. In these sessions, we will be doing that. We will also practice the correct way of managing breathing—we call it airflow—to speak fluently."	Emphasizes the need for systematic practice
Client	"Sounds good."	
Clinician	"The procedure is called fluency shaping. In this technique, you learn to breathe in, let a small amount of air through your mouth, and start talking very slowly. You can talk slowly by simply pausing between words. But we don't want that. In fact, I don't want you to pause between words at all. Instead, I want you to blend the words smoothly and stretch the syllables. It is a method of prolonging the syllables, which means mostly vowels." [demonstrates prolonged speech by saying "*youumaaytaalkliiikethiis*"]	Describes airflow Describes syllable prolongation
Client	"But I already prolong some of my sounds. What is the difference?"	
Clinician	"Well, typically you prolong an initial consonant. Like you may say *ssssoup*. But in this method, I want you to prolong the second vowel. You say *suuup*. To give you another example, you may say *lllllike* but I want you to say *laaaike*. Do you notice the difference?"	Demonstrates syllable prolongation
Client	"Yes I do."	
Clinician	"Right. The technique essentially is to breathe in, breathe out only a small bit of air, and then start talking by stretching the syllables."	Summarizes airflow management skills and prolonged speech
Client	"I think I know what you mean."	Shows understanding of the target skills
Clinician	"We will first practice the breathing part. Breathe in like this, and breathe out a tiny bit of air like this." [*demonstrates the airflow*]	Teaching begins with airflow management
Client	[*Performs the action correctly*]	
Clinician	"Good! Remember to breathe out only a small amount of air, like you did perfectly! Okay, one more time. Breathe in and breathe out a little."	Verbal praise

Establishing Stutter-Free Conversation, continued

Scripts for Establishing Stutter-Free Conversation		Note
Client	[*Takes a deep breath and holds the air*]	Mismanagement of airflow
Clinician	"That is one the problems that can occur. You forgot to breatheout a little bit. You shouldn't hold the air like that. If you do, starting the speech will be difficult. Please try again. Breathe in and breathe out a little. Like this." [*demonstrates the airflow*]	Prompt corrective feedback
Client	[*Performs the action correctly*]	Correct airflow management
Clinician	"Very good!" "Now that you know how to breathe in and breathe out a little bit of air before talking, we are ready to move on. You now have to add speech to your breathing. It should be smooth and fluent. As you begin to breathe out, you should start talking. It should be sloooow and streeeeetched out like that. [*stretches out the two words*] Stretched words should blend into each other. Your speech should sound like a string of syllables, not individual word productions." "I will ask you a series of questions you answer with single words. This way, you practice airflow and slow speech together in simple word productions. Please tell me your first name; remember airflow and stretched speech."	Verbal praise **If judged essential, the clinician may provide additional practice trials on airflow management. Some clients do need more trials**
Client	[*no airflow*] "Jhaaa . . ."	Mismanaged airflow
Clinician	"Stop! You forgot the airflow. First breathe in, breathe out a little, and then say Jhaaaaan. Like this." [*models airflow and slow speech on the client's name*]	Corrective feedback for mismanaged airflow. Stops the client from speaking; models the target skills
Client	[*correct airflow*] "Jhaaaan."	Correct response
Clinician	"Excellent! You managed both the airflow and the stretched speech. Now tell me your last name. Say, Jhaaaanson." [*demonstrates airflow management and slow rate*]	Verbal praise and initiation of the next trial
Client	[*correct airflow*] "Joh . . ."	Failure to stretch
Clinician	"Stop! Airflow was fine, but you didn't stretch the syllables. Try it again. Jhaaaanson." [*demonstrates airflow management and slow rate*]	Corrective feedback and modeling
Client	[*correct airflow*] "Jhaaaanson."	Prolonged and stutter-free speech

Establishing Stutter-Free Conversation, continued

Scripts for Establishing Stutter-Free Conversation		Note
Clinician	"Excellent! You did everything right! Tell me your wife's first name. Airflow plus syllable stretching."	Verbal praise and the initiation of the next trial
Client	[*no airflow*] "Maaa . . ."	Mismanagement of airflow
Clinician	"No! You forgot the airflow. Try it again."	Corrective feedback
Client	[*correct airflow*] "Maaaara."	Prolonged and stutter-free speech
Clinician	"Great! Now tell me your Dad's first name."	Verbal praise; next trial
Client	[*correct airflow*] "Taaaam."	Prolonged and stutter-free speech
Clinician	"Good! Correct airflow and syllable stretching. Now tell me your Mom's first name."	Verbal praise; next trial
Client	[*correct airflow*] "Loooora."	Prolonged and stutter-free speech
Clinician	"Wonderful! You are doing really well! How many brothers do you have? Just say one word—a number."	Verbal praise; the next question
Client	[*correct airflow*] "Two."	No stretching, though fluent
Clinician	"Not correct! You forgot to slow down. Try it again."	Corrective feedback
Client	[*correct airflow*] "Twooo."	Prolonged and stutter-free speech
Clinician	"I like that! You did it correctly! What is your first brother's name?"	Verbal praise
Client	[*correct airflow*] "Mmmm . . ."	Sound prolongation
Clinician	"Stop! You stuttered. You have to quickly open your mouth and prolong the next sound. Try it again."	Corrective feedback; instruction
Client	[*correct airflow*] "Maaaany."	Prolonged and stutter-free speech
Clinician	"Very good! See, when you quickly move to a prolonged vowel, you don't stutter. What's your second brother's name?"	Verbal praise; points out the reason for success
Client	[*no airflow*] "Erick."	No airflow management, no slow speech
Clinician	"Oops! Please say that again with airflow and stretching."	Corrective feedback
Client	[*correct airflow*] "Eeeeerik."	Prolonged and stutter-free speech

Establishing Stutter-Free Conversation, continued

Scripts for Establishing Stutter-Free Conversation		Note
Clinician	"Excellent! Do you have sisters?"	Verbal praise
Client	[*correct airflow*] "Yeeees. Juuust oooone."	Stutter-free
Clinician	"Excellent! You said it right and you didn't stutter! What is your sister's name?"	Verbal praise; next question
Client	[*correct airflow*] "Maaaanica."	Prolonged and stutter-free speech
Clinician	"Very good! Everything correct! How old is Monica?"	Verbal praise; next question
Client	[*no airflow*] "T-t-t . . ."	Sound prolongation; missing fluency skills
Clinician	"Stop! You forgot breathing and stretching. When you forget, you stutter, you see! Try that again."	Corrective feedback
Client	[*correct airflow*] "Tweeeenty niiiine."	Prolonged and stutter-free speech
Clinician	"Excellent! You have been doing well. Now, maybe you can say two or three words at a time. Tell me your full name. Breathe-and-stretch"	Verbal praise **Treatment shifted to the phrase level; additional trials on single words may be needed**
Client	[*correct airflow*] "Jhaaaan Jhaaaanson."	Prolonged and stutter-free speech
Clinician	"That was great! Correct airflow and syllable stretching. Now, tell me your Mom's full name."	Verbal praise
Client	"Loo . . ."	Missed airflow management
Clinician	"Stop! You forgot the airflow. Try again."	Corrective feedback
Client	[*correct airflow*] "Looora Jhaaaanson."	Prolonged and stutter-free speech
Clinician	"Excellent! Tell me your Dad's full name."	Verbal praise
Client	[*correct airflow*] "Taaaam Jhaaaanson."	Correct response
Clinician	"Perfect! Tell me your first brother's full name."	Verbal praise
Client	[*correct airflow*] "Maaaany Jhaaaanson."	Correct response
Clinician	"Good airflow and stretching! Now, tell me your second brother's full name."	Verbal praise
Client	[*correct airflow*] "Eeeerick Jhaaaanson."	Prolonged and stutter-free speech
Clinician	"Very good! You are breathing and stretching correctly! Now, tell me your sister's full name."	Verbal praise

Establishing Stutter-Free Conversation, continued

Scripts for Establishing Stutter-Free Conversation		Note
Client	[*no airflow*] "Mmm . . ."	Mismanages airflow; sound prolongation
Clinician	"Stop! Did you forget something?"	Corrective feedback. Prompts self-evaluation
Client	"Airflow!"	Correct self-evaluation
Clinician	"You know what went wrong! Now try that again. Your sister's full name."	Reinforces self-evaluation
Client	[*correct airflow*] "Maaaanica Nuuuneeeez."	Prolonged and stutter-free speech
Clinician	"Very good job! Maybe you can now try to say more words each time. Perhaps you can try some simple sentences. Where do you live?"	Verbal praise **Treatment shifts to short sentences of longer phrases.** **Additional trials on two-word phrases may be needed**
Client	[*correct airflow and syllable stretching*] "I live in Modesto."	Correct response; **from here on, for ease of reading, syllable stretching is not shown orthographically**
Clinician	"Excellent! You said four words, all with good airflow and syllable stretching. Do you rent or own your place?"	Verbal praise
Client	[*correct airflow and stretching*] "I own my house."	Prolonged and stutter-free speech
Clinician	"Excellent! You are saying more words correctly! What do you do for living?"	Verbal praise; next trial
Client	[*correct airflow*] "I own a lllll . . ."	Sound prolongation due to lack of syllable stretching
Clinician	"No, you didn't stretch it enough. That's why you stuttered. Try that again; prolong the next sound in that word you were trying to say."	Corrective feedback
Client	[*correct airflow and stretching*] "I own a landscape nursery."	Prolonged and stutter-free speech
Clinician	"Good airflow and stretching! That was a long sentence! Well, you must have a green thumb! Do you like working with plants and trees?"	Verbal praise
Client	[*correct airflow and stretching*] "I love it."	Prolonged and stutter-free speech

Establishing Stutter-Free Conversation, continued

Scripts for Establishing Stutter-Free Conversation		Note
Clinician	"Very good! Does your nursery specialize in certain kinds of landscaping? You can just say, *yes, it does*."	Verbal praise
Client	[*correct airflow and stretching*] "Yes it does."	Prolonged and stutter-free speech
Clinician	"Excellent! Good airflow and syllable stretching. No stuttering! Okay, what kind of specialty plants can I buy at your nursery?"	Verbal praise
Client	[*correct airflow*] "Water saving p-p-p-p . . ."	Part-word repletion; failure to stretch
Clinician	"Oops! That was a stutter. You didn't quickly move to the next, stretched sound. Say the *p* sound softly, and quickly move to the next sound, and stretch it well. Try that again."	Corrective feedback
Client	[*correct airflow and stretching*] "Water saving plants."	Prolonged and stutter-free speech
Clinician	"Excellent! That soft and quick *p* and prolonged *læ* eliminated stuttering, didn't it?"	Verbal praise and an explanation
Client	[*correct airflow and stretching*] "Yes!"	Prolonged and stutter-free speech
Clinician	"Good. Do you also sell non-allergenic plants?"	Verbal praise
Client	[*correct airflow and stretching*] "Yes, I do."	Stutter-free
Clinician	"Very good. You are doing well. Maybe you can try saying more words at a time. When you try it, stop after a few words and do the airflow before starting again. If a sentence is too long, you can break it. Every time you restart, do the breathing part. Do you have some people working for you?"	Verbal praise; introducing longer utterances
Client	[*correct airflow and stretching*] "Yes, I have four people working for me. [*correct airflow and stretching*] Two are full-time and two are part-time."	Prolonged and stutter-free speech; does the airflow at the beginning of a new sentence
Clinician	"That's the way to handle it! You stopped and did the airflow before starting again. How many acres of land do you have?"	Verbal praise
Client	[*correct airflow and stretching*] "My nursery has some five acres."	Prolonged and stutter-free
Clinician	"Excellent! Good airflow and syllable stretching! Is your nursery open on Sundays?"	Verbal praise

Establishing Stutter-Free Conversation, continued

Scripts for Establishing Stutter-Free Conversation		Note
Client	[*correct airflow and stretching*] "Yes, it is open. [*no airflow or stretching*] S-s-s- . . ."	Incorrect responses; sound repetition
Clinician	"Oops! You were trying to say *Sunday*? Make the *s* sound soft and quickly move to the next sound. Stretch it. [*modeling*] Suuunday."	Corrective feedback; models airflow and syllable prolongation
Client	[*correct airflow and stretching*] "Suuuunday is our busiest day."	Prolonged and stutter-free speech
Clinician	"Good stretching! What is the busiest season of the year? Make it a long sentence."	Verbal praise
Client	[*correct airflow and stretching*] "Our busiest season of the year is spring."	Prolonged and stutter-free speech
Clinician	"Excellent! You are getting a good hang of it! "I am switching topics now. You said you have two brothers. Are they older or younger than you? And, what do they do? Don't forget the airflow in between sentences."	Verbal praise; new topic initiation No modeling; evoking multiple questions
Client	[*correct airflow and stretching*] "Both of my brothers are older than me. [*correct airflow and stretching*] Manny is a civil engineer and works for the county [*correct airflow and stretching*] Erick owns a bookstore in downtown Visalia."	Correct fluency skill management; airflow in between sentences; stutter-free speech
Clinician	"That's great! What kind of work does your engineer brother do for the county?"	Verbal praise
Client	[*correct airflow and stretching*] "He is a supervisor for the county transportation department. [*correct airflow*] He is in charge of road maintenance throughout the county."	Prolonged and stutter-free speech
Clinician	"Good management of airflow and syllable prolongation! What kind of books does Erick carry in his bookstore?"	Verbal praise
Client	[*correct airflow and stretching*] "All kinds, but it is a good place for some old books. [*correct airflow*] He has a back room where he keeps out-of-print books. [*correct airflow*] I love to browse through the books in that room."	Correct fluency skill management; airflow in between sentences; stutter-free speech

Establishing Stutter-Free Conversation, continued

Scripts for Establishing Stutter-Free Conversation		Note
Clinician	"I like the way you are using your airflow and syllable prolongation! Now let us talk a little bit about your own family. Do you have any children?"	Verbal praise
Client	[*correct airflow and stretching*] "Yes, I do. [*correct airflow*] I have two children. A boy and a girl."	Correct fluency skill management; airflow in between sentences; stutter-free speech
Clinician	"Tell me about your children. How old are they? In what grades are they studying? What school do they go to?"	Asks a series of questions to induce more continuous speech
Client	[*correct airflow and stretching*] "My daughter is the older of the two. [*no airflow*] Mmm . . ."	Lack of airflow management; sound prolongation
Clinician	"Stop! You forgot something."	Corrective feedback; prompts self-evaluation
Client	[*correct airflow and stretching*] "Yes, I forgot airflow. I was about to say that my daughter is 10 and my son is 8. [*correct airflow*] My daughter is in the fourth grade and my son is in the second. [*correct airflow*] Both go to the same school. [*correct airflow*] They go to the Gettysburg elementary school."	Correct management of fluency skills; stutter-free speech
Clinician	"How do they get to their school every morning?"	
Client	[*correct airflow and stretching*] "The school bus stops just around the corner from my house. [*correct airflow*] Most of the days they take the bus. [*correct airflow*] On some days when they get up late or something I give them a ride to school."	Maintains stutter-free speech in longer sentences
Clinician	"What does your wife do?"	
Client	[*correct airflow and stretching*] "My wife is a tax accountant."	Stutter-free speech
Clinician	"Does she work for a consulting firm?"	
Client	[*correct airflow*] "No, she has her own practice. She has an associate who works for her. [*correct airflow*] But it is pretty much a solo practice."	Stutter-free speech

The clinician continues to teach the fluency skills in conversational speech to establish stutter-free speech. The number of sessions in this phase will be client-specific. When the client has sustained fluency skills as well as stutter-free speech in conversational speech across three or more sessions, the clinician shifts training to the next phase, which involves narrative speech.

Treatment of Stuttering in Adults:
I. Comprehensive Fluency Shaping Procedure

Establishing Stutter-Free Narrative Speech

Overview

To establish narrative speech in adults within the fluency shaping treatment program, the clinician should have the client talk continuously on a single topic. Instead of the conversational format used in the previous protocols, the clinician would ask the client to talk on a topic for extended duration. The clinician would only occasionally ask questions or offer comments to stimulate continuous speech from the client.

General Treatment Strategy

The topic selected for narrative speech should be client-selected. Perhaps the client will talk about varied topics over several sessions. Because the clients choose their topics and talk about them, it is not productive to write protocols for multiple topics. A single topic is illustrated in the protocol. Using this protocol, the clinician can have the client talk on several topics to establish stutter-free speech in narrative or continuous speech.

The clinician should continue to verbally reinforce fluency skills and the resulting stutter-free speech in all sessions. In this stage of treatment, the airflow management will not be as explicit or obvious as in the beginning stage. The client will learn to manage the airflow in a subtle manner. The degree of syllable prolongation, although not at the clinician's request, may also become somewhat shortened. Continuous speech that includes longer sentences and utterances tend to be prolonged less. This is acceptable as long as the client still maintains a slower rate compared to his or her baseline speech rate and the speech is stutter-free.

When the client begins to manage the airflow in a subtle manner and the speech rate increases somewhat during continuous speech, the speech will sound less unnatural. The clinician may reinforce this outcome as in the next stage of treatment, more natural-sounding speech will be the specific target.

Treatment of Stuttering in Adults:
I. Comprehensive Fluency Shaping Procedure

Treatment Protocol for Narrative Speech

Scripts for Establishing Stutter-Free Narration		Note
Clinician	"I think you have been managing the fluency skills in conversation quite well. Your speech is mostly stutter-free. You efficiently do the airflow and prolong syllables to produce continuous, stutter-free conversational speech. Now I think it's time to move on to even more continuous speech in which you practice your fluency skills. In each treatment session from now on, I would like you to talk on specific topics of your interest for extended periods of time. I will be talking less and you will be talking most of the time on topics of your choice. When you come for therapy next time, you may want to bring a list of topics on which you would like to talk. If you prefer, you can bring topic cards. Each index card will contain a topic and you talk on one topic at a time. On each card, you also may make notes to yourself, if you wish, so you can tell me more about each of them. "For today, is there a topic you want to talk about?"	Explains the next stage of treatment; suggests strategies for topic selection
Client	[*correct airflow and stretching*] "Yes. I can talk about our recent trip to Grand Canyon."	Suggests a topic
Clinician	"That's great! Tell me all about your trip in detail. Starting with who all went with you and how you got there and everything else."	
Client	[*correct airflow and stretching throughout the narration*] "Well, I made the trip with my wife and my two children. My wife Mara has been dreaming of this trip for many years. We just never had time to do it until last summer. I have been wanting to go to Las Vegas. We thought we would combine the two trips. So we flew into Las Vegas and spent a couple of days there. For my kids, it was their first airplane trip. They were thrilled. They thought they arrived in Las Vegas too soon! Yes, we had a great time in Las Vegas. It has changed a lot since the 90s when I had gone there *(continued)*	Although not indicated in the script, the client initiates airflow at the beginning of each sentence; maintains both syllable stretching and stutter-free speech Periodically, hears clinician's brief questions (e.g., "Did you have a good time?" "How was your stay in that place?" "Did you hike?") Periodically, hears clinician say, "You are doing well! or "You are speaking correctly!" and so forth

Establishing Stutter-Free Narration, continued

Scripts for Establishing Stutter-Free Narration		Note
Client *(continues)*	once. Now the town has a lot for kids, too. We stayed in MGM grand. Yeah, we enjoyed our stay in that huge hotel. They gave us a nice large room. After two days of fun in Las Vegas, we rented a car at the airport and drove to the Grand Canyon. It took only a few hours. Yes, my kids are good auto travelers. They don't bug me or my wife too much with the typical *are we there yet* sort of questions. They usually read a book or listen to their CD players. If we keep their stomachs filled, they are usually happy travelers! [*forgets airflow and syllable stretching*] Well . . ."	Continues with narrative speech. Manages fluency skills well and maintains stutter-free speech Mismanagement of fluency skills
Clinician	"Stop!"	Corrective feedback
Client	[*correct airflow and stretching*] "Oh yes! I got carried away with my story! Well, we arrived at the Grand Canyon late in the afternoon. We checked into a motel. No, we didn't stay right inside the park. The rooms inside the park were either not available or too expensive. We stayed right outside. No more than ten minutes from the center of the park. It was a nice place. It had a big swimming pool—very important for my kids. They got into it right away. Mara and I had something to drink and watched the kids in the pool as we relaxed and they swam and played in the water. Before the sunset, we all went to the park. It was a bright sunny day. And the views of the canyon! Out of this world! The ever-changing colors and shapes were fascinating. Even my normally talkative kids were quiet. They simply stared down the canyon in awe. We took long walks along the rim of the canyon until it was almost dark. We then went into the Grand Canyon Lodge and sat in the magnificent lobby for a while. Checked out the usual gift store and the book store. When our kids began to demand dinner, we went back to our hotel. Yes, they had a nice restaurant. We ate our dinner there. We were all tired and I think we all went to bed early, hoping to get up early and see the canyon again in the morning light."	Continues with narration Maintains the fluency skills and stutter-free speech Receives periodic verbal praise from the clinician
Clinician	"Thank you! That was a good story! I noticed that your syllable stretching is reduced somewhat, but that is fine. We may continue like this a few more times before we start working on speech that sounds more natural."	Offers periodic verbal praise throughout the narration Draws attention to a slight reduction in the extent of syllable prolongation

Establishing Stutter-Free Narration, continued

Scripts for Establishing Stutter-Free Narration		Note
Clinician	"You did well last time in talking stutter-free on selected topics. We will continue to do the same. Okay, do you have some topics for today?"	Feedback on previous performance
Client	[*correct airflow and stretching*] "Yes I do. I have several I can talk about."	Stutter-free speech
Clinician	"That's very good! Tell me all about the first topic you have selected for today. Make sure you maintain your fluency skills."	Prompts narrative speech on the first topic
Client	[*talks about the chosen topic for extended duration of time while maintaining fluency skills. Receives prompts, occasional questions, comments, statements of agreement, and so forth that facilitate continuous talking.*]	Following the clinician's feedback, stops talking when skills are mismanaged or when stuttering occurs
Clinician	[*monitors the client's fluency skills. Offers prompts, occasional questions, comments, statements of agreement, and so forth to keep the client talking continuously. Initiates speech on new topics as found necessary.*]	Gives corrective feedback when the fluency skills are mismanaged or when the client stutters

Treatment for narrative speech continues in this manner. Some clients need to talk on more topics and over several sessions than other clients. The clinician may move treatment to the next stage when the client sustains 98% stutter-free speech in at least three consecutive sessions. In the next stage of treatment, the clinician will explicitly target natural-sounding fluent speech.

Following protocols help establish normal prosodic features essential for natural-sounding speech.

Treatment of Stuttering in Adults:
I. Comprehensive Fluency Shaping Procedure

Stabilizing Natural-Sounding Fluency

Overview

- The immediate effects of fluency shaping is speech that is free of stuttering but unnatural-sounding. The stutter-free speech is too slow, sometimes too soft, and always too monotonous to be socially acceptable.

- Adults who are treated with fluency shaping believe that their stutter-free and unnatural-sounding speech is unacceptable to listeners. But it is even more unacceptable to themselves—those who stuttered but no longer do because of fluency shaping. The slow, deliberate speech takes personal tolls on the speaker. It reduces spontaneity in conversation. The need to constantly monitor a slow speech rate and to explicitly manage an otherwise automatic airflow is tiring and aversive to the speaker. While a slightly faster speech rate comes naturally to most speakers, a noticeably slower rate comes only from an all-absorbing attention to it. Treated stuttering clients sometimes say that it is easier to stutter than to maintain stutter-free speech. Many even believe, perhaps with good justification, that their listeners may be more tolerant of stuttering than their stutter-free slow speech. They believe that their slow and monotonous speech may be even more attention-grabbing than their stuttering.

- Because of those problems associated with fluency shaping, it is essential to shape normal-sounding speech before the client is dismissed. Normal-sounding speech is most effectively reinstated with a rate that approximates the client's typical, pretreatment rate. Most listeners do not quantitatively measure a speaker's rate of speech. They make global judgments as to whether the speech sounds natural or not. The clinician and the significant others in the client's life also can make judgments about speech naturalness. This judgment may include not only the rare but also the intonational patterns (pitch and loudness variations). Clinicians may invite comments about the client's speech naturalness from friends, colleagues, and family members. Generally, family members are the best judges of speech naturalness. Adult clients themselves can judge whether their fluency sounds natural or not.

- Natural-sounding fluency is induced essentially in a shaping program. In this procedure, the client may be asked to:
  ➢ gradually increase the rate of speech
  ➢ increase and vary the loudness of voice
  ➢ vary the vocal pitch throughout an utterance

- In instating natural-sounding speech, the clinician will:
  ➢ frequently model faster rate and improved intonation
  ➢ systematically reinforce any movement toward more natural-sounding speech
  ➢ give prompt corrective feedback when the client exhibits slower and monotonous speech

The protocols to follow are written to achieve these goals of natural-sounding speech.

Treatment of Stuttering in Adults:
I. Comprehensive Fluency Shaping Procedure

Treatment Protocol for Natural-Sounding Fluency

Scripts for Stabilizing Natural-Sounding Speech		Note
Clinician	"You have been doing really well in managing your fluency skills. Your management of airflow is more subtle. Your speech is also a little bit faster, although it is still slower than we want it to be. You have hardly stuttered in the last few sessions. Now that your fluency skills and stutter-free speech are well established, we need to start working on making your speech more natural sounding. The airflow management and syllable prolongation makes your speech monotonous. I know that this is a big concern to you. But by gradually talking a bit faster each time, you can make your speech sound more natural. It is possible that you should always talk a bit slower than before, but not too much slower. When you start talking a bit faster, you will notice that the ups and downs in your voice—we call it intonation—also will improve. A comfortably fast rate that does not bring on stuttering and good intonation will make your speech sound natural. Sometimes, when you talk very slowly, speech is too soft. We want to take care of this problem, too. Speech should be sufficiently loud. That's what we need to work on now. Do you agree?"	Explains the need for the next stage of treatment Describes the problems associated with slow speech Sets the new treatment targets
Client	"Yes, I do! I have been wanting to do that because I don't stutter that much any more."	
Clinician	"Very good. That's what we will practice now. No stuttering, but faster, more natural speech with good intonation and acceptable loudness of voice. [*begins to speak at a slightly faster rate than the client's clinical rate*] Now let us start with a slightly faster speech. You can talk, maybe more like this, and try what happens. Your goal is not to stutter when you speed up. Therefore, you have to increase the speed of your speech gradually. If you suddenly go too fast, you may lose control of your fluency skills. It's like driving too fast and losing control of the car."	Models a slightly faster rate for the client to imitate
Client	[*speaks at a slightly faster rate*] "Yeah, I get it. That's what I have been doing all my life, I guess."	

Stabilizing Natural-Sounding Speech, continued

Scripts for Stabilizing Natural-Sounding Speech		Note
Clinician	[*still speaking at only a slightly higher rate than the client's clinical rate*] "To practice more natural speech, we can have a conversation about anything. Now, tell me what did you do this past weekend. Talk slightly faster like this, but without stuttering."	Initiates treatment
Client	[*speaks at a slightly faster rate*] "Last Saturday and Sunday I spent time in a ski resort, reading books, magazines, newspapers, and eating good food! And sleeping a lot."	Increased speech rate and improved intonation
Clinician	[*modeling the target rate*] "You spoke slightly faster as I wanted! Very good. You mean to say you didn't ski? Did your wife and kids go with you?"	Verbal praise
Client	[*speaks at a slightly faster rate*] "No, I didn't ski I don't like skiing at all. Actually, I went with my wife and my two kids. You could say I was their chauffeur. My wife loves skiing. My kids, too, are learning to ski. While they work hard on the snowy slopes, I relax in the cozy room or the lovely wood-paneled lounge with a fireplace."	Increased speech rate and improved intonation
Clinician	[*modeling the target rate*] "Very good! You are talking a little bit faster, but you are not stuttering! Did you notice that your intonation, too, is improving?"	Verbal praise; maintains conversation
Client	[*speaks at a slightly faster rate*] "Yes, I did. It's nice!"	Maintains increased speech rate
Clinician	[*modeling the target rate*] "Good! Do you watch your wife and kids ski?"	Evoking speech
Client	[*speaks at a slightly faster rate*] "Sometimes I do. I spend as much time as I can outdoors, but it is not a whole lot of time. I just don't like to be out in winter. Mara understands that being out in that cold and muddling through snow is not fun for me. [*speeds up excessively*] Taking pity on me . . . "	Maintains the target speech rate and improved patterns of intonation
Clinician	"Stop! That is a bit too fast. Maintain the rate at which you have been talking!"	Corrective feedback
Client	[*speaks with the target rate*] "Taking pity on me, my wife and children discourage me from accompanying them to the ski area. I think they have more fun there without seeing my puppy-sad face!"	Returns to an appropriate rate
Clinician	"Which suits you anyway! I like the rate at which you are talking now. It's slightly faster, has more intonation, but it is not too fast to bring on the stuttering. "Did you like the ski lodge you stayed there?"	Verbal praise

Stabilizing Natural-Sounding Speech, continued

Scripts for Stabilizing Natural-Sounding Speech		Note
Client	[*speaks with the target rate*] "Very much. It's on a lake. Beautiful surroundings. Snow everywhere, of course, but I like watching the snow-filled hills sloping all the way down to this big lake with sparkling blue water. We manage to get a room with a view. [*speeds up excessively*] Mmmm . . ."	Excessively fast speech rate and a sound prolongation
Clinician	"Stop! Now you know what happens when you go too fast!"	Corrective feedback
Client	[*speaks with the target rate*] "Oh boy! What was I going to say? Yes, my wife plans it way ahead of time. She made reservations for the next year when we checked-out last Sunday. That way, a nice room is guaranteed."	
Clinician	[*Continues conversation. Asks questions, prompts details, periodically reinforces the increased speech rate, and stops when the client's rate increases too fast or when the client stutters.*] "Okay, you have been doing really well at that rate of speech. I think it is now time to try a bit faster rate of speech. [*modeling the new and faster target rate*] Maybe you can talk more like this now. "Do they have a good restaurant in that ski resort? Maybe you can tell me about the kinds of food they have and your favorite food there."	Provides verbal praise and corrective feedback as needed Shifts training to a faster speech rate with greater intonation Continues conversation
Client	[*speaks with the new and faster rate*] "They actually have two restaurants there. The one downstairs is a casual place for lunch. You can order nice salads, gourmet sandwiches, a variety of soups, pizza, and some Mexican fare. The other is a more formal and upscale restaurant on the second floor with fantastic views of the lake and the hills. It's open for breakfast and dinner only. They have a huge breakfast buffet in the morning. They have a variety of items on their dinner menu, and all are exceptionally good. Many are unique preparations, I would think. I like their steak as well their various seafood items. Their salad is out of this world and a meal by itself."	Maintains the new target speech rate and improved intonation
Clinician	"Excellent! See how your speech is sounding more and more normal as you increase your speed and bring back your intonation!"	Verbal praise continues to shape natural-sounding speech in this manner

The number of sessions in which the clinician stabilizes natural-sounding speech will be client-specific. The client is ready for dismissal only when probes in which reinforcement and corrective feedback are kept to a minimum and yet the client maintains a desirable rate and natural-sounding speech with few or no dysfluencies.

Treatment of Stuttering in Adults:
I. Comprehensive Fluency Shaping Procedure

Treatment Recording Sheet

Personalize and print this page from the CD.

Name of the client:	DOB:
Address:	Phone:
Diagnosis: Stuttering	Session date(s):
Clinician:	Comments:

Chart the client's progress for each session with your preferred method. You may calculate a percent dysfluency or stuttering rate based on the number of words spoken. If more detailed data are warranted, score the individual dysfluency types and add them up to calculate the dysfluency rate.

Essential Measures		Optional Measures: Frequency of Specific Dysfluency Types					
Dates of Service	Percent Stuttering	Prolongations	Pauses	Repetitions	Interjections	Revisions	Incomplete Phrases

Treatment of Stuttering in Adults:
I. Comprehensive Fluency Shaping Procedure

Probe Protocol

Probe Procedure

- Record two conversational speech samples, each 5 to 7 minutes in duration
- Record a 3-minute monologue; ask the client to talk about a topic such as:
  - ➢ favorite sports
  - ➢ favorite vacations
  - ➢ favorite movies
  - ➢ favorite TV shows
  - ➢ weekend activities
  - ➢ current events of interest
  - ➢ the nature of work and work-related experiences
  - ➢ hobbies
  - ➢ newspaper articles
  - ➢ books recently read
  - ➢ any other client-specific topic
- Obtain a 5-minute home speech sample
- Record one or more extraclinic speech samples in such places as the client's work place and a restaurant
- Make a phone call and measure dysfluency rates in telephone conversations
- Analyze the percent dysfluency or stuttering rate
- Personalize the *Probe Recording Sheet* and record the dysfluency or stuttering rates; print the sheet for client's clinical file

Treatment of Stuttering in Adults:
I. Comprehensive Fluency Shaping Procedure

Probe Recording Sheet

Personalize and print this page from the CD.

Name of the client:	DOB:
Address:	Phone:
Diagnosis: Stuttering	Session date(s):
Clinician:	Comments:

Analyze the probe speech samples with your preferred method. You may calculate a percent dysfluency or stuttering rate based on the number of words spoken. If more detailed data are warranted, score the individual dysfluency types and add them up to calculate the dysfluency rate.

Take at least three clinic probe samples. If possible, obtain three extraclinic probe samples.

Essential Measures		Optional Measures: Frequency of Specific Dysfluency Types					
Dates/Setting of Probe	Percent Stuttering	PRO	PAU	REP	INT	REV	INC
1. /mm/dd/yy/ Clinic							
2. /mm/dd/yy/ Clinic							
3. /mm/dd/yy/ Clinic							
1. /mm/dd/yy/ Home							
2. /mm/dd/yy/ Office							
3. /mm/dd/yy/ A public place							

PRO (Prolongations); PAU (Pauses); REP (Repetitions); INT (Interjections); REV (Revisions); INC (Incomplete phrases).

Dismiss the client from current services when the client's stuttering or dysfluency rate stays below the target percentage in conversational probes. Schedule follow-ups and booster treatments as needed.

Treatment of Stuttering in Adults:
II. Prolonged Speech

Overview

Prolonged speech is a well-established treatment for older children and adults who stutter (Cordes & Ingham, 1998; Curlee, 1999a; Conture, 2001; Gregory, 2003; Guitar, 2006; Shapiro, 1999). Prolonged speech may be used with or without airflow management. For several decades, fluency shaping has been used around the world as a standard treatment for adults who stutter. Although pause-and-talk (time-out) is a better alternative to fluency shaping, the latter technique has been popular with clinicians. Its origin is in the effects of delayed auditory feedback (DAF) which induces slower rate of speech and syllable prolongations (Goldiamond, 1965). It soon became evident that delayed auditory feedback is not necessary to induce a slower and prolonged speech in people who stutter. Instructions and modeling are just as effective and are attractive because they do not cost anything to the client or the clinician.

The limitations of prolonged speech are the same as the comprehensive fluency shaping that includes airflow management. The most significant limitations include an unnatural-sounding speech and poor maintenance of fluency (Curlee, 1999a; Conture, 2001; Gregory, 2003; Guitar, 2006; Shapiro, 1999). Prolonged speech produces stutter-free speech, not normal fluency. Clients who have learned to avoid stuttering by this method feel that they need to constantly monitor their speech rate, instead of what they want to say. They believe that their slow and monotonous speech is socially unacceptable. Consequently, they begin to speak at rates that are not conducive to maintaining their stutter-free speech; the result is a relapse of stuttering.

Because the procedure induces unnatural-sounding speech, normal prosodic features are also a treatment target. By reinstating normal prosodic features, the unnaturalness of speech can be minimized and by periodic booster treatment, maintenance may be enhanced.

Syllable prolongation has the following two treatment targets:

- **Slower Speech Rate with Syllable Prolongation:** Prolonging syllable duration is an effective strategy to reduce or even totally eliminate stuttering. There is considerable replicated evidence (some controlled and some uncontrolled) to support its effectiveness. When the vowel following an initial consonant (the syllable nucleus) is prolonged, dysfluencies are almost always eliminated. This prolongation is different from the typical prolongation (a form of stuttering) of people who stutter. Typically, people who stutter prolong the initial consonant (e.g., *ssss*up); in prolonged speech treatment, they prolong the following vowel (e.g., s*ooo*p).

- **Normal Prosodic Features:** Because of syllable prolongation, speech will sound excessively slow and monotonous. Speech may also be too soft. Therefore, to reduce the social consequences of an unnatural-sounding speech, normal prosodic features—including normal speech rates, intonation, and loudness variations—are targeted as well. If the speech continues to sound unnatural, social acceptance will be extremely limited, and as a consequence, stuttering may relapse.

To begin with, the clinician describes the syllable prolongation to the client and frequently models the slow and syllable-stretched rate of speech. Making modifications as found necessary for a given client, the clinician:

- Establishes baserates of dysfluencies or stuttering as the clinician defines them. To obtain reliable baserates of dysfluencies in older students, adolescents, and adults, the clinician tape-records an extended conversational speech. Topic cards which suggest various topics of conversation (e.g., *favorite games and sports, vacations, current social and political issues, work-related experiences, hobbies, movies, TV shows*) may be useful with most older clients. An oral reading sample also may be obtained to assess the differential dysfluency rates in oral reading versus conversational speech. A 3- to 5-minute monologue on a topic of interest also may be recorded. If practical, the clinician may obtain a home speech sample for analysis of dysfluencies or stuttering. After establishing baserates, the clinician initiates treatment.

- Describes and models a slower speech rate achieved through syllable prolongation. The clinician teaches the client to extend the duration of vowels following the initial consonants. The optimal duration of prolongation is client-specific; but it should result in stutter-free speech. For each client, the clinician should find a rate that is slow enough to eliminate dysfluencies. A few successful trials at the single word level should be sufficient to move on to the next step.

- Moves on to the phrase level training when the client successfully produces a number of words, stretching syllable durations. In learning to prolong syllables in two-word phrases, the client adds a new word to the already practiced single word. For instance, an adult man who has been practicing fluency skills in saying his first name (e.g., *Jhaaan*") may be asked to say his first and the last name (e.g., "*Jhaaan Jeeekəəəb*"). It is not essential to move from single words to two-word phrases in all cases; the number of words in practice phrases will depend on the client. Some clients may succeed at three to four word phrases at the beginning of this stage.

- Manages the behavioral treatment contingencies promptly and strictly. It may be noted that syllable stretching or prolonged speech is the target skill the client learns to produce. Prolonged speech does not specify a new treatment procedure; it specifies the target skill the client has to learn. A description of how that skill is taught and learned constitutes treatment. In this technical sense, treatment is still the same behavioral procedures that include instructions, demonstrations, modeling, prompting, positive reinforcement for correct production of targeted skill resulting in fluency, and corrective feedback for errors in managing the skill and for dysfluencies.

- Targets normal prosodic features when the client sustains stutter-free speech (perhaps a 98% fluency, though it may sound unnatural) across a few sessions. The clinician models a slightly faster rate for the client to imitate. As the client learns to sustain stutter-free speech at the initial faster rate, the clinician models progressively faster rates and varied intonational patterns for the client to imitate. Eventually, the clinician may stabilize a slightly slower than the client's habitual speech rate that still sounds natural.

- Trains family members, friends, and client-selected colleagues to recognize various forms of dysfluencies and to prompt and reinforce slower rate to sustain natural-sounding fluency in home, office, and other nonclinical settings. Spouses or other family members may be trained to hold informal treatment sessions at home. Such training may begin as soon as the client sustains stutter-free speech in the clinic. These steps are essential to maintain fluency.

- Conducts follow-up assessments and arranges for booster treatment when the results of a follow-up warrant additional treatment. The initial follow-up may be scheduled for 3 months following the dismissal. Additional follow-ups may be scheduled at 6- or 12-month intervals. In all follow-up sessions, the clinician takes an extended speech sample without treatment to calculate the percent stuttering or dysfluency rates.

The following prolonged speech treatment protocols have been written to establish stutter-free speech and to stabilizing natural-sounding fluency:

1. Protocols to establish stutter-free speech in conversational speech
2. Protocols to establish stutter-free speech in narrative speech
3. Protocols to stabilize natural-sounding fluency

Treatment of Stuttering in Adults: II. Prolonged Speech

Establishing Stutter-Free Conversational Speech

Overview

- With older students and adult clients, the **syllable prolongation** may be initiated at the word and phrase level or the sentence level, depending on the individual. The strategy is to initiate treatment at the highest level of response topography possible (e.g., shorter or longer sentences), not necessarily at the lowest level (e.g., single words). Because the treatment has to move through the different levels of response complexity, starting treatment at a higher level the client can perform is more efficient than routinely starting at the lowest level.

- Even when the lowest level of single words seems to be needed for a given client, the clinician should swiftly move on to phrases and sentences. Lingering for too long at the single word level is both inefficient and suggestive of potential misapplication of the treatment procedure. Most older students, adolescents, and adults who stutter may master syllable prolongation at the short sentence level at the very beginning. A low stuttering frequency and severity may be another factor that suggests the possibility of starting treatment at the sentence level.

- The clinician may use various topic cards the client brings to the clinic to evoke sustained monologues or conversational speech. The clinician may prompt, instruct, or otherwise encourage the client to produce shorter and longer sentences.

- Frequent modeling of syllable prolongation is essential in treating most clients, including otherwise verbally competent adults. Clinicians may also reduce their own speech rates while teaching the fluency skills. Clinicians who talk fast may find it hard to control the speech rates in clients they work with.

- If dysfluencies persist, it is typically because the client has failed to prolong syllables to a sufficient extent.

- With most adolescents and adults, verbal reinforcement is effective. An informative feedback at the end of the session that summarizes the client's progress in comparison with progress in previous sessions may be additionally useful. Verbal praise may take several forms:
  - ➤ Wonderful! You stretched your sounds well!
  - ➤ Very good! I like the way you are talking very slowly!
  - ➤ Fantastic! You are talking at a nice, slow rate!
  - ➤ I like your speech with no stuttering in it!
  - ➤ Good job! Your speech is completely stutter-free!

- Positive reinforcement should be prompt, natural, and should follow all syllable-stretched productions in the beginning stage of treatment. For instance, the clinician should promptly praise the client for prolongation of syllables. This initial continuous reinforcement may be changed to one of intermittent schedule during natural conversational exchanges.

- Verbal corrective feedback should be offered immediately when the client fails to prolong the syllables. Regardless of whether syllables were prolonged or not, the clinician should immediately give corrective feedback for all dysfluent productions. The feedback should be prompt, clear, and objective in tone. The client should stop when he or she fails to prolong syllables or produces a dysfluency; the client should correct the error and then continue. The clinician may use several forms of corrective feedback; each should point out what went wrong:
  - ➢ Stop, you didn't stretch the syllables long enough!
  - ➢ Stop, that was too fast! Stretch your speech more!
  - ➢ No, you should slow down some more!
  - ➢ Stop, you stuttered!
- The same stimulus materials used in baserating dysfluencies in sentences may be appropriate for treatment sessions. Topics of interest to the client may more readily evoke speech from older students and adult. Therefore, conversations and discussion of topics should be client-selected.
- To evaluate the client's progress in treatment, the clinician may tape-record each session and later calculate the percent dysfluency or stuttering rate.
- If a correctly implemented syllable prolongation approach does not produce satisfactory results, the clinician may consider alternative procedures (e.g., a comprehensive fluency shaping, pause-and-talk, or a combination of pause-and-talk and a slight syllable prolongation). Although there will be individual differences, speech should be nearly stutter-free in a matter of few sessions. If not, the progress may be judged unsatisfactory, leading to a change in the treatment procedure.

Treatment of Stuttering in Adults:
II. Prolonged Speech

Treatment Protocol for Conversational Speech

Scripts for Establishing Stutter-Free Conversation		Note
Clinician	"There are a few options for you to speak more fluently than you do now. In the treatment procedure I have selected for you, you master a fluency skill that helps you speak more fluently. In fact, the skill that you will practice in these sessions will be incompatible with stuttering. This means that you can't stutter and perform this skill simultaneously. The skill that will most likely eliminate most of your stuttering is a slow speech. Have you sometimes used this technique of slowing down to speak more fluently?"	Gives an overview of the procedure selected for the client
Client	"Yes. I sometimes deliberately speak slowly to avoid stuttering."	Shows awareness of slow speech
Clinician	"Has it worked?"	
Client	"Yes, it has. But the problem is to remember to slow down."	
Clinician	"That's right. Even a simple task like that needs to be systematically practiced. In these sessions, you will be doing that."	Emphasizes the need for systematic practice
Client	"Sounds good."	
Clinician	"The procedure is called prolonged speech. In this technique, you learn to talk very slowly. You can talk slowly by simply pausing between words. But we don't want that. In fact, I don't want you to pause between words at all. Instead, I want you to blend the words smoothly and stretch the syllables. It is a method of prolonging the syllables, which means mostly vowels." [*demonstrates prolonged speech by saying "youumaaytaalkliiikethiis"*]	Introduces syllable prolongation

Describes and models syllable prolongation |
| Client | "But I already prolong some of my sounds. What is the difference?" | |

Establishing Stutter-Free Conversation, continued

Scripts for Establishing Stutter-Free Conversation		Note
Clinician	"Well, typically you prolong an initial consonant. Like you may say *sssssoup*. But in this method, I want you to prolong the second vowel. You say *suuup*. Not the *s* sound, but the *ooo* sound that you prolong in this case. To give you another example, you may say *lllllike* but I want you to say *laaaike*. Again, not the *l* sound that you may prolong, but the *ai* sound that follows that you prolong here. Do you notice the difference?"	Demonstrates syllable prolongation
Client	"Yes I do."	
Clinician	"Right. The technique essentially is to stretch all the syllables of each word and then to blend the words. You should say the stretched words without pauses in between them. It's like talking in one long string of syllables with no break."	Summarizes the essential feature of prolonged speech
Client	"I think I know what you mean."	Shows understanding of prolonged speech
Clinician	"Very good! "Your speech should be sloooow and streeeeetched out like that. [*stretches out the two words*] [*continues to talk with syllable stretching*] Stretched words should blend into each other like I am talking now. There shouldn't even be a slight pause in between words. "I will ask you a series of questions you answer with single words. This way, you practice slow speech in simple word productions. Please tell me your first name; stretch your syllables."	Verbal praise Additional instruction and demonstration
Client	"Ja . . ." [*Javier*]	Mismanaged airflow
Clinician	"Stop! You forgot to stretch. Say Jaaaavieeer." [*models slow speech on the client's name*]	Corrective feedback and modeling of slow speech
Client	[*correct syllable stretching*] "Jaaaavieeer."	Prolonged, stutter-free speech
Clinician	"Excellent! That was good stretching. Now tell me your last name. Say, Nuuuneeez." [*models syllable stretching on Nunez*]	Verbal praise and initiation of the next modeled trial
Client	"Nun . . ."	Failure to stretch
Clinician	"Stop! You didn't stretch the syllables. Try it again. Nuuuneeez."	Corrective feedback and modeling
Client	"Nuuuneeez."	Prolonged, stutter-free speech

Establishing Stutter-Free Conversation, continued

Scripts for Establishing Stutter-Free Conversation		Note
Clinician	"Excellent! You did everything right! Tell me your wife's first name. Please stretch the syllables."	Verbal praise and the initiation of the next trial
Client	"Maaarleeene" [*Marlene*]	Prolonged, stutter-free speech
Clinician	"Excellent. Nice stretching of the syllables. Now tell me your Dad's first name."	Verbal praise
Client	"Aaaarmaaando." [*Armando*]	Prolonged and stutter-free speech
Clinician	"Good! Correct syllable stretching. Now tell me your Mom's first name."	Verbal praise; next trial
Client	"Jaaaceeenta." [*Jacinta*]	Prolonged and stutter-free speech
Clinician	"Wonderful! You are doing really well! How many brothers do you have? Just say one word—a number."	Verbal praise; the next question
Client	"Two."	No stretching, though fluent
Clinician	"Not correct! You forgot to prolong the word. Try it again."	Corrective feedback
Client	"Twooo."	Prolonged and stutter-free speech
Clinician	"I like that! You did it correctly! What is your first brother's name?"	Verbal praise
Client	"C-c- . . . "	Sound repetition
Clinician	"Stop! You stuttered. You have to quickly open your mouth and prolong the next sound. Try it again."	Corrective feedback; instruction
Client	"Caaaarloos." [*Carlos*]	Prolonged and stutter-free speech
Clinician	"Very good! See, when you quickly moved to a prolonged vowel, you don't stutter. What's your second brother's name?"	Verbal praise; points out the reason for success
Client	"Aaalfreeedo." [*Alfredo*]	Prolonged, stutter-free speech
Clinician	"I like the way you stretched the syllables. Are your brothers older or younger than you?"	Verbal praise
Client	"Ooolder." [*older*]	Prolonged, stutter-free speech
Clinician	"Good stretching. So you are the youngest of the three brothers."	Verbal praise
Client	"Yeeees." [*yes*]	Prolonged, stutter-free speech

Establishing Stutter-Free Conversation, continued

Scripts for Establishing Stutter-Free Conversation		Note
Clinician	"Excellent! Good syllable stretching. Do you have sisters? If so, how many?"	Verbal praise
Client	"Aaaai dooo. Twooo seesters." [*I do. Two sisters*]	Prolonged, stutter-free speech
Clinician	"Excellent! You said it right and you didn't stutter! What is your first sister's name?"	Verbal praise; next question
Client	"Ooooliviiia." [*Olivia*]	Prolonged and stutter-free speech
Clinician	"Very good! What's your second sister's name?"	Verbal praise; next question
Client	"Rrrr . . . "	Sound prolongation
Clinician	"Stop! You didn't move quickly to the next sound to prolong it. Try that again."	Corrective feedback
Client	"Rooosiiita." [*Rosita*]	Prolonged and stutter-free speech
Clinician	"Very good. Are your sisters older or younger than you?"	Verbal praise
Client	"Youuuunger." [*younger*]	Prolonged, stutter-free speech
Clinician	"Excellent! You have been doing well in saying single words. Now, may be you can say two or three words at a time. Tell me your full name. Stretch it out."	Verbal praise **Treatment shifted to the phrase level; additional trials on single-words may be needed in some cases**
Client	"Jaaavieeer Nuuuuneeez." [*Javier Nunez*]	Prolonged and stutter-free speech
Clinician	"That was great! Good syllable stretching. Now, tell me your Mom's full name."	Verbal praise
Client	"Jac . . . "	No prolongation
Clinician	"Stop! You forgot to prolong. Try again."	Corrective feedback
Client	"Jaaacinta Nuuuneez." [*Jacinta Nunez*]	Prolonged and stutter-free speech
Clinician	"Excellent! Tell me your Dad's full name."	Verbal praise
Client	"Aaaarmaaandoo Nuuuneez." [*Armando Nunez*]	Prolonged, stutter-free speech
Clinician	"Perfect! Tell me your first brother's full name."	Verbal praise
Client	[*correct airflow*] "Caaarloos Nuuuneez."	Prolonged, stutter-free speech
Clinician	"Good stretching! Now, tell me your second brother's full name."	Verbal praise

Establishing Stutter-Free Conversation, continued

Scripts for Establishing Stutter-Free Conversation		Note
Client	"Aaalfreeedoo Nuuuneez." [*Alfredo Nunez*]	Prolonged and stutter-free speech
Clinician	"Very good! You are breathing and stretching correctly! Now, tell me your first sister's full name."	Verbal praise
Client	"Oooliviiia Nuuuneez." [*Olivia Nunez*]	Prolonged, stutter-free speech
Clinician	"Excellent. And your second sister's full name?"	Verbal praise
Client	"Rooosiiita Nuuuneez." [*Rosita Nunez*]	Prolonged, stutter-free speech
Clinician	"Very good job! Maybe you can now try to say more words each time. Perhaps you can try some simple sentences. Do you have any children? Make it a sentence and stretch syllables and blend words."	Verbal praise **Treatment shifted to short sentences of longer phrases.** **Additional trials on two-word phrases may be needed in some cases**
Client	[*correct syllable stretching*] "I have two children."	Prolonged, stutter-free speech **From here on, for ease of reading, syllable stretching is not shown orthographically**
Clinician	"Good stretching! Tell me their names."	Verbal praise
Client	[*correct syllable stretching*] "My son's name is Mario. [*fails to stretch*] Mmmm . . . "	Sound prolongation (dysfluency)
Clinician	"Stop! You should move to the next syllable and prolong it."	Corrective feedback
Client	"My [pause] daughter . . . "	Prolonged speech, but too much pausing between words
Clinician	"Stop! You are not blending the words. Say, maaaidaaughteer's . . . "	Models word blending
Client	[*syllable stretching*] "My daughter's name is Cecilia."	Stretched syllables and blended words; stutter-free speech
Clinician	"Good stretching and blending of words! Where do you live?"	Verbal praise
Client	[*syllable stretching*] "I live in Chowchilla."	Prolonged and stutter-free speech
Clinician	"Excellent! You said four words, all with good syllable stretching. For how long have you lived in Chowchilla?"	Verbal praise

Establishing Stutter-Free Conversation, continued

Scripts for Establishing Stutter-Free Conversation		Note
Client	[*syllable stretching*] "For about 5 years."	Prolonged and stutter-free speech
Clinician	"Excellent! You are saying more words correctly! What do you do for living?"	Verbal praise; next trial
Client	[*fails to stretch*] "I-I . . ."	Sound prolongation due to lack of syllable stretching
Clinician	"No, you didn't stretch it enough. That's why you stuttered. Try that again."	Corrective feedback
Client	[*syllable stretching*] "I am a high school teacher."	Prolonged and stutter-free speech
Clinician	"Good stretching! That was a long sentence, too! Okay, what do you teach? What is the name of your school? Make it one sentence."	Verbal praise
Client	[*syllable stretching*] "I teach science at the Chowchilla High."	Prolonged and stutter-free speech
Clinician	"Very good! How big is the school?"	Verbal praise
Client	[*syllable stretching*] "Not too big, we only have two hundred students."	Prolonged and stutter-free speech
Clinician	"Excellent! Good syllable stretching. How big are your classes?"	Verbal praise
Client	[*syllable stretching until the stutter*] "I would have s-s- . . ."	Part-word repletion; failure to stretch
Clinician	"Oops! That was a stutter. You didn't quickly move to the next, stretched sound. Say the *s* sound softly, and quickly move to the next sound, and stretch it well. Try that again."	Corrective feedback
Client	[*syllable stretching*] "I have some thirty students in my classes."	Prolonged and stutter-free speech
Clinician	"Excellent! That soft and quick *s* and prolonged *uuum* in *some* eliminated stuttering, didn't it?"	Verbal praise and an explanation
Client	[*syllable stretching*] "Yes!"	Prolonged and stutter-free speech
Clinician	"Good. What science subjects do you teach?"	Verbal praise
Client	[*syllable stretching*] "I teach biology."	Stutter-free
Clinician	"Very good. You are doing well. May be you can try saying more than one sentence at a time. Do you teach anything besides biology?"	Verbal praise; introducing longer utterances

Establishing Stutter-Free Conversation, continued

Scripts for Establishing Stutter-Free Conversation		Note
Client	[*syllable stretching*] "Yes, I do. On occasion, I teach physics and even early American history."	Prolonged and stutter-free speech
Clinician	"That's the way to handle it! What was your major in college?"	Verbal praise
Client	[*syllable stretching*] "I majored in teacher education, but took some courses in biology and physics."	Prolonged and stutter-free
Clinician	"Excellent! What college or university did you attend?"	Verbal praise
Client	[*stretching until the stutter*] "I graduated from S-s-s-. . . "	Incorrect responses; sound repetition
Clinician	"Oops! Make the *s* sound soft and quickly move to the next sound. Stretch it."	Corrective feedback and instruction
Client	[*syllable stretching*] "I graduated from Sonoma State in Northern California."	Prolonged and stutter-free speech
Clinician	"Good stretching! Did you like Sonoma State?"	Verbal praise
Client	[*syllable stretching*] "Yes, I liked it a lot. It is a small campus in a pretty surrounding."	Prolonged and stutter-free speech
Clinician	"Excellent! You are getting a good hang of syllable stretching! I am switching topics now. You said you have two brothers. What do they do?"	Verbal praise; new topic initiation No modeling; evoking multiple questions
Client	[*syllable stretching*] "Carlos is a police officer in San Francisco. Alfredo is a medical technician. He is a paramedic with an ambulance company in Oakland."	Prolonged and stutter-free speech
Clinician	"That's great! Do they have families?"	Verbal praise
Client	[*syllable stretching*] "Yes, both are married and have children. Carlos has a son and Alfredo has a daughter. Both are young, like ten or eleven I think."	Prolonged and stutter-free speech
Clinician	"Very good! What about your sisters? What do they do? Where do they live?"	Verbal praise
Client	[*syllable stretching*] "My two younger sisters are in college. They are not in the same college, though. Olivia is attending Pomona State and Rosita is attending UC Irvine. Olivia wants to be an elementary school teacher. She is almost finished, should graduate this year. Rosita just started. She is a freshman. She is not sure of her major yet."	Prolonged and stutter-free speech

Establishing Stutter-Free Conversation, continued

Scripts for Establishing Stutter-Free Conversation		Note
Clinician	"I like the way you are prolonging your syllables! Now let us talk a little bit about your own family. Tell me about your children. How old are they? In what grades are they studying? What schools do they go to?"	Verbal praise; prompts multiple sentence productions
Client	[*syllable stretching until the stutter*] "My son Mario is the older of the two. He is eight. Mmm . . ."	Sound prolongation
Clinician	"Stop! You forgot something."	Corrective feedback; prompts self-evaluation
Client	[*syllable stretching*] "Yes, I forgot to stretch! I was about to say that my daughter Cecilia is 6. Mario is in the second grade and Cecilia is in the first. Both go to the same school. They go to the Clark elementary school in town."	Correct management of fluency skills; stutter-free speech
Clinician	"How do they get to their school every morning?"	
Client	[*syllable stretching*] "The school bus stops just around the corner from my house. Most of the days, they take the bus. On some days when they get up late or something I give them a ride to school."	Maintains stutter-free speech in longer sentences
Clinician	"Good! You are maintaining slow speech in multiple sentences! What does your wife do?"	Verbal praise
Client	[*syllable stretching*] "My wife is a dental hygienist."	Stutter-free speech
Clinician	"Does she work in a dentist's office?"	
Client	[*syllable stretching*] "Yes, she works for a dentist in town. The dentist must be very happy with Marlene's work because she has worked there for almost 10 years now."	Stutter-free speech
Clinician	"Well, that is really excellent. You can now talk very well with syllable stretching. You notice that you hardly stutter!"	Verbal praise

The clinician continues to teach the fluency skills in conversational speech to establish stutter-free speech. The number of sessions in this phase will be client-specific. When the client has sustained fluency skills as well as stutter-free speech in conversational speech across three or more sessions, the clinician shifts training to the next phase, which involves narrative speech.

Treatment of Stuttering in Adults:
II. Prolonged Speech

Establishing Stutter-Free Narrative Speech

Overview

To establish stutter-free narrative speech with syllable prolongation, the clinician should have the client talk continuously on a single topic. Instead of the conversational format used in the previous protocols, the clinician would ask the client to talk on a topic for extended duration. The clinician would only occasionally ask questions or offer comments to stimulate continuous speech from the client.

General Treatment Strategy

The topic selected for narrative speech should be client-selected. Perhaps the client will talk about varied topics over several sessions. Because the clients choose their topics and talk about them, it is not productive to write protocols for multiple topics. A single topic is illustrated in the protocol. Using this protocol, the clinician can have the client talk on several topics to establish stutter-free speech in narrative or continuous speech.

In all sessions, the clinician should continue to verbally reinforce slower rate of speech that eliminates most, if not all, stuttering. In this stage of treatment, the duration of syllable prolongations will be reduced to some extent. The speech will not be as slow as in the initial stage of treatment. Continuous speech that includes longer sentences and utterances tend to be prolonged less. This is acceptable as long as the client still speaks at a slower rate compared to his or her baseline speech rate and maintains stutter-free speech.

It is likely that toward the end of this phase of treatment, the client begins to speak at a faster rate (still slower than his or her typical rate). The clinician may reinforce this outcome as in the following stage of treatment, more natural-sounding speech will be the specific target.

Treatment of Stuttering in Adults:
II. Prolonged Speech

Treatment Protocol for Narrative Speech

Scripts for Establishing Stutter-Free Narration		Note
Clinician	"I think you have been managing the fluency skills in conversation quite well. Your speech is mostly stutter-free. You systematically prolong syllables to produce continuous, stutter-free conversational speech. Now I think it's time to move on to even more continuous speech in which you practice speaking at a slower-than-the-usual rate. In each treatment session from now on, I would like you to talk for extended periods of time on topics of your interest. I will be talking less and you will be talking most of the time on a topic of your choice. When you come for therapy next time, you may want to bring a list of topics on which you would like to talk. If you prefer, you can bring topic cards. Each index card will contain a topic and you talk on one topic at a time. On each card, you also may make notes to yourself, if you wish, so you can tell me more about each of them. For today, is there a topic you want to talk about? Don't forget syllable stretching."	Explains the next stage of treatment; suggests strategies for topic selection
Client	[*syllable stretching*] "Well, let me see. My wife and I love to travel. We can talk about our recent travels."	Suggests a topic
Clinician	"That's great! Tell me all about your recent trips. Do you travel in the U.S. or do you travel abroad? Do you take your children on your travels?"	
Client	[*syllable stretching throughout the narration*] "Yes, we all four travel together. My teaching job is great for travel. Marlene usually off from work during July and August. Her boss has been very supportive of her. He has a part-timer who goes full-time during those two months. Kids are out of the school, so it all works out really well. Come May of each year, we are all bitten by the travel bug. Maybe I got the bug from my parents. They took us on extended vacations to see relatives in Mexico and Nicaragua. My grandpa—Dad's dad, was from Mexico City. He married my Grandma, *(continued)*	Maintains both syllable stretching and stutter-free speech Periodically, hears clinician's brief questions (e.g., did you have a good time? How was your stay in that place? What else did you do there?) Periodically, hears clinician say, "you are doing well! or "you are speaking correctly!" and so forth

Establishing Stutter-Free Narration, continued

Scripts for Establishing Stutter-Free Narration		Note
Client *(continues)*	who was from Nicaragua. So my parents often took us to see relatives in both the countries. We still have relatives there, but we don't see them that often. Well . . . " [*shows slight hesitation*]	Gets prompted from the clinician
Clinician	"Do you guys travel to other countries now?"	Prompts continued speech
Client	[*syllable stretching*] "Yes, after several visits to Mexico City and Managua in Nicaragua, we thought we should see other parts of the world. My wife Marlene is from Portugal, so the first trip out of the Americas was to Portugal. Our first visit to Portugal was many years ago, before we had children. We went there about a year after we got married. I just loved Portugal. Lisbon is a beautiful city, easy to navigate. Good public transportation. It has a lot of old, historic buildings. Great museums. We found the people to be very friendly to foreigners. Both of us loved Portuguese food because Marlene cooks that kind of food at home. I love Port, so went to Porto, the city after which the drink is named. We visited a few wineries that produce Port. Traveling within the country was easy. Years ago when we went, Portugal was very affordable. It still is, we have gone there some three times in the last 10 years. I don't mind living there for a couple of months every summer!" [*pauses briefly*]	Continues with narration

Maintains a slower rate and stutter-free speech

Receives periodic verbal praise from the clinician

A pause in narration |
| Clinician | "That's great! You are doing well. You are not stretching the syllables as much, but that's Okay. You just have to maintain stutter-free speech. Continue to stretch the syllables at the beginning of each sentence, even if it is to a lesser extent. If you didn't stretch syllables in the final words of sentences, that may be Okay, too, as long as you maintain fluency.

It looks like you have really enjoyed Portugal. Do you or Marlene speak Portuguese? Also, tell me what other countries have you visited." | Offers periodic verbal praise throughout the narration

Draws attention to a slight reduction in the extent of syllable prolongation |
| Client | "Marlene knows Portuguese well. She can read and write in that language. She was around 10 when her Mom and Dad immigrated to the United States. Her parents continued to talk in Portuguese, so she never forgot the language. She tried to teach it to our children, *(continued)* | |

Establishing Stutter-Free Narration, continued

Scripts for Establishing Stutter-Free Narration		Note
Client *(continues)*	but not with great success. Both Mario and Cecilia understand some common expressions. They can't speak the language. "Well, lll . . . "	Lack of stretching, a sound prolongation
Clinician	"Stop! What happened?"	Encourages self-evaluation
Client	[*syllable stretching*] "I didn't stretch enough. I was going to say, *let me see.* I was trying to think about the other countries we visited. Over the years, we have visited Canada, England, Italy, India, Greece, Turkey, Thailand, South Africa, Egypt, and Brazil."	Good self-evaluation Continues narrative speech
Clinician	"Excellent! You are stretching even less, and yet you are not stuttering! That's great. "Of all those countries you visited, is there one that is your favorite?"	Feedback on previous performance
Client	[*syllable stretching*] "That's a tough question. Marlene and I find that each country offers something different. In terms of incomparable ancient architecture, Egypt stands out. Quaint beautiful villages dot the English countryside. Greek islands offer best relaxation. Italian art treasure is exhausting! India's Rajasthan is the most colorful place on earth, with more castles than most other countries. African animal parks will take your breath away. So I can go on like this, but I can't pick one favorite place."	Stutter-free speech
Clinician	"That's very good! You have maintained stutter-free speech very well! We will continue this type narrative speech when you return next time. "	Verbal praise
Client [*in subsequent sessions*]	[*talks about new topics for extended duration of time while maintaining stutter-free speech*]	Continues to practice stutter-free speech production
Clinician [*in subsequent sessions*]	[*monitors the client's fluency; offers prompts, occasional questions, comments, statements of agreement, and so forth to keep the client talking continuously; initiates speech on new topics as found necessary*]	Gives corrective feedback when the client speeds up excessively or stutters

Treatment for narrative speech continues in this manner. Some clients need to talk on more topics and over several sessions than other clients. The clinician may move treatment to the next stage when the client sustains 98% stutter-free speech in at least three consecutive sessions. In the next stage of treatment, the clinician will explicitly target natural-sounding fluent speech.

Following protocols help establish natural-sounding speech.

Treatment of Stuttering in Adults:
II. Prolonged Speech

Stabilizing Natural-Sounding Fluency

Overview

- The immediate effects of syllable prolongation is stutter-free but unnatural-sounding speech. The speech that is devoid of stuttering is too slow, sometimes too soft, and always too monotonous to be socially acceptable.

- Adults who are treated with prolonged speech believe that their stutter-free and unnatural-sounding speech is unacceptable to listeners. But it is even more unacceptable to themselves—those who stuttered but no longer do because of prolonged speech treatment. The slow, deliberate speech takes personal tolls on the speaker. It reduces spontaneity in conversation. The need to constantly monitor a slow speech rate is tiring and aversive to the speaker. While a slightly faster speech rate comes naturally to most speakers, a noticeably slower rate comes only from an all-absorbing attention to it. Treated stuttering clients sometimes say that it is easier to stutter than to maintain stutter-free speech. Many even believe, perhaps with good justification, that their listeners may be more tolerant of stuttering than their stutter-free slow speech. They believe that their slow and monotonous speech may be even more attention-grabbing than their stuttering.

- Because of those problems associated with prolonged speech treatment, it is essential to shape natural-sounding speech before the client is dismissed. Natural-sounding speech is most effectively reinstated with a rate that approximates the client's typical, pretreatment rate. Most listeners do not quantitatively measure a speaker's rate of speech. They make global judgments as to whether the speech sounds natural or not. The clinician and the significant others in the client's life also can make judgments about speech naturalness. This judgment may include not only the rate but also the intonational patterns (pitch and loudness variations). Clinicians may invite comments about the client's speech naturalness from friends, colleagues, and family members. Generally, family members are the best judges of speech naturalness. Adult clients themselves can judge whether their fluency sounds natural or not.

- Natural-sounding fluency is induced essentially in a shaping program. In this procedure, the client may be asked to:
  - gradually increase the rate of speech by minimizing the duration of syllable prolongations
  - increase and vary the loudness of voice
  - vary the vocal pitch throughout an utterance
- In instating natural-sounding speech, the clinician will:
  - frequently model faster rate and improved intonation
  - systematically reinforce any movement toward more natural-sounding speech
  - give prompt corrective feedback when the client exhibits slower and monotonous speech

The protocols to follow are written to achieve these goals of natural-sounding speech.

Treatment of Stuttering in Adults:
II. Prolonged Speech

Treatment Protocol for Natural-Sounding Speech

Scripts for Stabilizing Natural-Sounding Speech		Note
Clinician	"You have been doing really well in maintaining stutter-free speech with syllable prolongation. You have even managed to speak a bit faster, although it is still slower than we want it to be. You have hardly stuttered in the last few sessions. Now that your stutter-free speech is well established, we need to start working on making your speech more natural sounding.	Explains the need for the next stage of treatment
	It is the syllable prolongation that makes your speech monotonous. I know that this is a big concern to you. But by gradually talking a bit faster each time, you can make your speech sound more natural. It is possible that you should always talk a bit slower than before, but not too much slower. When you start talking a bit faster, you will notice that the ups and downs in your voice—we call it intonation—also will improve. A comfortably fast rate that does not bring on stuttering and good intonation will make your speech sound natural. Sometimes, when you talk very slowly, speech is too soft. We want to take care of this problem, too. Speech should be sufficiently loud. That's what we need to work on now. Do you agree?"	Describes the problems associated with slow speech

Sets the new treatment targets |
Client	"Yes, I do! I don't stutter that much any more, and I am eager to talk more naturally!"	
Clinician	"Very good. That's what we will practice now. No stuttering, but faster, more natural speech with good intonation and acceptable loudness of voice. [*begins to speak at a slightly faster rate than the client's clinical rate*] Now let us start with a slightly faster speech. You can talk, maybe more like this, and try what happens. Your goal is not to stutter when you speed up. Therefore, you have to increase the speed of your speech gradually. If you suddenly go too fast, you may lose control of your fluency skills. It's like driving too fast and losing control of the car."	Models a slightly faster rate for the client to imitate
Client	[*speaks at a slightly faster rate*] "Yeah, I get it. That's what I have been doing all my life, I guess."	

Stabilizing Natural-Sounding Speech, continued

Scripts for Stabilizing Natural-Sounding Speech		Note
Clinician	[*still speaking at only a slightly higher rate than the client's clinical rate*] "To practice more natural speech, we can have a conversation about anything. Now, tell me what did you do this last weekend. Talk slightly faster like this, but without stuttering."	Initiates treatment
Client	[*speaks at a slightly faster rate*] "Last Saturday and Sunday I spent time in a ski resort, reading books, magazines, newspapers, and eating good food! And sleeping a lot."	Increased speech rate and improved intonation
Clinician	[*modeling the target rate*] "You spoke slightly faster as I wanted! Very good. You mean to say you didn't ski? Did your wife and kids go with you?"	Verbal praise
Client	[*speaks at a slightly faster rate*] "No, I didn't ski I don't like skiing at all. Actually, *I* went with my wife and my two kids. You could say I was their chauffeur. My wife loves skiing. My kids, too, are learning to ski. While they work hard on the snowy slopes, I relax in the cozy room."	Increased speech rate and improved intonation
Clinician	[*modeling the target rate*] "Very good! You are talking a little bit faster, but you are not stuttering! Did you notice that your intonation, too, is improving?"	Verbal praise; maintains conversation
Client	[*speaks at a slightly faster rate*] "Yes, I did. It's nice!"	Maintains increased speech rate
Clinician	[*modeling the target rate*] "Good! Do you watch your wife and kids ski?"	Evoking speech
Client	[*speaks at a slightly faster rate*] "Sometimes I do. I spend as much time as I can outdoors, but it is not a whole lot of time. I just don't like to be out in the snow. Marlene understands that being out in that cold and muddling through snow is not fun for me. [*speeds up excessively*] Taking pity on me . . ."	Maintains the target speech rate and improved patterns of intonation
Clinician	"Stop! That is a bit too fast. Maintain the rate at which you have been talking!"	Corrective feedback
Client	[*speaks with the target rate*] "Taking pity on me, my wife and children discourage me from accompanying them to the ski area. I think they have more fun there without seeing my puppy-sad face!"	Returns to an appropriate rate
Clinician	"Which suits you anyway! I like the rate at which you are talking now. It's slightly faster, has more intonation, but it is not too fast to bring on the stuttering. "Did you like the ski lodge you stayed there?"	Verbal praise

Stabilizing Natural-Sounding Speech, continued

Scripts for Stabilizing Natural-Sounding Speech		Note
Client	[*speaks with the target rate*] "Very much. It's on a lake. Beautiful surroundings. Snow everywhere, of course, but I like watching the snow-filled hills sloping all the way down to this big lake with sparkling blue water. We manage to get a room with a view. [*speeds up excessively*] Mmmm . . ."	Excessively fast speech rate and a sound prolongation
Clinician	"Stop! Now you know what happens when you go too fast!"	Corrective feedback
Client	[*speaks with the target rate*] "Oh boy! What was I going to say? Yes, my wife plans it way ahead of time. She made reservations for the next year when we checked-out last Sunday. That way, a nice room is guaranteed."	
Clinician	[*Continues conversation. Asks questions, prompts details, periodically reinforces the increased speech rate, and stops when the client's rate increases too fast or when the client stutters.*] "Okay, you have been doing really well at that rate of speech. I think it is now time to try a bit faster rate of speech. [*modeling the new and faster target rate*] Maybe you can talk more like this now. "Do they have a good restaurant in that ski resort? Maybe you can tell me about the kinds of food they have and your favorite food there."	Provides verbal praise and corrective feedback as needed Shifts training to a faster speech rate with greater intonation Continues conversation
Client	[*speaks with the new and faster rate*] "They actually have two restaurants there. The one downstairs is a casual place for lunch. You can order nice salads, gourmet sandwiches, a variety of soups, pizza, and some Mexican fare. The other is a more formal and upscale restaurant on the second floor with fantastic views of the lake and the hills. It's open for breakfast and dinner only. They have a huge breakfast buffet in the morning. They have a variety of items on their dinner menu, and all are exceptionally good. Many are unique preparations, I would think. I like their steak as well their various seafood items. Their salad is out of this world and a meal by itself."	Maintains the new target speech rate and improved intonation
Clinician	"Excellent! See how your speech is sounding more and more normal as you increase your speed and bring back your intonation!"	Verbal praise continues to shape natural-sounding speech in this manner

The number of sessions in which the clinician stabilizes natural-sounding speech will be client-specific. The client is ready for dismissal only when probes in which reinforcement and corrective feedback are kept to a minimum and yet the client maintains a desirable rate and natural-sounding speech with few or no dysfluencies.

Treatment of Stuttering in Adults:
II. Prolonged Speech

Treatment Recording Sheet

Personalize and print this page from the CD.

Name of the client:	DOB:
Address:	Phone:
Diagnosis: Stuttering	Session date(s):
Clinician:	Comments:

Chart the client's progress for each session with your preferred method. You may calculate a percent dysfluency or stuttering rate based on the number of words spoken. If more detailed data are warranted, score the individual dysfluency types and add them up to calculate the dysfluency rate.

Essential Measures		Optional Measures: Frequency of Specific Dysfluency Types					
Dates of Service	Percent Stuttering	Prolongations	Pauses	Repetitions	Interjections	Revisions	Incomplete Phrases

Treatment of Stuttering in Adults:
II. Prolonged Speech

Probe Protocol

Probe Procedure

- Record two conversational speech samples, each 5 to 7 minutes in duration
- Record a 3-minute monologue; ask the client to talk about a topic such as:
  - favorite sports
  - favorite vacations
  - favorites movies
  - favorite TV shows
  - weekend activities
  - current events of interest
  - the nature of work and work-related experiences
  - hobbies
  - newspaper articles
  - books recently read
  - any other client-specific topic
- Obtain a 5-minute home speech sample
- Record one or more extraclinic speech samples in such places as the client's work place and a restaurant
- Make a phone call and measure dysfluency rates in telephone conversations
- Analyze the percent dysfluency or stuttering rate
- Personalize the *Probe Recording Sheet* on the CD and record the dysfluency or stuttering rates; print the sheet for client's clinical file

Treatment of Stuttering in Adults: II. Prolonged Speech

Probe Recording Sheet

Personalize and print this page from the CD.

Name of the client:	DOB:
Address:	Phone:
Diagnosis: Stuttering	Session date(s):
Clinician:	Comments:

Analyze the probe speech samples with your preferred method. You may calculate a percent dysfluency or stuttering rate based on the number of words spoken. If more detailed data are warranted, score the individual dysfluency types and add them up to calculate the dysfluency rate.

Take at least three clinic probe samples. If possible, obtain three extraclinic probe samples.

Essential Measures		Optional Measures: Frequency of Specific Dysfluency Types					
Dates/Setting of Probe	Percent Stuttering	PRO	PAU	REP	INT	REV	INC
1. /mm/dd/yy/ Clinic							
2. /mm/dd/yy/ Clinic							
3. /mm/dd/yy/ Clinic							
1. /mm/dd/yy/ Home							
2. /mm/dd/yy/ Office							
3. /mm/dd/yy/ A public place							

PRO (Prolongations); PAU (Pauses); REP (Repetitions); INT (Interjections); REV (Revisions); INC (Incomplete phrases).

Dismiss the client from current services when the client's stuttering or dysfluency rate stays below the target percentage in conversational probes. Schedule follow-ups and booster treatments as needed.

Treatment of Stuttering in Adults:
III. Pause-and-Talk (Time-Out)

Overview

Since the 1970s, fluency shaping has been the main treatment technique for adults who stutter. With or without modified airflow, slow speech has been the major method of inducing stutter-free speech. The fluency shaping technique has been used with school-age children as well. But the limitations of the fluency shaping has been a concern all along. As noted in the protocols on fluency shaping, the slow and prolonged speech induces a monotonous and unnatural-sounding speech. Stutter-free speech that fluency shaping induces is socially unacceptable and unacceptable to the clients themselves. Maintenance of normal-sounding fluency in adults who have been treated with prolonged speech has been poor. Therefore, in recent years, dissatisfaction with the prolonged speech outcomes has encouraged some clinicians to explore alternative treatments.

An effective alternative to fluency shaping is pause-and-talk, more often described as *time-out* in behavioral research (Hegde, 1998). Pause-and-talk was originally investigated in 1968 by Haroldson, Martin, and Starr, and studies demonstrating its effectiveness continued to be published in subsequent years (e.g., James, 1976, 1981; Onslow et al., 1997). Nonetheless, fluency shaping gained greater popularity among clinicians. A potential misconception among clinicians that time-out, technically classified as a punishment procedure, is socially unacceptable, may be the reason why clinicians have not used it more frequently (Ahlander & Hegde, 2000). When parents of children who stutter were given a complete description of time-out and then asked whether they would approve the technique for their children, no parent voiced objections (Ahlander & Hegde, 2000). There is enough controlled experimental evidence to show that pause-and-talk is effective and that it does not induce unnatural-sounding speech. Although maintenance data are limited, available evidence suggests that pause-and-talk may promote better maintenance than fluency shaping.

Pause-and talk includes reinforcement for fluency and reinforcer withdrawal for stuttering. The technique is similar to response cost, which is more efficiently and effectively administered to children who stutter. The main difference between the two procedures is that in the response cost procedure, the clinician offers tokens and back-up reinforcers for fluency; in the pause-and-talk procedure, the clinician offers attention as reinforcer for fluency. In the response cost procedure, each dysfluency results in a loss of a token for the client; in the pause-and-talk procedure, each dysfluency results in a withdrawal of attention (being paid for fluent speech) for a brief period of 5 seconds. In both the procedures, the clinician places contingencies on fluent as well as dysfluent productions.

In pause-and-talk, the positive reinforcement the client receives for fluency is not as explicit as it is in response cost. The clinician does not explicitly and specifically reinforce fluent productions in pause-and-talk. The client receives the same kind of attention that two conversational partners pay to each other in normal discourse. Even though this attention is contingent on fluent speech, it is not explicitly stated, nor is it accompanied by verbal reinforcement that points out fluency. Sudden and complete withdrawal of attention is specifically contingent on each stuttering or dysfluency, however.

Before starting treatment with pause-and-talk, the clinician should establish the base-rates of dysfluencies in sentences, conversational speech, and narratives as described in a previous section. Regardless of the treatment procedures used, the baserate protocols remain the same for adults who stutter. After establishing the baserates, the clinician may chose either the fluency shaping procedure, syllable prolongation, or pause-and-talk. A combination of slight syllable prolongation and pause-and-talk is also an option to consider. In this section, protocols for the pause-and-talk method are described.

Student clinicians and parents can be relatively easily trained to administer the pause-and-talk procedure. An experimental single-subject design study has demonstrated the feasibility of training parents to exclusively administer treatment at home (Carter-Wagner & Hegde, 1998). The result suggests that other family members, such as spouses of adults who stutter, may be efficiently trained to administer pause-and-talk at home. Family members of adults who stutter may initially conduct brief but formal sessions but eventually maintain fluency by paying social attention to fluent speech without an explicit time-out duration.

Appropriate for Older Students and Adolescents

Pause-and-talk may be effectively used to treat stuttering in older students and adolescents as well. Pause-and-talk may be inappropriate for preschoolers. Treating preschoolers requires toys, picture cards, storybooks, and so forth to keep them talking. When speech is evoked with such stimulus materials, the eye contact between the child and the clinician is not constant. Furthermore, contingent on stuttering, it is difficult to stop a 3-year-old child from talking because the child is also engrossed in stimulus manipulations. For older children and adolescents who can be engaged in conversational speech, pause-and-talk will work as well as it does with adults. Several studies have shown effectiveness of pause-and-talk with older students and adolescents (e.g., Ahlander & Hegde, 2000; Hegde & Parson, 1989; Onslow et al., 1997). Therefore, although the protocols that follow are more specifically written for adults, they may be used with older children with modifications in conversational topics to suit the child.

Limitations of Pause-and-Talk

Clinical experience suggests that pause-and-talk may be less effective with clients whose stuttering is very severe. In the author's experience, if dysfluency or stuttering rates are as high as 50% or more, the client will fail to move at a desirable pace in the treatment process. Too many time-out periods and limited opportunities to positively reinforce fluent conversation with attention will result in an inefficient administration of the procedure. Possibly, the client will be frustrated with the method. In such cases, the clinician has two options: either use the comprehensive fluency shaping procedure described in a previous section or use a combination of slight syllable prolongation and pause-and-talk, described in a later section.

Protocols using pause-and-talk have been written at two levels of training:

1. Treatment at the conversational speech level
2. Treatment at the narrative speech level

Because pause-and-talk is initiated at the conversational speech level, it involves fewer levels of training than some of the other procedures.

Treatment of Stuttering in Adults:
III. Pause-and-Talk

Treatment in Conversational Speech

Overview

- Pause-and-talk is most efficiently administered in conversational speech. Older students, adolescents, and adults who stutter may be engaged in conversation in all treatment sessions. The method requires eye contact between the clinician and the client; therefore, conversational speech is essential for this method to work effectively.

- Frequent modeling of fluent productions for the client to imitate—a common characteristic of most stuttering treatment procedures—is not a typical part of pause-and-talk. The clients are rarely asked to imitatively produce fluent speech in pause-and-talk procedure.

- Pause-and-talk has two components: Reinforcement for fluency and reinforcement withdrawal for stuttering.

- **To reinforce fluency**, the clinician:
  - Maintains eye contact as the client talks fluently
  - Pays attention to what the client is saying
  - Maintains a pleasant facial expression, including smiling
  - Makes comments typical of everyday conversation, including expressions of agreement and disagreement; nods and shakes head as found appropriate
  - Asks questions, prompts responses, suggests topics of conversation, and uses any device that keeps the client talking
  - Minimizes his or her own speech to what is necessary to stimulate and maintain conversational speech in the client

- **To withdraw reinforcement for stuttering**, the clinician:
  - Says "Stop" to the client at the earliest sign of a dysfluency or stutter; makes sure the client stops talking
  - Terminates the eye contact
  - Looks at his or her watch to count five seconds
  - Alternatively, looks elsewhere and estimates the five seconds of time-out duration
  - Remains still for the duration of time-out
  - Maintains a neutral facial expression
  - Reestablishes the eye contact at the end of the time-out duration
  - Says something that will encourage the client to resume talking (e.g., "You were saying . . . ," "Please continue," "You can talk now," etc.)
  - Alternatively, gestures the client to continue talking, especially in the latter stages of treatment (e.g., a hand gesture that suggests *please continue*)

- The time-out duration should never be too long. A 5-second time-out is effective.

- To evaluate the client's progress in treatment, the clinician may tape-record each session and later calculate the percentages of dysfluency or stuttering.

- If a correctly implemented pause-and-talk procedure does not produce satisfactory results, the clinician may consider other options, described earlier. Although there will be individual differences, stuttering frequency should be significantly reduced in a matter of few sessions. If not, the progress may be judged unsatisfactory, leading to a change in the treatment procedure.

- As with any behavioral treatment, attention should be contingent strictly on fluent speech. The clinician should not continue to pay attention when a dysfluent production is in progress. As soon as the earliest sign of a dysfluent speech production is noticed, the clinician should say "Stop" and make sure the client stops talking. Some of the early signs of stuttering include the following:
  - ➤ Quivering or puckering of the lips
  - ➤ Knitting of the eyebrows
  - ➤ Suddenly increased tension in the facial, shoulder, or chest muscles
  - ➤ A slight hesitation that may mushroom into a full-fledged stutter
  - ➤ An attempt to avoid eye contact
  - ➤ Tensed movements of hand or feet

- The time-out duration should never follow a fluent production because of a slowness in recognizing a dysfluent production.

- The clinician should take note that in the pause-and-talk procedure, such fluency shaping skills as gentle phonatory onset, airflow management, and slower rate of speech are not targeted. A common error to be avoided is to inadvertently induce slower speech. Modeling of fluent speech is not frequently used in the pause-and-talk method, but if it ever becomes necessary, it should be done at a normal rate of speech. Strictly implemented pause-and talk procedure does not negatively alter speech prosody, including rate of speech. In fact, the speech rate may, within the normal range, slightly increase when the method consistently reduces stuttering.

- If the client begins to speak slowly to increase fluency and thus avoid the time-out periods, the clinician may instruct the client to speak faster. A normally fast rate may be occasionally modeled for the client to imitate.

Treatment of Stuttering in Adults:
III. Pause-and-Talk

Treatment Protocol for Conversational Speech

Scripts for Pause-and-Talk in Conversation		Note
Clinician	"There are a few effective options to treat stuttering in adults like you. The procedure I have selected for you is called pause-and-talk. Research has shown that it is effective in treating stuttering in older students, adolescents, and adults. It is a simple procedure, but it has to be done very precisely to be effective. In all treatment sessions, we will be talking as two conversational partners. As long as you are talking fluently—without a stutter—I will listen to you with my full attention. You can continue to talk as long as you are fluent. But the instant I notice a stutter, I will ask you to stop talking. You must stop talking when I say "Stop!" It is very important that you don't continue to stutter, and that you terminate speech instantly. As soon as I say "Stop," I will look away from your face for about five seconds. I may look at my watch, or simply avoid eye contact with you and stay quiet for those five seconds. Those five seconds are your pause period. You pause after every stutter; actually, you pause when it appears like you are going to stutter. I might say "stop" even as I find a slight indication of a stutter. For instance, if I see a slight tension in your lips or forehead, I might say "Stop," and you immediately stop talking. At the end of the pause duration, which, as I said, is about five seconds, I will look at your face again to reestablish our eye contact. You can then talk again. I might say something like 'you may talk now,' or 'please continue,' but as soon as I look at you, it means the pause duration is over and that you can begin talking immediately. So, you stop talking when you begin to stutter and pause for five seconds. You then start talking again. You now see why this method is called *pause-and-talk*. Easy to remember what you have to do when you and I are talking here."	The clinician introduces and describes the pause-and-talk method to the client Emphasizes the importance of stop talking at the very onset of a dysfluency

Pause-and-Talk in Conversation, continued

Scripts for Pause-and-Talk in Conversation		Note
Client	"Yes, I do."	Understands
Clinician	"We will start with conversational speech. When you have sustained fluency in conversation for a few sessions, I will be asking you to talk on a topic for extended periods of time. For now, it will be usual conversation. I want you to look at me when you talk. I will ask a series of simple questions about you and your family and your work; it's all for the sake of conversation. Okay?"	Sets the stage for conversational speech
Client	"Okay."	
Clinician	"Do you often have difficulty saying your name when someone asks you?"	Initiates conversation
Client	"Yes, I do. Mm . . ."	Sound prolongation
Clinician	"Stop." [*Avoids eye contact; sits motionless*] "You were about say . . ."	5-sec time-out Re-establishes eye contact
Client	"My name is often the most difficult to say. It is harder to say when sss . . ."	Eye contact with the clinician Sound prolongation; cessation of eye contact
Clinician	"Stop." [*Avoids eye contact; sits motionless*] "Please continue."	5-sec time-out Re-establishes eye contact
Client	"When someone asks for my name, it is especially difficult. It's not only saying my name, but also to responding when my name is called out. Answering the teacher's roll call has been a dreaded thing for me. In my-my . . ."	Fluent speech; maintains eye contact with the clinician Word repetition
Clinician	"Stop." [*Avoids eye contact; sits motionless*] "Okay, in your . . ."	5-sec time-out Re-establishes eye contact
Client	"In my grade school classes, I was just terrified when the teacher's roll call approached my name. I knew the previous four or five names! It was a terrible count-down for me! No matter how I answered—sometimes I would attempt a *yes* and at other times I would try to say *here*, but I almost always stuttered. I preferred to raise my hand, but some of my teachers wouldn't look at the class when they called the names out. One teacher wanted us to shout *here* at her when she called the names out. Her eyes were fixed on the roll-call print-out."	Fluent speech; no time-out

Pause-and-Talk in Conversation, continued

Scripts for Pause-and-Talk in Conversation		Note
Clinician	"Did you have any therapy in grade schools for your stuttering?"	Initiates a new topic of conversation
Client	"I-I . . ."	Dysfluency; cessation of eye contact
Clinician	"Stop." [*Avoids eye contact; sits motionless*] "Yes, continue."	5-sec time-out Re-establishes eye contact
Client	"I had several years of therapy in my elementary and intermediate schools. I remember going to my school speech teachers once a week and sometimes maybe twice a week. I don't remember what we did in my elementary school, but when I was eleven or twelve, I remember them asking me to speak slowly. Something about breathing, too, that I am not sure now. Maybe I was asked to take a deep breath and talk slowly. I did that for a couple of years."	Fluent speech; no time-out
Clinician	"Did that therapy help? If so, how long did the improvement last?"	Continues conversation Maintains eye contact
Client	"I think I stuttered less when I was doing it during my therapy time. But it was really hard for me to speak slowly in other situations. I don't think I ever was fluent at school and home like most other kids. Oh, I just remembered! I had some therapy during my first year in high school, too! The th-th . . ."	Fluent speech Part-word repetition; cessation of eye contact
Clinician	"Stop." [*Avoids eye contact; sits motionless*] "Go ahead!"	5-sec time-out Re-establishes eye contact
Client	"The therapist in high school was a much older woman than my earlier therapists. We talked a lot about my stuttering, how I felt about it, and how others reacted to it, what I did about other people's reaction—and all that. It was mostly about my feelings. We may have talked about the same things for several sessions. I felt like my stuttering was something I had to somehow manage. I just didn't like going for therapy in my high school years. I think I stopped going after a while. My parents didn't press me about it and my stuttering didn't seem to bother my friends."	Fluent speech; no time-out
Clinician	"I see. What about your college years? Did you have much trouble speaking? Did you have any therapy?"	Continues conversation

Pause-and-Talk in Conversation, continued

Scripts for Pause-and-Talk in Conversation		Note
Client	"Yes, my stuttering was quite noticeable in college. I was terrified about making presentations in front of the class. When I had to take that mandatory speech class, I went to my professor to see if there was a way to avoid that dreaded speech to the class. I confessed my fear of speaking in front of the class due to my stuttering problem. My professor bluntly told me there was no way to avoid the speech. It's a speech class!—he reminded me. He then told me there is a speech clinic on campus where I can get help. I k-k- . . . "	Fluent speech Dysfluency; cessation of eye contact
Clinician	"Stop." [*Avoids eye contact; sits motionless*] "Okay, tell me."	5-sec time-out Re-establishes eye contact
Client	"I kind of considered going to the speech clinic on campus, but never really felt comfortable seeking help. I can't explain it. It's almost 10 years since I graduated from college. Now I think I should have gotten help then. Maybe it would have been more effective than my previous therapies in schools."	Fluent speech; no time-out
Clinician	"Perhaps. Now let me ask you this. What was your major in college? Also tell me about your job now."	Suggests new topics
Client	"I-I-I . . . "	Word repetition; cessation of eye contact
Clinician	"Stop." "You were saying . . . "	5-sec time-out Re-establishes eye contact
Client	"I majored in journalism. I always wanted to be a journalist. I was not so much interested in reporting from the field, but I was very interested in the editorial aspects of newspaper publishing. Nn . . . "	Fluent speech; no time-out Dysfluency; cessation of eye contact
Clinician	"Stop." [*gestures to continue*]	5-sec time-out Re-establishes eye contact
Client	"Now I am working as an assistant editor of a large newspaper. It's a lot of fun. I enjoy my job very much, although I have very little free time. I get to write some editorials and edit most major news reports."	Fluent speech; no time-out
Clinician	"That sounds like a nice job!"	

Continue to administer pause-and-talk in this manner until the client's stuttering is reduced signifi-cantly. When the stuttering rate is well under 5%, initiate pause-and-talk treatment at the level of narrative speech.

Treatment of Stuttering in Adults:
III. Pause-and-Talk

Establishing Fluency in Narrative Speech

Overview

To establish fluent narrative speech in adults with the pause-and-talk method, the clinician should have the client talk continuously on a single topic. Instead of the conversational format used in the previous protocols, the clinician would ask the client to talk on a topic for extended duration. The clinician would only occasionally ask questions or offer comments to stimulate continuous speech from the client.

General Treatment Strategy

The topic selected for narrative speech should be client-specific. Perhaps the client will talk about varied topics over several sessions. Because the clients choose their topics to talk about, it is not productive to write protocols for multiple topics. A single topic is illustrated in the protocol. Using this protocol, the clinician can have the client talk on several topics to establish stutter-free speech in narrative or continuous speech.

In this stage of treatment, the clinician should continue to maintain normal communicative interactions during fluent productions and impose the time-out duration for each dysfluency. Encouraging the client to talk on multiple topics, the clinician will seek to strengthen fluency in spontaneous and extended speech.

Treatment of Stuttering in Adults:
III. Pause-and-Talk

Treatment Protocol for Narrative Speech

Scripts for Pause-and-Talk in Narration		Note
Clinician	"You have been doing really well in speaking fluently. Have you noticed your stuttering is way down? Your speech has been very fluent for several sessions now. I think it is time that we moved on to the next, more complex, stage of treatment. Now I want you to speak continuously on a topic of your choice. I may ask a few questions or make a comment here and there, but I will let you talk continuously. Today we will find topics to talk about, but from next time on, you may want to bring a list of topics on which you will talk. It is all up to your interest. I will give you my full attention. As before, anytime you begin to stutter, I will stop you. Can you think of a topic on which you can talk for a while? You have not told me much about your family. Maybe you can fill me in. You can narrate details about your childhood, where you were born, your parents, their occupations, your siblings, and so forth. But remember to talk for an extended period of time, like you are giving a brief lecture."	Introduces the new narrative task
Client	"Okay. My wife and I have lived in California for the past ten years. But I am originally from Minnesota. I was born in a small town called Winona, Minnesota. There were maybe some 10,000 people living in that town, just south of Rochester where they have the Mayo Clinic. But the town had three colleges. Two private Catholic colleges and one state university campus. So there were a lot of young, wide-eyed, vibrant students in town, which made it kind of nice. Without the colleges, Winona would have been a little sleepy village. During my childhood days, we had no shopping malls. No big stores, except for JC Penneys. Even that wasn't too big. There was a tiny Sears, which carried no merchandise, because it was only a catalog store. J-j-j- . . . "	Talks continuously and fluently for a while; no time-out A part-word repetition
Clinician	"Stop." [gestures to continue]	5-sec time-out Re-establishes eye contact

Pause-and-Talk in Narration, continued

Scripts for Pause-and-Talk in Narration		Note
Client	"Just a few locally owned stores in downtown. The usual grocery shops, auto repair shops, a Radio Shack, a downtown movie theatre, a hardware store, one nursery, a few small stores that sold clothes . . . and that was mostly it. Now they have shopping malls with all the usual big stores like Wall Mart and Target and Mervyns. "Let me see. What more can I say about Winona. Oh yeah, when I was growing up there, there were hardly any restaurants in town. McDonalds and Kentucky Fried Chicken, of course. But there was one very nice seafood restaurant. Everyone went there, dressed up to eat. I think there was one more formal restaurant in a Holiday Inn, the classiest hotel in town. They have several new restaurants now. Including some Mexican and Chinese places."	Fluent speech; no time-out A slight pause, which prompts the clinician to ask questions
Clinician	"I have never been to Minnesota. What is the area like? Flat or hilly? I suspect the winters must be awful. Well, at least for a Californian like me."	Stimulates more continuous speech
Client	"Yes, you will find the winters quite unbearable. Below zero wind-chill factor is quite common. Tons of snow, but it is white powdery, pretty snow. Another nice thing about it is that it may snow for a day or two, and then the sun comes out, bright and shiny. Clear sunlight reflected from that pure white stuff! I tell you, you need your sunglasses. You plug your car into electric outlets in apartment parking lots!"	Fluent speech; no time-out
Clinician	"What? You plug-in cars in parking lots? How do you do that?"	
Client	"Yes, you do! If not, there is often no way to start your car in the morning. An electric cord hangs out of your radiator. You plug that into one of the outlets lined up in parking lots. It keeps the radiator warm. I liked the winters there. It's really beautiful. Fall is wonderful, too. Winona is in a beautiful setting. High bluffs on either side of the town. On one side flows the mighty Mississippi river and on the other side you see beautiful hills. Gorgeous color in fall. Like Monet covered the hills with a huge painting. There is a small lake in the middle of the town. Freezes in winter, so *(continued)*	Fluent speech; no time-out

Pause-and-Talk in Narration, continued

Scripts for Pause-and-Talk in Narration		Note
Client *(continues)*	"you can see dedicated fishermen in the middle of the lake, ice fishing. Their vehicles parked right on what used to be a lake earlier in the season. Once in a few years, too eager a fisherman, usually from out of town, would drive on thin ice and qui-qui . . . "	Dysfluency; cessation of eye contact
Clinician	"Stop." [*Avoids eye contact; sits motionless*] "Alright. Tell me now."	5-sec time-out Re-establishes eye contact
Client	" . . . quickly sink to the bottom of the lake. The highway from Winona to La Crosse, Wisconsin area is one of the most scenic roads in the area. It may even rank as one of the most scenic in the entire country. At various places, the road parallels the Mississippi. I loved driving up and down that beautiful highway."	A slight pause, which prompts the clinician to ask a question
Clinician	"Do you have family in Winona?"	Prompts more speech
Client	"Yes, I do. My parents still live there. My Mom taught at Winona High and my Dad managed an independently owned hardware store downtown. Both are now retired, but they still live in the same large house on a tree-lined street where they raised the three of us. I have one brother and one sister. My brother Todd is older than me and he now lives with his family in Minneapolis. He studied at the University of Minnesota, earned a degree in agriculture, and got a job in a large grain company. He married his high school sweetheart. Belinda, his wife, works at a bank and they have two teenage children. My sister Katie is younger than me, so that makes me the middle man! Katie just graduated from University of Illinois at Urbana-Champaign, with a degree in computer science. She is a software specialist and works for some big computer company in Chicago. She loves the city and wants to live there forever. Maybe she also thinks that Chi-chi- . . . "	Fluent speech; no time-out A part-word repetition
Clinician	"Stop." [*Avoids eye contact; sits motionless*] "Okay." [*gestures to continue*]	5-sec time-out Re-establishes eye contact
Client	"Maybe she also thinks that Chicago is not a bad place to find a husband. She has a nice *(continued)*	

Pause-and-Talk in Narration, continued

Scripts for Pause-and-Talk in Narration		Note
Client *(continues)*	apartment in a high-rise building, overlooking Lake Michigan. I get to stay in her apartment whenever I go to Chicago on business. The view of the lake from her living room and dining area is spectacular."	Fluent production; no time-out

A slight pause, which prompts the clinician to ask a question |
| Clinician | "Do you travel much on business?" | Prompts continued speech |
| Client | "Not much, now that I am in the editorial department. Previously, I used to travel to other cities regularly where we have sister newspapers. Our company owns newspapers in several states. I would visit the offices of individual newspapers for a variety of reasons and various kinds of meetings. Ever since I moved to the editorial department, my travel is limited to Chicago. I go once in two or three months to Chicago because our corporate headquarters is housed there. I attend some editorial meetings. Editors from other parts of the country also come to the Chicago office. It's entirely fine that I have to go there, because I love to see my sister regularly. Typically my office meetings are on a Thursday and Friday. If I can manage it, I might stay over Saturday and spend time with Katie. Of course, not during winter. I think Chicago dishes it out much worse than Minnesota does. Man, that bone-chilling wind from the lake!" | Fluent production; no time-out

A slight pause, which prompts the clinician to ask a question |
| Clinician | "How often do you go back to Minnesota to see your parents? And to see your brother and his family?" | Prompts continued speech |
| Client | "I wish it were more often than it really is. We have the typical Thanksgiving or Christmas get-together at my parents' house in Winona. One year it is Christmas and the other year it is Thanksgiving. That means at least once a year. My sister shows up and my brother and his family usually arrive a day earlier because they live within driving distance. One of the two annual get-togethers is always at my house. They all enjoy visiting me in sunny California during the winter. Last Christmas, they all visited me and found themselves under gloomy and rainy skies." | Fluent speech; no time-out

A slight pause, which prompts the clinician to ask a question |
| Clinician | "Well you haven't told me about yourself. Do you have a family of your own?" | Prompts continued speech |

Pause-and-Talk in Narration, continued

Scripts for Pause-and-Talk in Narration		Note
Client	"I thought you would never ask! Well, mmmm . . ."	Sound prolongation
Clinician	"Stop." [*Avoids eye contact; sits motionless*] "Okay." [*gestures to continue*]	5-sec time-out Re-establishes eye contact
Client	"Well, my family is limited to my parents, my sister, and my brother and his family. I never married. I started working as soon as I graduated and I have been as happy as I have been busy."	Fluent production
Clinician	"How do you spend your free time? What are your hobbies? Do you have a lot of friends in town?"	Asks a series of questions to prompt continuous speech
Client	"Free time? What's that? Newspaper editors have very little free time. We have to work nonstop. On paper, I get a day off in a week, but often I end up working at home. These computers and high-speed internet connections are killers. What they do is to kill anyone's free time. It's like being in your office all the time! You are always in touch with your boss, it feels like. But I am very particular about taking a two-week vacation each year. I love to travel abroad. My favorite continent is Africa. I have visited Africa some 10 times now. I have been to most all the countries and to every great national wildlife park in Africa. I love to watch the animals in their natural habitat. With all the tourists and luxury lodges and everything, I don't know how natural their habitats are any more, but it is still very nice to see them over there. Nothing like seeing them in a zoo, no matter how nice, large, and naturalistic the zoo is."	Fluent speech
Clinician	[*continues to administer the pause-and-talk procedure for additional time and sessions with narrative speech*]	

To stabilize fluency, continue to treat the client in the manner described. Revert to conversational speech if necessary. Offer additional narrative experiences to the client. Probe for fluency and stuttering when the client has maintained fluency at 98% or better across three sessions.

Treatment of Stuttering in Adults:
III. Pause-and-Talk

Treatment Recording Sheet

Personalize and print this page from the CD.

Name of the client:	DOB:
Address:	Phone:
Diagnosis: Stuttering	Session date(s):
Clinician:	Comments:

Chart the client's progress for each session with your preferred method. You may calculate a percent dysfluency or stuttering rate based on the number of words spoken. If more detailed data are warranted, score the individual dysfluency types and add them up to calculate the dysfluency rate.

Essential Measures		Optional Measures: Frequency of Specific Dysfluency Types					
Dates of Service	Percent Stuttering	Prolongations	Pauses	Repetitions	Interjections	Revisions	Incomplete Phrases

Treatment of Stuttering in Adult:
III. Pause-and-Talk

Probe Protocol

Probe Procedure

- Record two conversational speech samples, each 5 to 7 minutes in duration
- Record a 3-minute monologue; ask the client to talk about a topic such as:
  - Vacations
  - Job-related experiences
  - Favorite games, TV shows, or movies
  - Hobbies and weekend activities
  - Current events
  - Family and friends
  - Recently read books
  - Any other client-specific topic
- Obtain a 5-minute home speech sample
- Have the client bring a 5 to 10-minute home speech sample
- Analyze the percent dysfluency or stuttering rate
- Personalize the *Probe Recording Sheet* and record the dysfluency or stuttering rates; print the sheet for client's clinical file

Treatment of Stuttering in Adults:
III. Pause-and-Talk

Probe Recording Sheet

Personalize and print this page from the CD.

Name of the client:	DOB:
Address:	Phone:
Diagnosis: Stuttering	Session date(s):
Clinician:	Comments:

Analyze the probe speech samples with your preferred method. You may calculate a percent dysfluency or stuttering rate based on the number of words spoken. If more detailed data are warranted, score the individual dysfluency types and add them up to calculate the dysfluency rate.

Take at least three clinic probe samples. If possible, obtain three extraclinic probe samples.

Essential Measures		Optional Measures: Frequency of Specific Dysfluency Types					
Dates/Setting of Probe	Percent Stuttering	PRO	PAU	REP	INT	REV	INC
1. /mm/dd/yy/ Clinic							
2. /mm/dd/yy/ Clinic							
3. /mm/dd/yy/ Clinic							
1. /mm/dd/yy/ Home							
2. /mm/dd/yy/ Office							
3. /mm/dd/yy/ A public place							

PRO (Prolongations); PAU (Pauses); REP (Repetitions); INT (Interjections); REV (Revisions); INC (Incomplete phrases).

Dismiss the client from current services when the client's stuttering or dysfluency rate stays below the target percentage in conversational probes. Suggested criterion is less than 2% dysfluency rate in the clinic and less than 5% in natural settings. Schedule follow-ups and booster treatments as needed.

Treatment of Stuttering in Adults:
IV. Minimal Prolongation Plus Pause-and-Talk

Overview

For several decades, fluency shaping has been used around the world as a standard treatment for adults who stutter. Its origin is in the effects of delayed auditory feedback (DAF) which induces slower rate of speech and syllable prolongations (Goldiamond, 1965). It soon became evident that delayed auditory feedback is not necessary to induce a slower and prolonged speech in people who stutter. Instructions and modeling are just as effective and are more attractive because they do not cost anything to the client or the clinician.

Fluency shaping is a general term that includes airflow management, gentle phonatory onset, and syllable prolongation. This procedure has several limitations. The most significant limitations include an unnatural-sounding speech and poor maintenance of fluency. Essentially, fluency shaping does not immediately result in normal fluency; it generates stutter-free speech. Clients who have learned to avoid stuttering by this method feel that they need to constantly monitor their speech rate, instead of what they want to say. They believe that their slow and monotonous speech is socially unacceptable. Consequently, they begin to speak at rates that are not conducive to maintain their stutter-free speech; the result is a relapse of stuttering.

An effective alternative for fluency shaping is pause-and-talk (time-out). In this procedure, the clinician pays attention to speech that is fluent, but terminates attention immediately when stuttering is imminent, or a stuttering has just begun. The clinician says "Stop!" at the earliest sign of a stutter, terminates eye contact, sits motionless for 5 seconds, and then re-establishes eye contact to suggest that the client may continue to talk. This procedure, though very effective, may be problematic with clients who have a high dysfluency rate. If a person's stuttering is very severe (e.g., in excess of 30% dysfluency rate), the technique may be inefficient, even if it reduces stuttering. Such a client is likely to experience more time-out periods than fluent speech durations that receive positive social reinforcement. Consequently the method may be both inefficient and unpleasant to administer; it may be frustrating to clients.

Persons with very severe stuttering may be excellent candidates for an experimental type of treatment in which a very slight syllable prolongation is combined with pause-and-talk (Ahlander, 1999). The method does not include the full-fledged fluency shaping; it includes only one of its components, that too, in a severely truncated form: a very slight prolongation of the initial syllable of the initial word of utterances. The method does not force blending of words or prolongation of all syllables in an utterance. The degree of prolongation used in this combined treatment is always minimal enough to eliminate most stuttering. Because a majority of stuttering tends to occur on the first word in a phrase or sentence, a slight prolongation of the initial syllable of the first word is often effective in eliminating most stuttering. This reduction then lets the pause-and-talk procedure to play its role effectively: reduce the remaining dysfluencies effectively.

Advantages of Minimal Prolongation Plus Pause-and-Talk

A significant advantage is that the technique helps avoid the negative side effects of a comprehensive or full-fledged fluency shaping procedure. By inducing only a minimal prolongation of the initial syllable of the first words of each utterance, the method minimizes the devastating effects of the traditional prolonged speech on speech prosody and naturalness. By itself, such a minimal prolongation may be inefficient, ineffective, or both. But when combined with the other effective procedure—pause-and talk, the technique may be effective in inducing natural-sounding speech from the very beginning of treatment.

The combination enhances the effectiveness of pause-and-talk as well. As noted earlier, pause-and-talk may be inefficient, unpleasant, or both in cases of severe stuttering. By reducing most of the stutterings on the initial position of words, the technique makes pause-and-talk a much more pleasant, as well as effective, procedure.

In essence, the combination of minimal prolongation and pause-and-talk avoids the limitations of both and amplifies the advantages of each.

Treatment of Stuttering in Adults:
IV. Minimal Prolongation Plus Pause-and-Talk

Establishing Fluency in Conversational Speech

Overview

- Treatment may be started with conversational speech
- The client is asked to prolong only the first syllable (or the first syllable following the initial consonant of a word)
- The degree of prolongation, unlike in the comprehensive fluency shaping, is kept to a minimum
- The client does not prolong all syllables in the first word nor any syllables in subsequent words produced in an utterance; there is no insistence that the client blend words into a smooth string of syllables (which is done in the comprehensive fluency shaping procedure)
- The clinician tells the client to stop talking at the earliest sign of a stutter and avoids eye contact for 5 seconds. The clinician sits motionless during this time-out duration.
- At the end of the duration of no positive reinforcement, the clinician re-establishes eye contact, suggests verbally or nonverbally that the client now can continue to talk

To begin with, the clinician describes the minimal prolongation plus pause-and-talk. Making modifications as found necessary for a given client, and following a general sequence, the clinician:

- Establishes baserates of dysfluencies or stuttering as defined. To obtain reliable baserates of dysfluencies in adults, the clinician tape-records an extended conversational speech. Topic cards, which suggest various topics of conversation (e.g., *favorite games and sports, vacations, current social and political issues, work-related experiences, hobbies, movies, TV shows*), may be useful with most adults. An oral reading sample also may be obtained to assess the differential stuttering rates in oral reading versus conversational speech. A 3- to 5-minute monologue on a topic of interest also may be recorded. If practical, the clinician obtains a home speech sample for analysis of dysfluencies or stuttering. After establishing baserates, the clinician initiates treatment; begins with the slight syllable prolongation.

- Describes and models a slight prolongation of the initial syllable of the first word in phrases or sentences. Teaches this minimal prolongation as an isolated skill on a few trials. The clinician teaches the client to slightly extend the duration of vowels following the initial consonants. A few successful trials at the single word level should be sufficient to move on to the next step.

- Gives a quick overview of pause-and-talk. Emphasizes that the client will be asked to stop talking at the earliest sign of a stutter and that the client should cease talking for a duration of about 5 seconds.

- Conducts this treatment mostly in conversational speech and manages the behavioral treatment contingencies promptly and strictly. The clinician makes sure that the initial syllables are slightly prolonged and that the client does not talk during the time-out duration. The clinician offers positive verbal reinforcement for syllable prolongation, and offers only keenly interested attention for fluent speech (no verbal praise for being fluent as such); and sudden withdrawal of attention at the earliest sign of a stutter.

- Shifts treatment to narrative speech when the client has sustained adopted criterion of fluency (e.g., 98% fluency across three consecutive sessions).

- Dismisses the client when the client meets the adopted dismissal criterion (e.g., 95% fluency in natural settings).

- Trains family members, friends, and client-selected colleagues to recognize various forms of dysfluencies and to prompt and reinforce fluent speech in home, office, and other nonclinical settings. If practical, spouses or other family members may be trained to hold informal treatment sessions at home. Such training may begin as soon as the client sustains stutter-free speech in the clinic. These steps are essential for maintenance of fluency.

- Conducts follow-up assessments and arranges for booster treatment when the results of a follow-up warrant additional treatment. The initial follow-up may be scheduled for 3 months following the dismissal. Additional follow-ups may be scheduled at 6 or 12 month intervals. In all follow-up sessions, the clinician takes an extended speech sample without treatment to calculate the percent stuttering or dysfluency rates.

Treatment of Stuttering in Adults:
IV. Minimal Prolongation Plus Pause-and-Talk

Treatment Protocol for Conversational Speech

Scripts for Establishing Fluency in Conversation		Note
Clinician	"There are a few options for you to speak more fluently than you do now. I have selected a treatment procedure in which you will be doing two things. The procedure is a combination of two techniques, both known to be effective when applied individually. First, you will slightly prolong or stretch the initial syllable of the first word in a phrase or sentence. This stretching will slow your speech, but only minimally. You will not be stretching all the syllables you produce, although there is a technique in which you do that. Have you ever received therapy in which you have practice slow and stretched speech before?"	The clinician introduces the treatment procedure
Client	"No, I have not. I consulted with a psychologist once and we just talked about my stuttering and how I felt about it and the like."	
Clinician	[*modeling syllable stretching*] "Slow and stretched speech like this reduces stuttering. Have you sometimes used this technique of slowing down to speak more fluently?"	Models slow speech
Client	"Yes. I have tried slow speech to avoid stuttering."	
Clinician	"Has it worked?"	
Client	"Yes, it has, although it is difficult to do it all the time."	
Clinician	"That's right. Even a simple task like that needs to be systematically practiced. Although stretching all or most of the words one speaks is used as a therapy procedure, I will not be asking you to do that. I only want you to stretch the first syllable after the initial sound in a word. That, too, you don't have to stretch too much. [*stretching the syllable in* juust] Just a little like I just did. Although stretching most of the syllables eliminates stuttering, the resulting speech sounds unnatural. Therefore, I want you to stretch minimally and only the first syllable in the first word of a phrase or sentence you say."	Describes and demonstrates minimal syllable prolongation of the initial syllable

Establishing Fluency in Conversation, continued

Scripts for Establishing Fluency in Conversation		Note
Client	"Sounds good."	
Clinician	"Okay, then the second thing I want you to do is to stop talking for a brief duration anytime you stutter.	
	"This procedure is called *pause-and-talk*, the second component of treatment I have selected for you. Research has shown that it is effective in treating stuttering in older students, adolescents, and adults. It is a simple procedure, but it has to be done very precisely to be effective. In all treatment sessions, we will be talking as two conversational partners. You will stretch slightly the initial syllable of words that begin a phrase or a sentence. [*models*] *Laaike* this. This stretching will eliminate quite a few of your dysfluencies. As long as you are talking fluently—without a stutter—I will listen to you with my full attention. You can continue to talk as long as you are fluent. But the instant I notice a stutter, I will ask you to stop talking. You must stop talking when I say "Stop!" It is very important that you don't continue to stutter, and that you terminate speech instantly. As soon as I say "Stop," I will look away from your face for about five seconds. I may look at my watch, or simply avoid eye contact with you and stay quiet for those five seconds. Those five seconds are your pause period. You pause after every stutter; actually, you pause when it appears like you are going to stutter. I might say "Stop" even as I find a slight indication of a stutter. For instance, if I see a slight tension in your lips or forehead, I might say "Stop," and you immediately stop talking. At the end of the five-second pause duration, I will look at your face again to re-establish our eye contact. You can then talk again. I might say something like 'you may talk now,' or 'please continue,' but as soon as I look at you, it means the pause duration is over and that you can begin talking immediately. So, you stop talking when you begin to stutter and pause for five seconds. You then start talking again, but with a slight syllable stretching. Am I making it clear? Can you describe the procedure to me?"	Describes pause-and-talk

Establishing Fluency in Conversation, continued

Scripts for Establishing Fluency in Conversation		Note
Client	"Yes, you are clear. I should stretch the initial syllable and talk. If I stutter, you say "Stop!" and I should stop talking until you signal me to continue. I then start talking. I should stretch the first syllable as I begin to talk."	Understands the procedure
Clinician	"Exactly. And you stretch the first syllable of each new phrase or sentence you say. Even if you say just one word, you stretch the first syllable. In essence, the stretching will help eliminate stuttering on the first words of your utterances and pause-and-talk will help reduce the remaining stuttering."	Summarizes the procedure
Client	"Sounds good to me."	
Clinician	"We will start with conversational speech. When you have sustained fluency in conversation for a few sessions, I will be asking you to talk on a topic for extended periods of time. For now, it will be usual conversation. I want you to look at me when you talk. I will ask a series of simple questions about you and your family and your work; it's all for the sake of conversation. You should answer each question with the initial syllable stretch. Okay?"	Sets the stage for conversational speech
Client	"Okay."	
Clinician	"Where do you live? If you are starting with the word *I*, stretch and say it like this—*aaai*."	Initiates conversation; models syllable stretching
Client	"Aaai live in Modesto."	Correct initial syllable stretching; no other syllables stretched
Clinician	"Excellent! You stretched the initial syllable. That's exactly what I want you to do. "How far is Modesto from here ?"	Verbal praise for initial syllable stretching
Client	"Eeet [*it*] is an hour from here. Wheen [*when*] the traffic is not bad, that is. Duuuing [*during*] the rush hour, it may take up to 90 minutes. Haaiway ninety-nine is getting worse day-by-day. T-t- . . . "	Eye contact with the clinician Correct syllable stretching A sound repetition
Clinician	"Stop." [*Avoids eye contact; sits motionless*] "Please continue."	5-sec time-out Re-establishes eye contact

Establishing Fluency in Conversation, continued

Scripts for Establishing Fluency in Conversation		Note
Client	"Traaaffic was not bad today, though. I made it in 50 minutes."	Initial syllable stretching Fluent speech; maintains eye contact with the clinician
Clinician	"How long have you lived in Modesto? Where did you live before that?"	Continues conversation Maintains eye contact
Client	"Aaaai have lived in Modesto for the past 10 years. Beeefore that, I lived in Bakersfield for five years. Preeeviously [*previously*], I have lived in Los Angeles, Visalia, and San Diego as well."	Fluent speech; no time-out
Clinician	"Are you now kind of settled in Modesto now?"	Continues conversation Maintains eye contact
Client	"Yees [*yes*], I think so. Aaai better be! Tooo much moving around. Aaai think I have finally found a place I am comfortable with. Eeeet [*it*] is the right p-p-p . . . "	Initial syllable stretching Sound repetition
Clinician	"Stop." [*Avoids eye contact; sits motionless*] "Yes, continue."	5-sec time-out Re-establishes eye contact
Client	"Eeet is the right place for my business."	Initial syllable stretch; fluent speech
Clinician	"What kind of business do you have?"	Continues conversation Maintains eye contact
Client	"Aaai own a restaurant in town."	Initial syllable stretching
Clinician	"What kind of food do you serve at your restaurant?"	Continues conversation Maintains eye contact
Client	[*stretches the initial syllable*] "Mine is a Thai restaurant."	For ease of reading, **syllable stretching is not orthographically shown from here on**
Clinician	"Why did you settle on running a Thai restaurant, not being a Thai yourself?"	Continues conversation Maintains eye contact
Client	[*stretches the initial syllable*] "You can tell I am not Thai! My wife and I decided to open and manage a Thai restaurant because we love Thai food. [*stretches the initial syllable*] Plus, when we opened our restaurant, there were no Thai places in town. [*stretches the initial syllable*] It looked like a good business decision. [*stretches the initial syllable*] Of course, there are now at least half a dozen Thai restaurants in town. [*stretches the initial syllable*] But we were the pioneers! "	Initial syllable stretching; fluent speech; no time-out

Establishing Fluency in Conversation, continued

Scripts for Establishing Fluency in Conversation		Note
Clinician	"They sound like good reasons to open a new business. How did you and your wife first acquire a taste for Thai food?"	Continues conversation Maintains eye contact
Client	[*stretches the initial syllables of each initial word in sentences*] "We had eaten Thai food in some restaurants in Los Angeles and New York City before. [*fails to stretch*] B-b- . . ."	Correct initial syllable stretching until the stutter Part-word repetition
Clinician	"Stop." [*Avoids eye contact; sits motionless*] "Go ahead, please!"	5-sec time-out Re-establishes eye contact
Client	[*stretches the initial syllables of each initial word in sentences*] "But what really prompted us to venture into opening a Thai restaurant was our visit to Thailand. A few years ago, my wife Kendra and I vacationed for a few days in Thailand. We ate plenty of good Thai food there and fell in love with Thai cuisine. [*fails to stretch*] Sss . . ."	Correct initial syllable stretching in each sentence Sound prolongation
Clinician	"Stop." [*Avoids eye contact; sits motionless*] "Okay . . ."	5-sec time-out Re-establishes eye contact
Client	[*stretches the initial syllable*] "So we decided to open a Thai restaurant when we returned home."	Fluent speech; no time-out
Clinician	"What were you guys doing then? Before you went into the restaurant business, I mean."	Continues conversation Maintains eye contact
Client	[*stretches the initial syllables of each initial word in sentences*] "My wife and I are both teachers. I was teaching geography in Modesto High. My wife was teaching elementary school. But we were both burned out. We needed a career change. We had always fancied owning some kind of business. After our visit to Th-th- . . ."	Fluent speech; no time-out Part-word repetition
Clinician	"Stop." [*Avoids eye contact; sits motionless*] "After your visit to . . ."	5-sec time-out Re-establishes eye contact
Client	[*stretches the initial syllables of each initial word in sentences*] "After our visit to Thailand, we both resigned our jobs with the schools and opened the restaurant. We have never regretted it. Our restaurant business is quite successful, although now there are other Thai restaurants in town. I think the key to our success is consistently good food at a fair *(continued)*	Fluent speech; no time-out

Establishing Fluency in Conversation, continued

Scripts for Establishing Fluency in Conversation		Note
Client *(continues)*	price. We don't increase our prices frequently and our price increases are modest. Also, I think, because we were the first to open a Thai place in town, we have many loyal customers. Many of them we know by their name. They k-k- . . . "	Part-word repetition
Clinician	"Stop." [*Avoids eye contact; sits motionless*] [*Gestures the client to continue.*]	5-sec time-out Re-establishes eye contact
Client	[*stretches the initial syllables of each initial word in sentences*] "Our customers keep coming back to us. [*shows slight hesitation*]	Fluent speech; no time-out
Clinician	"When you go out to eat, what kinds of restaurants to you go to?"	Prompts more speech; maintains eye contact
Client	[*stretches the initial syllables of each initial word in sentences*] "As you might guess, we avoid all Thai restaurants in town! We smell it each day from morning to late night. Most of the time, we eat at our restaurant. Therefore, we have no interest in eating Thai food when we go out. Actually, the reason we go out is to s-s-s . . . "	Fluent speech and correct syllable stretching Part-word repetition
Clinician	"Stop." [*Avoids eye contact; sits motionless*] "You were saying . . . "	5-sec time-out Re-establishes eye contact
Client	[*stretches the initial syllables of each initial word in sentences*] "Yeah. We go out mostly to sample different kinds of food. Sometimes we go to an Indian restaurant in town. It's pretty good. Indian and Thai cuisines share many spices. Rice is common, too. So we like Indian food. But we also enjoy Mexican, Italian, and Mediterranean food. There is really llll . . . "	Fluent speech; correct syllable stretching of initial syllables of first words in a sentence
Clinician	"Stop." [*Avoids eye contact; sits motionless*] "Yeah." [*Gestures the client to continue.*]	5-sec time-out Re-establishes eye contact
Client	[*stretches the initial syllables of each initial word in sentences*] "There is really little that we don't like, as long as they are true to a tradition or tasty innovations."	Fluent speech; no time-out
Clinician	[*Continues conversation in this manner*]	

Continue to treat with the protocols for combining a slight initial syllable stretching of only the initial words of each sentence or utterance with pause-and-talk for all dysfluencies. When fluency is stabilized at 98% or better in conversational speech sustained across at least three sessions, shift treatment to narrative speech. Use the protocols that follow to stabilize fluency in narrative speech.

Treatment of Stuttering in Adults:
IV. Minimal Prolongation Plus Pause-and-Talk

Establishing Fluency in Narrative Speech

Overview

To establish fluent narrative speech within the combined minimal prolongation of initial syllables and pause-and-talk for dysfluencies, the clinician should have the client talk continuously on a single topic. Instead of the conversational format used in the previous protocols, the clinician would ask the client to talk on a topic for extended duration. The clinician would only occasionally ask questions or offer comments to stimulate continuous speech from the client.

General Treatment Strategy

The topic selected for narrative speech should be client-specific. Perhaps the client will talk about varied topics over several sessions. Because the clients choose their topics and talk about them, it is not productive to write protocols for multiple topics. A single topic is illustrated in the protocol. Using this protocol, the clinician can have the client talk on several topics to establish stutter-free speech in narrative or continuous speech.

The clinician should continue to pay interested and enthusiastic attention to fluent narrations in all sessions. The clinician also should promptly impose the 5-second time-out on each dysfluency. Because of the treatment up to this point will have stabilized fluency in conversational speech, the client is unlikely to stutter much. Therefore, the need for time-out will be minimal.

Treatment of Stuttering in Adults:
IV. Minimal Prolongation Plus Pause-and-Talk
Treatment Protocol for Narrative Speech

Scripts for Establishing Fluency in Narration		Note
Clinician	"I am pleased with your progress so far. You have been consistently prolonging the initial syllables of the first words in each sentence. You promptly stop when I say stop because of a stutter. Your stuttering frequency is way down. I think it's time now to move on to even more continuous speech. From now on, I would like you to talk on specific topics of your interest for extended periods of time. I will be talking less and you will be talking most of the time on a topic of your choice. When you come for therapy next time, you may bring a list of topics written on a sheet of paper or you can bring topic cards. Each index card will contain a topic and you talk on one topic at a time. You can also make notes to yourself on each card, if you wish, so you can tell me more about each of them.	Explains the next stage of treatment

Suggests strategies for topic selection |
| | "To get us started today, you can tell me what it takes to open a new restaurant. All the details you had to pay attention to; all the problems you had to face. You can be as detailed as possible so you speak in a the manner of a long monologue." | Suggests a topic |
| Client | [*stretches the initial syllables of each initial word in sentences*] "Okay, that's easy. When Kendra and I decided on opening a restaurant, we had to find a place. We had to apply to the city for a restaurant license. Most important of all, we had to find a chef. We advertised for a chef in newspapers in LA and San Francisco, hoping that someone who is tired of the big city will consider our offer. Luckily, and as we hoped for, two Thai chefs responded. Both were working in restaurants in the LA area, but wanted to move to a more affordable place to live. As soon as we found out the addresses of their restaurants, we drove to LA without letting them know. We had to find out how good they were! We went to the restaurants and ate two lunches and two dinners at each place. Kendra and I compared our notes. One *(continued)* | Correct stretching of the initial syllable of initial words of sentences

Fluent speech; no time out |

Establishing Fluency in Narrative Speech, continued

Scripts for Establishing Fluency in Narration		Note
Client *(continues)*	guy was clearly better than the other. His dishes tasted better, looked better. He not only balanced spices and flavors, but also color and texture. So we hired him. It turned out to be a good move. He is not only a great chef, he is also a thorough gentleman. He had just come from Thailand to LA. He needed to get his wife from Bangkok. We helped with his application to the immigration department. It took almost a year, but his wife finally joined him. He is very grateful for that. His wife also works as a chef in our restaurant. As the business grew, we needed additional hands. We eventually hired another Thai chef from a restaurant in town who fills in when my regular chef is out. He is also very good . . . " [*slight hesitation*]	Continues his narrative speech Stretches the initial syllable of the first words in each sentence Fluent speech
Clinician	"What about finding a place for your restaurant? Could you easily find a suitable building?"	Prompts speech on a related topic; maintains eye contact
Client	[*stretches the initial syllables of each initial word in sentences*] "Well that was not all that easy. We had a business leasing agent looking for a suitable place in town. We wanted a place near downtown but not too far from the nearby big shopping mall with a lot of foot traffic. We looked at other places in town, including a shopping center just outside the town. Finally, we found a place we liked and leased it. It is inbetween downtown and the big shopping mall—the llll . . . "	Continues with narration.
Clinician	"Stop." [*Avoids eye contact; sits motionless*] "You were telling about the location of your restaurant. Has the place worked out for you?"	5-sec time-out Re-establishes eye contact
Client	[*stretches the initial syllables of each initial word in sentences*] "Yes, it has been a good location. It was the location we preferred. We get a good lunch crowd from the nearby shopping center. Our dinner customers come from all parts of the town, including some nearby towns. We are always busy. So it has worked out really well. The building was new when we leased it. It has gone through three remodelings in 10 years. Our restaurant is spacious. People seem to like it the way we have set it up. We have a modern kitchen and the chef is pleased with it. The biggest problem in running a small business like ours is to find *(continued)*	Continues with narration Fluent speech

Establishing Fluency in Narrative Speech, continued

Scripts for Establishing Fluency in Narration		Note
Client *(continues)*	reliable employees. In the beginning, we had some problems with waiters and waitresses. The turnover was high. We would train them and they would leave us within a month. Many a times Kendra and I served our customers. I think in the beginning, we didn't offer them competitive wages. Well, we just couldn't. But as our customer base improved, we increased the hourly wages for waiters and waitresses. Then they began to stay longer. Besides better wages, our waiters and waitresses began to earn more money in tips. Now we have an older woman who is very reliable. She works more hours in a week than any other. We also have three college girls who work part-time. Then we have a retired mailman who wants to earn some extra cash. He comes in whenever we need an extra hand. He is always available, so it's kind of nice." [*shows a slight hesitation*]	Fluent speech Stretches the initial syllables of each initial word in sentences
Clinician	"What about advertising, promotion, account keeping, and all that?"	Prompts continued speech; maintains eye contact
Client	[*stretches the initial syllables of each initial word in sentences*] "We don't do much advertising now. In the beginning, we did some in the local newspaper. There is a college newspaper in which we occasionally advertise because many of our customers are college students. We offer discounts to both college students and senior citizens. Now because of our good customer base, word-of-mouth is sustaining our business. That's nice because advertising regularly in newspapers is an expensive proposition. [*slight hesitation*] Oh yes, you asked about accounting. My wife is the business accountant. She is very good at keeping accurate and detailed records. She has all the computer programs needed to keep accounting records. She also pays our employees, keeps track of their attendance, gives them bonuses during Christmas, and does everything. She also has accurate records of income and expenses for our tax consultant. Our tax man says very few people bring such well organized records. I think she easily handles the work of two employees. I can't imagine our restaurant without her management."	Fluent speech

Continue to treat the client in this manner until stutter-free speech is well established and the client can maintain it almost automatically across several sessions. Subsequently, begin fading the syllable prolongation.

Treatment of Stuttering in Adults:
IV. Minimal Prolongation Plus Pause-and-Talk

Fading Syllable Prolongation

Overview

- The immediate effect of syllable prolongation, even if it is slight, is to create stutter-free but somewhat unnatural-sounding speech. Although the speech under the minimal prolongation plus pause-and-talk will not sound as unnatural as it does under the comprehensive fluency shaping procedure, the clinician still needs to pay limited attention to speech naturalness.

- Before the client is dismissed, even the slight degree of initial syllable prolongation should be faded out. This task is much less extensive than it is in the comprehensive fluency shaping procedure. In the minimal prolongation plus pause-and-talk procedure, natural-sounding speech is most effectively reinstated by fading the syllable prolongation. Because of the minimal degree of syllable prolongation used, it is relatively easier to fade it than it is in the comprehensive fluency shaping procedure. As the degree of prolongation is reduced and eventually the syllable durations approximate the normal, the speech will sound natural. Because the pause-and-talk method will still be in effect, there is little danger of stuttering returning when the prolongation of the initial syllables is faded.

- Natural-sounding fluency is induced by gradually reducing the degree of syllable prolongation. This aspect of the treatment should not take as much time as it does in the comprehensive fluency shaping procedure. In most cases, instructions to reduce syllable prolongations throughout a few treatment sessions are effective. Most adult clients will happily oblige the clinician and promptly reduce and eventually eliminate syllable prolongation.

The protocols to follow are written to achieve these goals of natural-sounding speech.

Treatment of Stuttering in Adults:
IV. Minimal Prolongation Plus Pause-and-Talk

Treatment Protocol for Fading Syllable Prolongation

Scripts for Fading Syllable Prolongation		Note
Clinician	"You have been doing really well in talking fluently. You hardly are stuttering now. Your syllable stretching is somewhat less now than it was at the beginning. I have let it go because eventually we don't want that syllable stretching. I think it is now time to reduce the amount of stretching until you no longer do it. Begin talking with only a touch of stretching."	Instructs the client to start fading the initial syllable stretching
Client	[*begins talking with reduced stretching*] "I would like that very much! I know it helped me, but I don't like this stretching business!"	Maintains fluent speech as he reduces the amount of syllable stretching
Clinician	"I think you can do it with reduced stretching. Continue to talk with only a touch of stretching, like you just did. You described what your wife's responsibilities. What are your responsibilities?"	Maintains eye contact; encourages to talk fluently with reduced amount of syllable stretching
Client	[*begins talking with reduced stretching*] "I do all the purchasing. I make sure that the chefs have what they need. I have vendors for soft drinks, beer, and other restaurant supplies. I am always in touch with them to make sure that the place is well-stocked. Being a Thai restaurant, I have to buy a lot of rice every week! I have a wholesaler in San Francisco who supplies Thai Jasmine rice and a variety of spices. Every day, I go to a downtown seafood market to buy fresh fish and shrimp and all the rest. In the afternoons, I go shop for vegetables. Thai food needs a lot of fresh vegetables for all those popular vegetarian curries! Plus I supervise employees on a daily basis. Every d-d-d . . . "	Fluent speech with reduced syllable stretching Sound repetition
Clinician	"Stop." [*Avoids eye contact; sits motionless*] [*gestures to continue*]	5-sec time-out Re-establishes eye contact
Client	[*reduced stretching*] "Every day is a busy day. No time to get bored!"	Fluent speech
Clinician	"You are doing well in stretching less and less. Try to stretch even less. I think you still can be fluent. "Well, obviously, you and your wife enjoy running your restaurant. What are some of the downsides of owning such a business?"	Encourages further reduction in syllable stretching

Fading Syllable Stretching in Narrative Speech, continued

Scripts for Fading Syllable Prolongation		Note
Client	[*barely noticeable syllable stretching*] "Plenty of things to say! For the two of us who own the place, the biggest problem was lack of free time. We close the place only once a week—on Mondays. On Mondays, we are busy at home. Cleaning, washing, ironing, shopping for the home. All the household chores need to be finished on Mondays. For the first five or six years, we didn't take a vacation at all! That's depressing because Kendra and I love to travel. For the last few years, we have been able to take a week-long vacation a year. Sometimes twice a year. A huge improvement! This is now possible because of Kendra's cousin moved to town a few years ago. She doesn't work outside the home, but is willing to help us out. Kendra trained Jamie and her husband Tom to take care of the business for a few days each week. We pay them generously and they have been doing a great job of managing the place when we are gone. Their help has restored our mental health!"	Fluent speech with barely noticeable syllable stretching
Clinician	[*Continues treatment in this manner until the syllable stretching is completely faded out and the client's fluency sounds natural. Stabilizes natural-sounding fluency across several sessions until the client reports satisfactory fluency in natural settings.*]	Administers time-out if the client exhibits dysfluencies

Some clients need to talk on more topics and over several sessions than other clients. Some clients need to go at a slower pace in fading syllable stretching whereas others can move relatively fast.

Treatment of Stuttering in Adults:
IV. Minimal Prolongation Plus Pause-and-Talk

Treatment Recording Sheet

Personalize and print this page from the CD.

Name of the client:	DOB:
Address:	Phone:
Diagnosis: Stuttering	Session date(s):
Clinician:	Comments:

Chart the client's progress for each session with your preferred method. You may calculate a percent dysfluency or stuttering rate based on the number of words spoken. If more detailed data are warranted, score the individual dysfluency types and add them up to calculate the dysfluency rate.

Essential Measures		Optional Measures: Frequency of Specific Dysfluency Types					
Dates of Service	Percent Stuttering	Prolongations	Pauses	Repetitions	Interjections	Revisions	Incomplete Phrases

Treatment of Stuttering in Adults:
IV. Minimal Prolongation Plus Pause-and-Talk

Probe Protocol

Probe Procedure

- Record two conversational speech samples, each 5 to 7 minutes in duration
- Record a 3-minute monologue; ask the client to talk about a topic such as:
  - ➤ favorite sports
  - ➤ favorite vacations
  - ➤ favorite movies
  - ➤ favorite TV shows
  - ➤ weekend activities
  - ➤ current events of interest
  - ➤ the nature of work and work-related experiences
  - ➤ hobbies
  - ➤ newspaper articles
  - ➤ books recently read
  - ➤ any other client-specific topic
- Obtain a 5-minute home speech sample
- Record one or more extraclinic speech samples in such places as the client's work place or a restaurant
- Make a phone call and measure dysfluency rates in telephone conversations
- Analyze the percent dysfluency or stuttering rate
- Personalize the *Probe Recording Sheet* on the CD and record the dysfluency or stuttering rates; print the sheet for client's clinical file

Treatment of Stuttering in Adults:
IV. Minimal Prolongation Plus Pause-and-Talk

Probe Recording Sheet

Personalize and print this page from the CD.

Name of the client:	DOB:
Address:	Phone:
Diagnosis: Stuttering	Session date(s):
Clinician:	Comments:

Analyze the probe speech samples with your preferred method. You may calculate a percent dysfluency or stuttering rate based on the number of words spoken. If more detailed data are warranted, score the individual dysfluency types and add them up to calculate the dysfluency rate.

Take at least three clinic probe samples. If possible, obtain three extraclinic probe samples.

Essential Measures		Optional Measures: Frequency of Specific Dysfluency Types					
Dates/Setting of Probe	**Percent Stuttering**	**PRO**	**PAU**	**REP**	**INT**	**REV**	**INC**
1. /mm/dd/yy/ Clinic							
2. /mm/dd/yy/ Clinic							
3. /mm/dd/yy/ Clinic							
1. /mm/dd/yy/ Home							
2. /mm/dd/yy/ Office							
3. /mm/dd/yy/ A public place							

PRO (Prolongations); PAU (Pauses); REP (Repetitions); INT (Interjections); REV (Revisions); INC (Incomplete phrases).

Dismiss the client from current services when the client's stuttering or dysfluency rate stays below the target percentage in conversational probes. Schedule follow-ups and booster treatments as needed.

Treatment of Stuttering in Adults:
V. Promoting Maintenance of Fluency

Maintenance Strategies

Maintenance of fluency in adults who have been treated for their stuttering has been a difficult clinical problem. Maintenance following fluency shaping procedures has been especially troublesome. People who have received fluency shaping treatment, especially syllable prolongation, tend to experience a relapse of their stuttering when their constant monitoring of a slower rate of speech begins to fade. Therefore, the clinician should implement procedures designed to promote maintenance of fluency across situations and over time. The general strategies are common to most clients and applicable to all treatment procedures:

To promote maintenance of fluency, the clinician:

- Always selects the most effective procedure for the client; to improve chances of maintenance, the resulting fluency must be strong and stable and the stuttering frequency should be well below 3%; preferably, it should be below 1% at the time of dismissal.

- Gives sufficient treatment at the level of conversational speech and narrative speech; fluency not strengthened at these levels of complex speech is unlikely to be maintained.

- Teaches self-monitoring skills to the client. Instead of giving corrective feedback all the time, the clinician asks "What happened?" or "Did you forget something?" The client may say "Oh! I forgot syllable prolongation!" "I didn't breathe out!" "I didn't slow down," "I didn't pause when I stuttered" and so forth. The clinician verbally reinforces such self-monitoring skills. In using pause-and-talk, the clinician waits for a brief duration following a stutter to see if the client would stop on his or her own. When the client learns to pause on his or her own following a stutter, the clinician verbally reinforces the client for doing it (but only after the end of the time-out period).

- Initially, has a family member (or a friend or a trusted colleague) observe the treatment sessions and understand how it is implemented; responds fully to the questions the observer may have about the treatment procedure.

- Later, invites the family member into the treatment sessions; points out the important aspects of treatment and how the observer may help the client. In subsequent sessions, trains the family member to administer the treatment procedure that has worked well for the client. The clinician teaches the family member to:
  - ➢ Model fluent productions for the client
  - ➢ Verbally reinforce the client for fluent productions
  - ➢ Offer gentle corrective feedback for stutterings
  - ➢ Prompt a slower rate or airflow management before the client begins to talk
  - ➢ Remind the client to speak fluently before beginning to say something
  - ➢ Conduct home treatment at least twice a week; perhaps three times after dismissal

- Moves treatment to less structured, more naturalistic settings; takes the client out for a walk, and monitors fluency by offering verbal reinforcement and corrective feedback in a subtle manner; takes the client to shops or restaurants and asks the client to speak to strangers while monitoring one's own fluency.

- Asks the client and the family member to contact the clinic if there is an increase in stuttering rate; lets them know that a few sessions of booster treatment at a later date may help sustain fluency.
- Follows up the client and records a brief probe sample of conversational speech.
- Calculates the percent dysfluency or stuttering rate; if the rate is unacceptable, offers booster treatment.
- Encourages family members to resume treatment sessions at home.
- Schedules further follow-ups.

Treatment of Stuttering in Adults:
V. Maintenance of Fluency

Maintenance Probe Recording Sheet

Personalize and print this page from the CD.

Name of the client:	DOB:
Address:	Phone:
Diagnosis: Stuttering	Session date(s):
Clinician:	Comments:

Analyze the follow-up speech samples with your preferred method. You may calculate a percent dys-fluency or stuttering rate based on the number of words spoken. If more detailed data are warranted, score the individual dysfluency types and add them up to calculate the dysfluency rate.

Essential Measures		Optional Measures: Frequency of Specific Dysfluency Types					
Dates/setting of follow-up probe	Percent Stuttering	PRO	PAU	REP	INT	REV	INC
Follow-up #1 Date:							
Follow-up #2 Date:							
Follow-up #3 Date							

Offer booster treatment if the follow-up probe dysfluency rates are unacceptable. On completion of the booster treatment, schedule additional follow-up sessions.

Glossary

Baserates. The natural frequency of dysfluencies or stuttering (as defined by the clinician) before an intervention program is started; multiple observations often needed to establish their reliability; needed to show improvement under treatment; established through conversational speech samples.

Booster Treatment. Treatment offered to clients sometimes after they were discharged from their initial treatment; follows maintenance probes that show a need for additional treatment; the clients may receive the original treatment in a few sessions, or may receive a new and effective form of treatment; designed to promote maintenance of fluency in natural settings and across time.

Comprehensive Fluency Shaping Procedure. A treatment package that includes airflow management for producing fluent speech, reduced speech rate through syllable prolongation, blending of words, and natural-sounding speech; an effective procedure used worldwide for many decades; induces unnatural-sounding speech, hence, the need to reshape natural-sound speech in the later stages of treatment; associated with a high rate of stuttering relapse, which may be mitigated by systematic follow-up and periodic booster treatment; appropriate for older students, adolescents, and adults.

Corrective Feedback. Verbal statements that inform the client that a target fluency skill was not produced or that there was a stutter; a procedure designed to reduce errors in managing fluency skills and stuttering during treatment; may include such verbal statements as "Stop! You did not prolong the syllables!," "No, that was a stutter," and so forth.

Delayed Auditory Feedback. A treatment procedure in which the speaker's own speech is fed back to his or her ears through headphones after a brief delay; possible with small, portable, electronic units; results in slow and monotonous speech that is stutter-free; the origin of modern stutter-free prolonged speech treatment; not recommended because it is unnecessary; effect now achieved through instructions and modeling, as in the comprehensive fluency shaping procedure or the prolonged speech procedure.

Dysfluencies. Speech characteristics that impair fluency; include part-word, whole-word, and phrase repetitions; speech-sound prolongations, silent prolongations of articulatory postures; silent pauses; broken words or intralexical pauses; interjections of sounds, syllables, words, and phrases; revisions; and incomplete phrases; in diagnosing stuttering, some clinicians consider only part-word repetitions and speech-sound prolongations as stutterings; others count all kinds of dysfluencies; some clinicians use a quantitative criterion (e.g., 5% dysfluency rate) to diagnose stuttering; others make global and clinical judgments of stuttering.

Fading. Gradually reducing a response property (e.g., the degree of syllable prolongation) or the clinician's modeling of fluent productions; necessary to eliminate the special stimulus control of response properties or clinician's modeling; useful in inducing more natural-sounding speech and to promote more spontaneous speech.

Fluency Reinforcement. A direct procedure to increase fluency and as a concomitant effect, reduce stuttering; the clinician offers verbal praise for all fluent productions and ignores all stuttering; fluent speech may be modeled occasionally, but stuttering does not receive any systematic consequences; effective in treating preschool children who stutter; a minimal, simple approach to treating stuttering in young children; parents and clinicians easily trained in its application.

Maintenance Strategy. Procedures the clinician implements to promote maintenance of fluency in natural settings and over time; includes such tactics as teaching self-monitoring skills, self-charting of stuttering during treatment, delaying corrective feedback for stuttering to encourage self-evaluation, teaching clients to pause as soon as they stutter, asking the child to hand back a token when stuttering occurs, and so forth.

Masking Noise. Different intensities of white noise delivered through headphones to mask the client's hearing to varying degrees; a procedure that reduces stuttering in the short term; not a recommended treatment procedure because of poor long-term effects and potential health hazard associated with prolonged exposure to noise.

Minimal Prolongation. An experimental procedure that is combined with pause-and-talk; the client is asked to slightly prolong the initial vowel of initial words of sentences; no prolongation of other syllables; has minimal effect on speech naturalness; effective when combined with pause-and-talk; the slight prolongation is easily faded; helps enhance the effects of pause-and-talk; appropriate when a client's stuttering rate is high.

Modeling. Clinician's production of target behaviors (fluent productions) designed to encourage imitative production of such behaviors; often used in the initial stages of most treatment programs; helpful in establishing the skills; need to be faded in latter stages of treatment; often done soon after the client stutters.

Narrative Speech. A form of speech in which the client narrates personal experiences or stories; evoked in young children by telling them stories they are asked to retell; useful in stabilizing fluency in speech that is more continuous than conversational speech.

Natural-Sounding Speech. Speech produced with a normal rate and typical prosodic features (normal patterns of intonation and loudness variations); a final target of treatment when fluency shaping procedures are used.

Pause-and-Talk. An effective and direct stuttering reduction strategy without teaching any fluency skills (e.g., slow speech or airflow management); the client is asked to stop talking at the earliest sign of a stutter; the clinician then avoids eye contact and sits motionless for 5 seconds; the client is signaled to resume conversation after the pause duration; supported by experimental efficacy data; does not induce unnatural-sounding speech; limited data suggest good maintenance of fluency; preferred treatment for older students, adolescents, and adults.

Probe. A measure of stuttering or dysfluencies (as defined by the clinician) taken sometime after the treatment was applied, but with no treatment variables; measured in conversational speech samples, recorded without any form of treatment; needed to show that fluency is sustained without the treatment variables; samples and home and other natural settings enhance the validity of probes.

Prolonged Speech. A treatment procedure appropriate for older children, adolescents, and adults; a component of the comprehensive fluency shaping used in its own right; includes stretching of the syllables throughout all utterances and blending words in a smooth and slow manner; effective in inducing stutter-free but unnatural-sounding speech; supported by treatment research; needs additional treatment steps in which natural-sounding speech is the treatment target; relapse of stuttering a serious problem.

Prompts. Hints the clinician gives to encourage the production of any target response; always less than full modeling of the target response; may be verbal (e.g., "did you forget something?") or nonverbal (e.g., a gesture to slow down the speech rate).

Reinforcement Plus Corrective Feedback. A treatment procedure for preschool and school-age children; includes positive verbal reinforcement for fluency and corrective feedback for stuttering; involves frequent modeling of fluent productions for the child to imitate; prompt reinforcement and corrective feedback respectively contingent on fluent and dysfluent productions is the key element.

Response Cost. An effective and direct stuttering reduction strategy; the clinician reinforces fluent productions with verbal praise and token presentation and withdraws a token while giving corrective feedback for each dysfluent production; supported by experimental evidence; a preferred method for treating stuttering in preschool and school-age children; does not affect speech naturalness; clinicians and parents are easily trained in its application.

Role Reversal. A technique of mitigating negative emotional reaction an occasional child may show when a token is first withdrawn for stuttering in the response cost method; the clinician plays the role of a client who is earns tokens for fluent productions and loses them for stuttering; the child is allowed to play the role of a clinician who awards and removes tokens from the clinician; the clinician simulates stuttering to lose tokens; effective in permanently counteracting any negative reaction a child may show for the initial token withdrawal.

Stutter-Free Speech. An excessively slow and monotonous speech that is devoid of typical stuttering or dysfluencies; induced by syllable prolongation; result of both prolonged speech treatment and comprehensive fluency shaping procedure.

Stuttering. A disorder of fluency, characterized by an excessive amount of dysfluencies; unusual effort in speaking; abnormal management of airflow during dysfluent speech production; such associated motor behaviors as rapid eye blinks, hand and feet movements, wrinkling of the forehead, and tensed movement of the articulators; negative emotional reactions about speaking situations and one's own speech; and avoidance of speaking situations, certain sounds and words; not all clients exhibit all of the features; onset is typically in early childhood years.

Time-Out. See *pause-and-talk*.

Token Bankruptcy. Insufficient token retention by the end of a response cost treatment session, resulting in a failure to acquire the chosen back-up reinforcer; to be avoided at all costs; avoided by giving extra tokens for longer fluent productions, frequent modeling of fluent productions to increase the frequency of fluently imitated productions, and by extending the treatment sessions by a few minutes to allow for additional token earning.

Tokens. A form of conditioned generalized reinforcers backed up by tangible reinforcers; a part of the response cost method; involves the presentation of tokens of varied shapes and colors for fluent productions and their withdrawal for stutterings; always exchanged for the back-up gift at the end of the session.

Treatment at the Continuous Speech Level. Often a second or subsequent stage of treatment in which fluently produced connected speech is the treatment target; preceded by treatment at the sentence level; followed by treatment at the narrative speech level, although the sequence may be changed for individual clients.

Treatment at the Conversational Speech Level. An intermediate stage of treatment in which naturalistic conversation is targeted for stabilizing fluency or stutter-free speech, depending on the technique being selected; essential to stabilize fluency in social interactions; may be involved in promoting natural-sounding speech when fluency shaping techniques are used.

Treatment at the Narrative Speech Level. A latter of stage of treatment in which the clients are encouraged to narrate personal experiences or stories; a stage of treatment in which young children may be told stories and asked to retell them; useful in stabilizing fluency in extended speech segments.

Treatment at the Sentence Level. Often an initial stage of treatment with most intervention strategies and with most young children; involves evoking simple and isolated sentences to which the treatment variable is applied (e.g., slow speech, token presentation or withdrawal, application of pause-and-talk, reinforcement of fluency or corrective feedback for stuttering).

Treatment Protocols. Scripted scenarios that the clinician follows in treating a disorder; much more detailed than the usual textual description of treatment procedures; they assign and specify the role the clinician and the clients play in treatment sessions; include step-by-step instructions on completing the treatment process.

Unnatural-Sounding Speech. Speech that is stutter-free, but too slow and monotonous to be socially and personally acceptable; an initial result of the comprehensive fluency shaping and prolonged speech treatment; a presumed reason for stuttering relapse when such treatment has been used.

Verbal Praise (Reinforcement). Verbal statements of praise for correctly producing fluency skills (e.g., airflow management or slow speech) and fluent productions; a part of almost all kinds of treatment procedures.

References

Ahlander, E. (1999). *Effect of pause-and-talk and response cost on stuttering: Social and professional validity.* Master's thesis, California State University-Fresno.

Ahlander, E., & Hegde, M. N. (2000). The relative effects of time-out and response cost on the frequency of stuttering. Paper presented at the National Treatment Efficacy Research Conference, Vanderbilt University, Nashville, Tennessee (March).

Bloodstein, O. (1995). *A handbook on Stuttering* (5th ed.). Albany, NY: Thomson Learning.

Carter-Wagner, J., & Hegde, M. N. (1998). Effectiveness of parent-administered time-out in treating children who stutter. Paper presented at the National Treatment Efficacy Research Conference, Vanderbilt University (April).

Conture, E. (2001). *Stuttering: Its nature, diagnosis, and treatment.* Boston: Allyn & Bacon.

Cordes, A. K., & Ingham, R. J. (1998). *Treatment efficacy for stuttering: A search for empirical bases.* Albany, NY: Thomson Learning.

Curlee, R. F. (Ed.) (1999a). *Stuttering and related disorders of fluency* (2nd ed.). New York: Thieme.

Curlee, R. F. (1999b). Identification and case selection guidelines for early childhood stuttering. In R. F. Curlee (Ed.), *Stuttering and related disorders of fluency* (2nd ed.) (pp. 1–21). New York: Thieme.

Goldiamond, I. (1965). Stuttering and fluency as measurable operant response classes. In L. Krasner & L. P. Ullman (Eds.), *Research in behavior modification* (pp. 106–156). New York: Holt, Rinehart, & Winston.

Gregory, H. H. (2003). *Stuttering therapy: rationale and procedures.* Boston: Allyn & Bacon.

Gregory, H. H., & Hill, D. (1999). Differential evaluation—differential therapy for stuttering children. In R. F. Curlee (Ed.), *Stuttering and related disorders of fluency* (2nd ed.) (pp. 22–42). New York: Thieme.

Guitar, B. (2006). *Stuttering: An integrated approach* (3rd ed.). Philadelphia: Lippincott Williams & Wilkins.

Halvorson, J. A. (1971). The effects on stuttering frequency of pairing punishment (response cost) with reinforcement. *Journal of Speech and Hearing Research, 14,* 356–354.

Haroldson, S. K., Martin, R. R., & Starr, C. D. (1968). Time-out for punishment for stuttering. *Journal of Speech and Hearing Research, 11,* 560–566.

Harrison, E., & Onslow, M. (1999). Early intervention for stuttering: The Lidcombe program. In R. F. Curlee (Ed.), *Stuttering and related disorders of fluency* (2nd ed.) (pp. 65–79). New York: Thieme.

Hegde, M. N. (1998). *Treatment procedures in communicative disorders* (3rd ed.). Austin, TX: Pro-Ed.

Hegde, M. N. (2004). Treating stuttering in preschool and school-age children. Paper presented at the ASHA CID4 leadership conference (Portland, OR, July).

Hegde, M. N., & Parson, D. (1989). The relative effects of Type I and Type II punishment on stuttering. A paper presented at the conference on treatment efficacy (San Antonio, TX, March).

James, J. E. (1976). The influence of duration on the effects of time-out from speaking. *Journal of Speech and Hearing Research, 19,* 206–215.

James, J. E. (1981). Behavioral self-control of stuttering using time-out from speaking. *Journal of the Experimental Analysis of Behavior, 14,* 25–37.

Kazdin, A. E. (1973). The effect of response cost and aversive stimulation in suppressing punished and nonpunished speech dysfluencies. *Behavior Therapy, 4,* 73–82.

Manning, W. H. (1999). Management of adult stuttering. In R. F. Curlee (Ed.), *Stuttering and related disorders of fluency* (2nd ed., pp. 160–180). New York: Thieme.

Onslow, M. (1993). *Behavioral management of stuttering.* Albany, NY: Thomson Learning.

Onslow, M., Packman, A., & Harrison, E. (2003). *The Lidcombe program of early stuttering intervention.* Austin, TX: Pro-Ed.

Onslow, M., Packman, A., Stocker, S., van Dorn, J., & Siegel, G. M. (1997). Control of children's stuttering with response-contingent time-out: Behavioral, perceptual, and acoustic data. *Journal of Speech and Hearing Research, 40,* 121–133.

Ryan, B. (1998). Efficacy research to develop treatment programs for preschool children who stutter. In A. K. Cordes & R. J. Ingham (Eds.), *Treatment efficacy for stuttering: A search for empirical bases* (pp. 163–190). Albany, NY: Thomson Learning.

Salend, S. J., & Andress, M. J. (1984). Decreasing stuttering in an elementary-level student. *Language, Speech, and Hearing Services in the Schools, 15,* 16–21.

Siegel, G. M., Lenske, J. G., & Broen, P. (1969). Suppression of normal speech disfluencies through response cost. *Journal of Applied Behavior Analysis, 2,* 265–276.

Shapiro, D. A. (1999). *Stuttering intervention.* Austin, TX: Pro-Ed.

Yairi, E., & Ambrose, N. G. (2005). *Early childhood stuttering.* Austin, TX: Pro-Ed.

Appendix

Recording Sheets

Stuttering Baserate Recording Work Sheet

Print this page from the CD or photocopy this page for your clinical use.

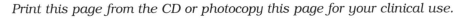

Name of the client:	DOB:
Diagnosis: Stuttering	Session date(s):

In its respective column, place a tally mark for each dysfluency you hear in the speech sample; add all the tally marks for each type of dysfluency; then add all dysfluencies for a total dysfluency count.

Types of Dysfluencies	Frequency
Prolongations	
Sound or syllable prolongations	
Silent prolongations	
Broken words (intralexical pauses)	
Pauses	
Silent pauses	
Repetitions	
Sound or syllable repetitions	
Word repetitions	
Phrase repetitions	
Interjections	
Schwa or *um* interjections	
Word interjections	
Phrase interjections	
Revisions	
Incomplete phrases	
Total number of dysfluencies	
Total number of words spoken	
Percent dysfluency rate	

Transfer the data to the Baserate Recording Form on the next page; personalize it and print it from the CD.

Baserate of Stuttering

Name of the client:	DOB:
Name of family member:	Phone:
Diagnosis: Stuttering	Session date(s):
Clinician:	Comments:

Types of Dysfluencies	Frequency
Prolongations	
Sound or syllable prolongations	
Silent prolongations	
Broken words (intralexical pauses)	
Pauses	
Silent pauses	
Repetitions	
Sound or syllable repetitions	
Word repetitions	
Phrase repetitions	
Interjections	
Schwa or *um* interjections	
Word interjections	
Phrase interjections	
Revisions	
Incomplete phrases	
Total number of dysfluencies	
Total number of words spoken	
Percent dysfluency rate	

Stuttering Treatment Recording Work Sheet

Print this page from the CD or photocopy this page for your clinical use.

Name of the client:	DOB:
Diagnosis: Stuttering	Session date(s):

In its respective column, place a tally mark for each dysfluency you hear in the speech sample; add all the tally marks for each type of dysfluency; then add all dysfluencies for a total dysfluency count.

Types of Dysfluencies	Frequency
Prolongations	
Sound or syllable prolongations	
Silent prolongations	
Broken words (intralexical pauses)	
Pauses	
Silent pauses	
Repetitions	
Sound or syllable repetitions	
Word repetitions	
Phrase repetitions	
Interjections	
Schwa or *um* interjections	
Word interjections	
Phrase interjections	
Revisions	
Incomplete phrases	
Total number of dysfluencies	
Total number of words spoken	
Percent dysfluency rate	

Progress in Treatment

Name of the client:	DOB:
Name of family member:	Phone:
Diagnosis: Stuttering	Session date(s):
Clinician:	Comments:

Types of Dysfluencies	Frequency
Prolongations	
Sound or syllable prolongations	
Silent prolongations	
Broken words (intralexical pauses)	
Pauses	
Silent pauses	
Repetitions	
Sound or syllable repetitions	
Word repetitions	
Phrase repetitions	
Interjections	
Schwa or *um* interjections	
Word interjections	
Phrase interjections	
Revisions	
Incomplete phrases	
Total number of dysfluencies	
Total number of words spoken	
Percent dysfluency rate	

Stuttering Probe Results Work Sheet

Print this page from the CD or photocopy this page for your clinical use.

Name of the client:	DOB:
Diagnosis: Stuttering	Session date(s):

In its respective column, place a tally mark for each dysfluency you hear in the speech sample; add all the tally marks for each type of dysfluency; then add all dysfluencies for a total dysfluency count.

Types of Dysfluencies	Frequency
Prolongations	
Sound or syllable prolongations	
Silent prolongations	
Broken words (intralexical pauses)	
Pauses	
Silent pauses	
Repetitions	
Sound or syllable repetitions	
Word repetitions	
Phrase repetitions©	
Interjections	
Schwa or *um* interjections	
Word interjections	
Phrase interjections	
Revisions	
Incomplete phrases	
Total number of dysfluencies	
Total number of words spoken	
Percent dysfluency rate	

Stuttering Probe Results

Name of the client:	DOB:
Name of family member:	Phone:
Diagnosis: Stuttering	Session date(s):
Clinician:	Comments:

Types of Dysfluencies	Frequency
Prolongations	
Sound or syllable prolongations	
Silent prolongations	
Broken words (intralexical pauses)	
Pauses	
Silent pauses	
Repetitions	
Sound or syllable repetitions	
Word repetitions	
Phrase repetitions	
Interjections	
Schwa or *um* interjections	
Word interjections	
Phrase interjections	
Revisions	
Incomplete phrases	
Total number of dysfluencies	
Total number of words spoken	
Percent dysfluency rate	

Index

A

Adults, treatment of stuttering for, 198–288
  Comprehensive fluency shaping procedure, 200–224
    establishing stutter-free conversational speech, 203–204
      treatment protocol for conversational speech, 205–213
    establishing stutter-free narrative speech, 214–217
      treatment protocol for narrative speech, 215–217
    probe protocol, 223
    probe recording sheet, 224
    stabilizing natural-sounding fluency, 218–221
      treatment protocol for natural-sounding fluency, 219–221
    treatment recording sheet, 222
  Maintenance probe recording sheet, 288
  Maintenance strategies, 286
  Minimal prolongation plus pause-and-talk, 266–285
    establishing fluency in conversational speech, 268–269
      treatment protocol for conversational speech, 270–275
    establishing fluency in narrative speech, 276
      treatment protocol for narrative speech, 277–279
    fading syllable prolongation, 280
      treatment protocol for fading syllable prolongation, 281–282
    probe protocol, 284
    probe recording sheet, 285
    treatment recording sheet, 283
  Pause-and-talk, 249–265
    probe protocol, 264
    probe recording sheet, 265
    treatment in conversational speech, 251–252
      treatment protocol for conversational speech, 253–256
    treatment in narrative speech, 257
      treatment protocol for narrative speech, 258–262
    treatment recording sheet, 263
  Prolonged speech, 225–248
    establishing stutter-free conversational speech, 228–229
      treatment protocol for conversational speech, 230–237
    establishing stutter-free narrative speech, 238
      treatment protocol for narrative speech, 239–241
    probe protocol, 247
    probe recording sheet, 248
    stabilizing natural-sounding fluency, 242
      treatment protocol for natural-sounding fluency, 243–245
    treatment recording sheet, 246
  Treatment options for, 198–199

B

Baserates of stuttering, 2–13, 190–196
  in adults, 190–196
    baserate protocol for conversational speech, 191–194
    baserate recording sheet, 196
    need for baserates in conversational speech, 190
    need for baserates in oral reading, 195
    recording an oral reading sample, 95
  in children, 2–13
    the need for, 2

protocols for continuous and
conversational speech, 6–8
protocols for narrative speech,
10–12
recording sheet, 13
for sentences, 4–5

C

Comprehensive fluency shaping
procedure, 85–113, 200–224
for adults and older students,
200–224
for school-age children, 85–113

F

Fluency reinforcement for
preschoolers, 17–35

M

Minimal prolongation plus pause-and-
talk in treating adults,
266–285

P

Pause-and-talk (time-out), 139–157,
249–265
in adults, 249–265
in school-age children, 139–157
Preschoolers, treatment of stuttering
for, 16–82
Fluency reinforcement, 17–35
continuous speech level, 23–25
treatment protocol for
continuous speech, 23–25
conversational speech level, 30
treatment protocol for
conversational speech, 31–32
narrative speech level, 26
treatment protocol for narrative
speech, 27–29
probe protocol, 34
probe recording sheet, 35

sentence level, 18–22
treatment protocol for
sentences, 19
treatment recording sheet, 33
Fluency reinforcement plus
corrective feedback, 37–55
continuous speech level, 43
treatment protocol for
continuous speech, 44–45
conversational speech level, 50
treatment protocol for
conversational speech, 51–52
narrative speech level, 46
treatment protocol for narrative
speech, 47–49
probe protocol, 54
probe recording sheet, 55
sentence level, 39–42
treatment protocol for
sentences,
treatment recording sheet, 53
Maintenance probe recording sheet,
82
Maintenance strategies, 81
Response cost, 56–80
continuous speech level, 66
treatment protocol for
continuous speech, 67–69
conversational speech level, 74
treatment protocol for
conversational speech, 75–77
narrative speech level, 70
treatment protocol for narrative
speech, 71–73
probe protocol, 79
probe recording sheet, 80
sentence level, 57–59
treatment protocol for
sentences, 60–65
treatment recording sheet, 78
Treatment options for, 16
Prolonged speech
in treating adults and older
students, 225–248
in treating school-age children,
114–138

R

Reinforcement plus corrective feedback in treating preschoolers, 37–55
Response cost
  in preschoolers, 56–80
  in school-age children, 158–186

S

School-age children, treatment of stuttering for, 84–188
  Comprehensive fluency shaping, 85–113
    establishing stutter-free conversational speech, 88–89
      treatment protocol for stutter-free conversational speech, 90–99
    establishing stutter-free narrative speech, 100
      treatment protocol for narrative speech, 101–105
    probe protocol, 112
    probe recording sheet, 113
    stabilizing natural-sounding fluency, 106
      treatment protocol for natural-sounding fluency, 107–110
    treatment recording sheet, 111
  Maintenance probe recording sheet, 188
  Maintenance strategies, 187
  Pause-and-talk, 139–157
    probe protocol, 156
    probe recording sheet, 157
    treatment in conversational speech, 141–142
      treatment protocol for conversational speech, 143–147
    treatment in narrative speech, 148
      treatment protocol for narrative speech, 149–154
    treatment recording sheet, 155
  Prolonged speech, 114–138
    establishing stutter-free conversational speech, 116–117
      treatment protocol for conversational speech, 118–124
    establishing stutter-free narrative speech, 125
      treatment protocol for narrative speech, 126–130
    probe protocol, 137
    probe recording sheet, 138
    stabilizing natural-sounding fluency, 131
      treatment protocol for natural-sounding fluency, 132–135
    treatment recording sheet, 136
  Response cost, 158–186
    continuous speech level, 168
      treatment protocol for continuous speech, 169–171
    conversational speech level, 180
      treatment protocol for conversational speech, 181–183
    narrative speech level, 172
      treatment protocol for narrative speech, 173–179
    probe protocol, 185
    probe recording sheet, 186
    sentence level, 160–162
      treatment protocol for sentences, 163–167
    treatment recording sheet, 184
  Treatment options for, 84

T

Tokens
  in treating preschoolers, 56–80
  in treating school-age children, 158–188